P9-DHB-985

The *Creole* Affair

The *Creole* Affair

The Slave Rebellion that Led the U.S. and Great Britain to the Brink of War

Arthur T. Downey

ROWMAN & LITTLEFIELD
Lanham • Boulder • New York • London

Published by Rowman & Littlefield
A wholly owned subsidiary of The Rowman & Littlefield Publishing Group, Inc.
4501 Forbes Boulevard, Suite 200, Lanham, Maryland 20706
www.rowman.com

16 Carlisle Street, London W1D 3BT, United Kingdom

British Library Cataloguing in Publication Information Available

Library of Congress Cataloging-in-Publication Data

Arthur T. Downey.
The Creole affair : the slave rebellion that led the U.S. and Great Britain to the brink of war / Arthur T. Downey.
p. cm.
Includes bibliographical references and index.
ISBN 978-1-4422-3661-5 (paperback) — ISBN 978-1-4422-3662-2 (electronic)
1. Creole (Brig) 2. Slave insurrections—United States—History—19th century. 3. Mutiny—United States—History—19th century. 4. Washington, Madison. 5. Slaves—Emancipation—Bahamas—History— 19th century. 6. United States—Foreign relations—Great Britain. 7. Great Britain—Foreign relations— United States. 8. Great Britain. Treaties, etc. United States, 1842 August 9. 9. Webster, Daniel, 1782– 1852. 10. Ashburton, Alexander Baring, Baron, 1774–1848. I. Title.
E447.D69 2014
327.7304109'034—dc23
2014009987

∞™ The paper used in this publication meets the minimum requirements of American National Standard for Information Sciences Permanence of Paper for Printed Library Materials, ANSI/NISO Z39.48-1992.

Printed in the United States of America

Contents

Preface

The most successful slave revolt in American history—on the high seas, on board the *Creole*—is an important event on its own, and deserves broad and deep scholarly study. The American and British diplomacy leading to the 1842 Webster-Ashburton Treaty was significant in deflecting the potential for a third US-UK war. This book tries to focus on the US domestic and diplomatic landscapes as seen from the viewpoint of the *Creole* affair. It also treats the various legal issues, domestic and international. The blending of these subjects enhances our understanding of that period, which is generally little known.

On the other hand, this book does not attempt to explore the impact of the *Creole* revolt on the slave and free black communities in the United States (or in the British Caribbean colonies). And it does not attempt to plow much new ground in diplomatic history; for example, it does not explore in depth the non-*Creole* issues surrounding the treaty, such as the delineation of the Maine boundary. It does attempt to provide an engaging and accurate story of the intersection of these two events, including their development over the following dozen years.

Fortunately, most of the basic documents are readily available: Presidential Messages to Congress, Opinions of the Attorney General, congressional debates, and the like. However, it proved necessary for me to carry on some research in the archives of the Bahamas in Nassau. Acquiring a personal sense for the physical surroundings of the harbor into which the *Creole* sailed on November 9, 1841, permitted me to develop a vivid picture of those events. Similarly, it was helpful to stand in "Ashburton House" across the park from the White House—now the parish house of St. John's Episcopal Church—and in the law office in Ohio of Congressman Joshua Reed Giddings, who offered the brilliant legal defense of the slaves' revolt.

The book begins with the facts of the revolt on the *Creole.* It then offers the context in which that event was set: in the United States, in terms of US-UK relations, and in the British Bahamas (part I). The story then returns to November 1841 in Nassau, and in the United States, and proceeds forward to the conclusion of the Webster-Ashburton Treaty (part II). Part III explores three events in the years following the diplomatic resolution, each event dealing with consequences flowing from the *Creole* affair. Finally, the epilogue traces the interesting lives in the period after the *Creole* affair of more than a dozen of the main characters. To assist the reader, there are three appendixes: a chronology of events, the relevant text of Tyler's Message to Congress in December 1841, and the complete texts of the Webster-Ashburton diplomatic notes dealing with the *Creole* affair.

All images are courtesy of the Prints and Photographs Division of the Library of Congress, unless otherwise noted.

Arthur T. Downey
2014

Introduction

For most of us, American history begins with the War of Independence and the establishment of the US Constitution, and then makes a brief stop at the Anglo-American War of 1812. At that point, most discussion of American history leaps forward to the Civil War, with no more than perhaps a glance at the Monroe Doctrine, Alexis de Tocqueville, the Mexican War, the acquisition of Texas, and the California gold rush. As a result, most Americans have missed the enormous growth in territory, strength, population, and social maturity during that half century between the War of 1812 and the Civil War. In the middle of that period, there was a real threat of yet another war—a third—with Great Britain.

America, slavery, and Great Britain formed a triangle of linked tension. The British introduced slavery into their American colonies, but at the time of the American Revolution, the slavery issue cut both ways for the British. In November 1775, the Royal Governor of Virginia, Lord Dunmore, promised freedom to slaves owned by rebels if those slaves would join His Majesty's troops.[1] The British were walking a bit of a tightrope, since they also wanted to leave untouched slaves owned by those colonialists who were loyal to the British Crown. In 1779, Sir Henry Clinton in New York declared that slaves who were captured by British forces while those slaves were serving the rebels would be sold for the benefit of the Crown; on the other hand, slaves who deserted the rebels would be offered "full security"—sort of a promise of freedom. By the end of the Revolutionary War, some 15,000 to 20,000 escaped slaves remained under British protection in the ports that had not yet been evacuated (New York, Charleston, and Savannah). Some 9,000 freed slaves accompanied the last British forces to leave.[2]

At the time of the establishment of the US government in 1789, 90 percent of blacks in the United States were slaves, and 40 percent of those lived in Virginia.[3] There were no slaves in Maine and Massachusetts, but as late as 1820, New York State had about the same number of slaves as Missouri; slavery remained legal in New York until 1827 and in Connecticut until 1848.

British action to free American slaves during the American Revolution had been driven by military necessity and clever political pragmatism. However, by the first decade of the new century, Britain had become the international star of the abolition movement. In 1806, Britain passed the Foreign Slave Trade Act, presented as a national security measure, rather than as a humanitarian one, which prohibited participating in the slave trade with current or former colonies and possessions of France.[4] Then, on February 23, 1807, Parliament passed the Act for the Abolition of the Slave Trade, which prohibited participation in the slave trade by British subjects, and the importation of slaves into British possessions, with effect on January 1, 1808. (This Act, of course, did not free any of the 600,000 slaves in the British Caribbean.) In December 1806, President Jefferson advised Congress of his support for legislation to ban the slave trade, and he signed a bill in March 1807, banning the import of slaves, effective ten months later. This nearly coterminous action against the slave trade was an occasion where the triangle of tension among the United States, slavery, and the United Kingdom was relaxed.

The War of 1812 revealed once again the British-American tension over slavery. British naval raids along the Chesapeake Bay created the opportunity for many slaves to escape and to enlist in British service, as sailors, laundresses, and so forth.[5] Hundreds of slaves enlisted. At the start of the war, the British were interested in only a few slaves—to serve as guides or pilots—but by 1814 the British encouraged mass escapes. Black marines permitted the British to raid deeper into American territory, and also allowed the black marines to "plunder their former masters and retrieve family members."[6] During the war, more than three thousand slaves from Maryland and Virginia alone fled to British ships. Not surprisingly, these events, as the great scholar of the period and 2014 Pulitzer Prize winner for history, Professor Alan Taylor, noted: "soured many Virginians on the Union because the national government did precious little to defend them and to prevent their slaves from escaping."[7] The British were "demonized" as "race traitors who allied with savage Indians on the frontier and fomented bloody slave uprisings in the South."[8]

The War of 1812 was concluded by the December 1814 Treaty of Ghent. The first article of that treaty required the British to withdraw promptly from American land and waters, and to leave behind any private property, including slaves. The British took a very narrow interpretation of this requirement, and the Royal Navy refused to return hundreds of freed slaves. President Monroe, a slaveholder, instructed the American minister to Britain, John

Quincy Adams, to demand compensation for those slaves. The British countered that the royal ships were their sovereign territory (even when within American territorial waters), and the slaves ceased to be "property" once on those vessels. The United States and United Kingdom finally agreed to submit the issue to Czar Alexander I of Russia, who in 1822 decided that the British had to compensate the Americans for those runaway slaves who were on board the navy's ships. Finally, in 1826, the United States accepted a British offer to settle the claims for $1.2 million.[9]

The United States tightened the screws on the international slave trade in 1819. In that year, Congress authorized the president to create the "Africa Squadron" of armed US vessels to cruise the African coast and interdict slaver traders.[10] The law provides that any slaves interdicted would be returned to Africa, rather than being sold in the United States. The law also provided an incentive for the US sailors in the squadron: a $25 bounty to be shared by the crew for every African rescued. In 1820, Congress ratcheted up the pressure: a new law provided that any American engaging in the African slave trade would be judged a pirate—and that carried a death penalty.[11] For a brief time in 1820, the United States had five navy ships off the coast of Africa. One of them, the USS *John Adams*, cooperated with a British Royal Navy ship in an effort to capture a slave ship, but the American ships were soon called to service elsewhere.[12]

At about the same time, Britain was also dramatically pressing to eliminate the international slave trade through diplomacy, backed by the Royal Navy. Thus, in 1817, Britain entered into treaties with The Netherlands, Portugal, and Spain banning the slave trade and permitting mutual rights of search of their vessels, and also established binational courts to adjudicate captured slave ships.[13] The robust enforcement mechanisms reflected a sea change in the effort to suppress the international slave trade. The British had made overtures to the Monroe administration at about the same time, but the United States rejected the idea. From the American perspective, the central problem was the issue of the "right of search." Secretary of State John Quincy Adams explained to the British Minister in Washington in 1819 that he simply could not listen to any proposal that would permit a right of search of American merchant vessels by foreign (UK) armed vessels—since it was too reminiscent of the impressment issue that was a trigger for the War of 1812.[14] The timing for the United States was also problematic, since it was dealing with the issue of the expansion of domestic slavery, a problem temporarily resolved by the famous Missouri Compromise of 1820, which preserved the exact balance between slave states and free states.

By 1823–1824, the United States and the United Kingdom were negotiating a treaty dealing with the slave trade, and they agreed that the two countries would stipulate that the penalties of piracy (death) would apply to the offense of participating in the slave trade by their respective citizens or subjects. The treaty was signed in London on March 13, 1824, but the Senate insisted that the waters off the American coast be excluded from the treaty. The British refused to accept that amendment, and the ratification failed in the Senate. In his message to both houses of Congress on December 7, 1824, President Monroe lamented the failure, but said he was suspending the negotiation of a new treaty until the definitive sentiments of Congress would be ascertained.[15] The British continued to conclude treaties with a host of countries, making the slave trade equal to piracy. (Indeed, in November 1840, the Republic of Texas signed such a slave trade treaty in London.)[16]

The British took a giant step forward with respect to slavery itself—not only the international slave trade. Effective August 1, 1834, the British abolished slavery throughout most of the Empire. Originally designed as a gradual emancipation, all the slaves were freed as of August 1, 1838. Southern slave owners were aghast at this nearby abolition, and, not surprisingly, this confirmed their view of the British as a menace. Professor Alan Taylor noted:

> Slaves overheard their masters denounce the British as a menace to the republic through their black proxies and abolitionist pawns. . . . American talk unwittingly had confirmed to listening blacks that the British offered their best chance to win freedom for all. Then, in the endless feedback of rhetorical dread, Americans regarded the Anglophilia of slaves as a special menace to the republic of white men.[17]

US-British relations were seriously strained for several years during the late 1830s. Most of those difficulties involved disputes along the northeast border areas, and did not directly involve slavery. There were, however, three instances—in 1830, 1834, and 1835—when American ships in the domestic slave trade were wrecked near British colonies in the Caribbean, and where the slaves gained their freedom to the anger of their owners. But a little-known event in late 1841 sparked a sharp deterioration in the US-UK relationship and brought America and Great Britain perilously close to their third war. Once again, the triangle of tension—the United States, slavery, and the United Kingdom—tightened. The event also exposed the sectional strains in the nation that, less than twenty years later, led to the Civil War. America's "original sin" of slavery began to dominate the public square during this period, when the politics and economics of slavery increasingly conflicted with the moral surge of abolitionism.

That 1841 event was a violent slave rebellion on board an American ship, the *Creole*, as it sailed with its human cargo from Richmond to New Orleans. It was the most successful slave revolt in American history.[18]

This is the story of that event, and that period.[19] It is a story of the horrors of slavery and the power of the drive for freedom. It is a story about diplomacy, particularly about how two extraordinary nonprofessional diplomats cleverly resolved the tensions that were pushing the United States and the United Kingdom toward war. And, it is a story about the role of law—domestic and international—with respect to the status of a slave, and the rights and obligations arising from that status. As was usual at that period, the key political leaders on the American side were all lawyers (President Tyler, Secretary of State Webster, Congressmen John Quincy Adams, Joshua Giddings, etc.).[20] On the British side, none of the leading figures were lawyers.

Even though the slave rebellion lasted only a few days in late November 1841, the struggles to grapple with specific issues continued into the mid-1850s, including an international claims tribunal in London, and a novella by the great abolitionist orator, Frederick Douglass.

Dramatis Personae

ON BOARD THE *CREOLE*

Robert Ensor, captain
Zephaniah C. Gifford, first mate
Lucius Stevens, second mate
John R. Hewell, agent for slave trader McCargo
William H. Merritt, one of the slaves' guards
Theophilus McCargo, nephew of slave trader
Mrs. Ensor, her daughter, and her niece
Six other crew members and one other passenger
Rebellious slaves: Madison Washington, Elijah Morris, Ben Johnstone, Pompey Garrison, and fifteen other slaves

IN NASSAU

John F. Bacon, American consul (1840–1842 and 1845–1850)
Timothy Darling, American consul (1842–1845)
William Woodside, master of the American brig *Congress*
Sir Francis Cockburn, governor general (1837–1844)
George Campbell Anderson, attorney general of the Bahamas

IN WASHINGTON

Andrew Jackson, president (1829–1837)
Martin van Buren, president (1837–1842)
William Henry Harrison, president (1842)

John Tyler, president (1841–1846)
John Forsyth, secretary of state (1834–1841)
Daniel Webster, secretary of state (1841–1843)
Hugh S. Legare, attorney general (1841–1843)
John Quincy Adams, congressman from Massachusetts (1831–1848) and president (1825–1829)
Joshua Reed Giddings, congressman from Ohio (1838–1859)
Henry A. Wise, congressman from Virginia (1833–1844)
Henry Clay, senator from Kentucky and Whig leader
John C. Calhoun, senator from South Carolina and former vice president
Roger B. Taney, chief justice (1836–1864)
Joseph Story, Supreme Court justice (1811–1845)
Winfield Scott, general, US Army (1814–1861)
Henry S. Fox, British minister to the United States (1836–1843)
Alexander Baring, Lord Ashburton, special British envoy (1842)

IN LONDON

William Lamb, Viscount Melbourne, prime minister (1834–1941)
Sir Robert Peel, prime minister (1834–1835 and 1841–1846)
Lord Palmerston, secretary of state for foreign affairs (1839–1841)
Lord Aberdeen, secretary of state for foreign affairs (1841–1846) and prime minister (1852–1855)
Lord John Russell, secretary of state for war and colonies (1839–1841) and prime minister (1846–1852 and 1865–1866)
Lord Stanley, secretary of state for war and colonies (1841–1845)
Martin Van Buren, American minister (1831–1832)
Andrew Stevenson, American minister (1836–1841)
Edward Everett, American minister (1841–1845)
Joshua Bates, umpire of the US-UK Claims Commission (1853–1855)

IN THE UNITED STATES

Charles Dickens, English author and visitor to the United States (1842 and 1867–1868)
Judah P. Benjamin, Louisiana attorney (1845)
Frederick Douglass, former slave and author of *The Heroic Slave* (1853)

The Rebellion

In late October 1841, the two-masted brig,[1] the *Creole*, lay at the dock in Richmond, Virginia's capital, as tobacco, supplies, and slaves were brought on board. The ship had been built only a year or so earlier and was owned by Johnson & Eperson of Richmond. Before loading, the slaves had been kept at a slave pen in Richmond. A slave described a Richmond slave pen where he had been held six months earlier:

> [T]here were two small houses standing at opposite corners within the yard. These houses are usually found within slave yards, being used as rooms for the examination of human chattels by purchasers before concluding a bargain. Unsoundness in a slave, as well as in a horse, detracts materially from his value. If no warranty is given, a close examination is a matter of particular importance to the negro jockey.[2]

At midnight, October 25, the *Creole* slipped away from the dock to begin her voyage to New Orleans under the command of Captain Robert Ensor of Richmond. His wife and their four-year-old daughter were on board, along with Ensor's fifteen-year-old niece. The crew was composed of a first mate, Zephaniah C. Gifford, who had been a seaman for thirteen years, and second mate, Lucius Stevens, and six crewmen. There were also four "passengers": (1) William H. Merritt, who had agreed to serve as a guard in exchange for free passage to New Orleans; (2) John Hewell, of Richmond, acting as a guard for the thirty-nine slaves owned by the local slave trader, Thomas McCargo; (3) Theophilus McCargo, a nephew of Thomas McCargo; and finally (4) Joseph Leitner (or Leidner), a Prussian acting as an assistant steward in exchange for passage. Thus, there were a total of sixteen nonslave crew and passengers. They were probably looking forward to leaving the chilled fall weather in Virginia, getting comfortable on the voyage in the warm Gulf Stream, and then basking in the relative heat of Louisiana.

As the ship sailed down the James River, the captain stopped a couple of times to pick up additional slaves. The brig passed Jamestown on the port side, where, in 1607, 102 men and boys landed and established the first English settlement in North America. Twelve years later, the first slaves were introduced: a British privateer had captured a Portuguese slave ship en route from Angola in southwest Africa, and it brought some twenty slaves to Jamestown, where they were traded for supplies.[3]

On October 29, the *Creole* finally transited the 110 miles from Richmond to Hampton Roads, where it lay over for one day and put additional slaves on board. The ship was close to Fort Monroe, the largest stone fort ever built in the United States, finally completed only seven years earlier. It was President Madison who, after the War of 1812, realized that the area needed to be protected from attack by the British, or any other sea power.[4] During the August 1831 Nat Turner slave rebellion in nearby Southampton County, Virginia, three companies were sent from Fort Monroe to thwart the rebellion.[5] Exactly thirty years later, during the first few months of the Civil War, Union General Ben Butler freed three Virginia slaves at Fort Monroe, claiming them as "contraband," almost three years before the Emancipation Proclamation. The *Creole* left Hampton Roads, Virginia, on October 30.

By the time the brig transited the Chesapeake Bay and entered the Atlantic Ocean, there were 135 slaves on board, about one-third of whom were women.[6] The male slaves were put in the forward hold, and the women slaves in the aft hold (except for six female "house servants" who were taken into the main cabin). In between the two holds were boxes of tobacco—the nonhuman cargo. The slaves were not chained or restrained, and could move about freely, although at night the men were not permitted to go into the women's aft hold. If they did, the ship's rule was that the men would be whipped. Undoubtedly, none of these slaves were looking forward to their arrival in New Orleans, and then their horrible—and short—life in a harsh climate on the large plantations.

The head slave cook was Madison Washington.[7] He and his slave assistants were responsible for cooking the salt pork and salt beef, and for the boiling of "coffee" made from parched grain. Twice a day, he supervised the distribution to the slaves of hardtack and other food. Thomas McCargo, a local slave trader in Richmond, had bought Washington.[8] McCargo's business was to buy slaves in Virginia, where there was an oversupply, and then, during the winter, move his "property" to the slave markets of New Orleans, where slaves were in demand for the cotton and sugar plantations, in time to get slaves in place for the coming planting season. McCargo shipped thirty-nine slaves on board the *Creole*; he insured them for about $800 each. While McCargo did not make this voyage himself, as he sometimes did, he sent an

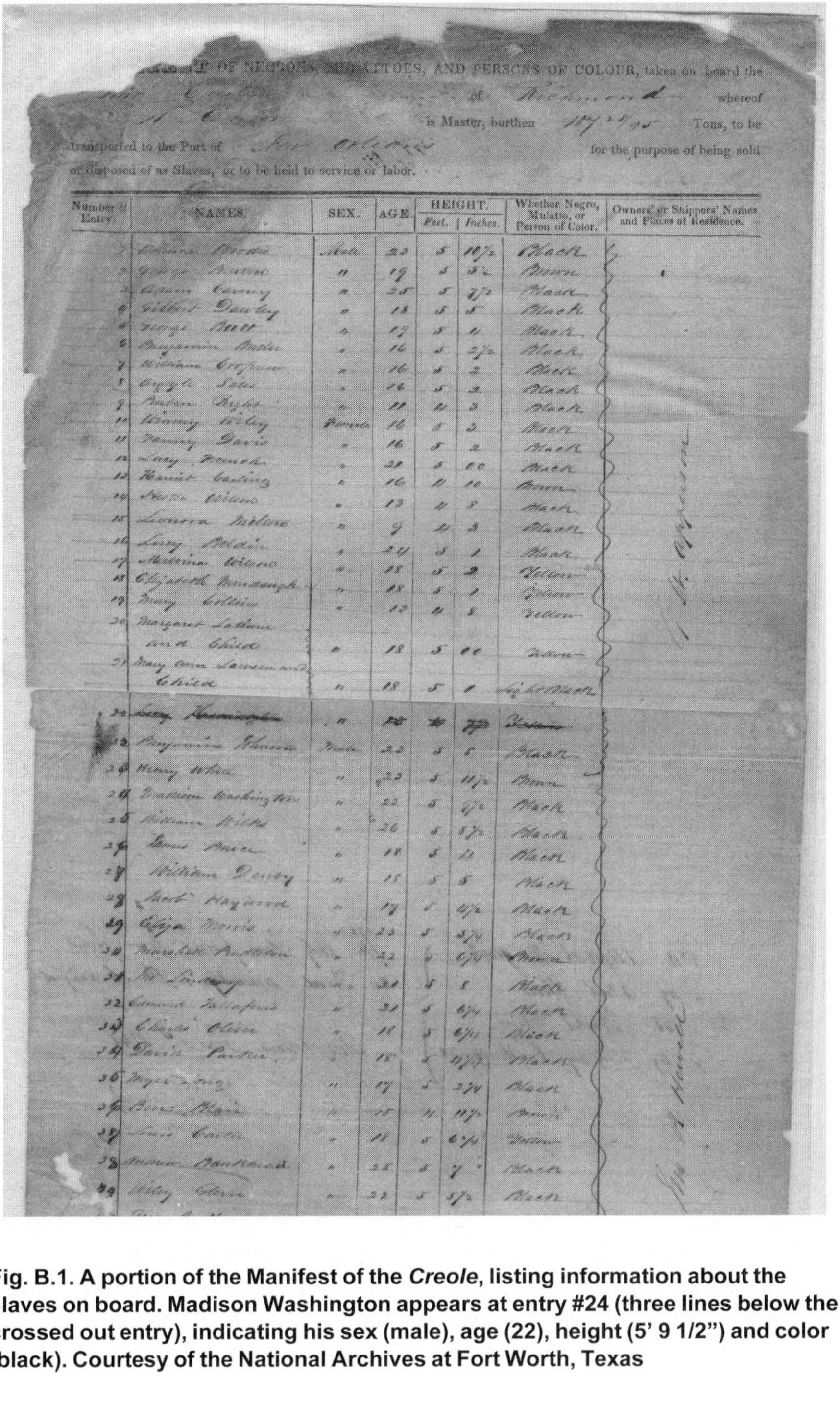

...OF NEGROES, MULATTOES, AND PERSONS OF COLOUR, taken on board the ... of ... whereof ... is Master, burthen ... Tons, to be transported to the Port of ... for the purpose of being sold or disposed of as Slaves, or to be held to service or labor.

Number of Entry.	NAMES.	SEX.	AGE.	HEIGHT. Feet.	HEIGHT. Inches.	Whether Negro, Mulatto, or Person of Color.	Owners' or Shippers' Names and Places of Residence.

Fig. B.1. A portion of the Manifest of the *Creole*, listing information about the slaves on board. Madison Washington appears at entry #24 (three lines below the crossed out entry), indicating his sex (male), age (22), height (5' 9 1/2") and color (black). Courtesy of the National Archives at Fort Worth, Texas

agent, John Hewell, to watch out for his interests and to guard his thirty-nine slaves. McCargo also sent his young nephew, Theophilus McCargo, on board the *Creole.*

Madison Washington had the lead role in planning a revolt. It is highly likely that he and the several other slave leaders had heard through the slave grapevine of earlier slave ships getting wrecked on some of the Caribbean Islands, and the slaves on board being liberated by the British. Washington's position as chief slave cook gave him a marvelous opportunity to speak to each of the slaves—to observe those whom he might try to recruit to his plan to revolt—and also to observe personalities and routines of the officers, crew, and guards. From that observation post, he may have been hatching a plot to take control of the ship.

The *Creole* sailed south, along the coast of the United States, heading toward Florida and eventually westward to New Orleans. On the night of November 7, 1841, the *Creole* was almost 200 miles northeast of Miami, about 130 miles northeast from the hamlet of Hole-in-the-Wall at the southern tip of the island of Abaco in the northern Bahamas, a British colony consisting of twenty-nine islands. At about 8:00 p.m., Captain Ensor ordered the ship to heave to.[9] Most of the people on board had turned in for the night, with the comfortable slow rocking movement of the ship in the warm waters of the Gulf Stream. The ship was dark, except for a lantern at the bow. The first mate, Zephaniah Gifford, was on watch duty.

One of the slaves, Elijah Morris, came forward to tell First Mate Gifford that one of the male slaves had gone aft into the female slave hold. Gifford called one of the guards (William Merritt), lit a lamp, and told Merritt to go down into the aft hold to see what was going on. Gifford remained at the hatch. Merritt suddenly found twenty-two-year-old Madison Washington, a large (five feet, nine inches) and strong slave belonging to Thomas McCargo, standing at his back. Washington jumped out of the hold; both Gifford and Merritt tried to hold him back, but Washington ran forward. Elijah Morris suddenly appeared with a pistol and fired it at Gifford, grazing the back of Gifford's head. Washington shouted at the male slaves in the forward hold: "We have commenced, and must go through; rush boys, rush aft; we have got them now. Come up, every damned one of you; if you don't lend a hand, I will kill you all and throw you overboard."[10]

Gifford rushed to the main cabin to arouse the captain and the others. The slaves ran aft and surrounded the main cabin. In the meantime, Merritt came on deck from out of the aft hold and was caught by one of the slaves, who shouted: "Kill him, God damn him, he's one of them." The slave tried to hit him with a handspike, but Merritt escaped, ran to his cabin. John Hewell, a "passenger" and McCargo's agent, grabbed a musket from the second mate's room and confronted the slaves. Hewell fired it from the companionway, but the gun had no powder and was useless. The slaves then "fell on him with clubs, handspikes and knives; they knocked him down and stabbed him less than twenty times." Several of the slaves had weapons: Ben Johnstone had the captain's bowie knife, Washington had a jackknife taken from Hewell, and Morris had a sheath knife belonging to one of the crew that he had taken from the forecastle. Hewell staggered into one of the staterooms, where he died. His body, nearly decapitated, was thrown overboard by order of Madison Washington, Johnstone, and Morris.

Captain Ensor grabbed a bowie knife and ran on deck. The slaves stabbed him and beat him severely, but he managed to climb up to the maintop, where he found temporary safety. (First Mate Gifford later found Captain Ensor passed out, and he lashed the captain to the rigging to prevent him from falling.) The second mate, Stevens, later found his way to the foreroyal yard—the smallest and highest horizontal beam—and joined the captain and first mate. The captain's wife and the children were not harmed. McCargo's young nephew, Theophilus McCargo, grabbed his pistols from a case, but they misfired, and he was taken prisoner. It looked as though he was to be killed, but two slaves intervened and pleaded with Elijah Morris and Ben Johnstone not to kill "Master Theo," and they agreed and sent young McCargo to the hold. The captain's wife, her child, and her niece begged for their lives. Two of the slave leaders, Elijah Morris and Pompey Garrison, were about to kill the helmsman, who was French. Madison Washington intervened, explaining that the helmsman did not speak English, and Washington told them not to kill him.

William Merritt, who was serving as a guard in exchange for passage, hid for a while, but the slaves finally found him. Elijah Morris and Ben Johnstone dragged him from hiding and, along with others, "surrounded him with knives, half-handspikes, muskets, and pistols, and raised their weapons to kill him." Just in time, and in desperation, Merritt told his captors that he used to be a mate and that he had enough experience to navigate the ship for them. One of the cabin servants, Mary, urged Madison Washington to intervene. Madison Washington ordered the men to stop threatening Merritt and took him into a stateroom, accompanied by some of the other slave leaders. Washington told Merritt that he wanted the ship to go to Liberia, an area on the west coast of Africa that was being developed as a colony mostly populated by freed American slaves. But Merritt explained that was not feasible, since there was not enough water or provisions on board for the long passage to the African coast. Ben Johnstone and several other slaves said they wanted to go to the British islands, where the *Hermosa* wrecked the previous year and whose slaves were then freed. Merritt then showed Washington and the others, using the ship's chart, that he could navigate to the British port of Nassau, where they would be freed. The slaves agreed that they would spare his life *if* he got the ship to that port.

By 1:00 a.m., the revolt was over. Madison Washington and his mutineers were in control of the *Creole*. Shouts and threats continued, but there were no more injuries or deaths.

At about 5:00 a.m., one of the slaves informed Merritt that Gifford and the captain were in the rigging. (Gifford had tied the captain in place there, because the vessel was rolling heavily.) The slaves found the captain, Gifford (the first mate), and Stevens (the second mate) hiding in the topsail, and Madison Washington ordered them to get them down on the deck. Ben Johnstone put a musket to Gifford's chest, and Madison Washington threatened to kill him if he would not take them to a British island, as Merritt had promised. They forced Stevens, the second mate, to make the same promise. The captain, under armed guard, was allowed to be treated by his wife. At daybreak, Washington ordered Gifford and Stevens to set sail. The slave leaders maintained a watch on the compass, and ordered that Gifford and Merritt not communicate with anyone, or else they would be thrown overboard.

During the voyage southward, the captain, his family, and the second mate (Stevens) were confined in the forward hold where the male slaves had been kept at night. Two of the five members of the crew who were wounded during the outbreak were kept in the main cabin. The other crew members were not restrained. The nineteen slaves involved in the rebellion moved into the main cabin, where they ate; all the other slaves ate on deck, as usual. The assistant steward, Joseph Leitner, was instructed to hand out the ship's supply of liquor, whereupon he brought out "four bottles of brandy, a jug of whiskey, and a demijohn of Madeira wine . . . [and the slaves] drank all the brandy, and most of the whiskey and wine."[11] The slaves opened the trunks of the passengers, and took out money and clothes; some of them put on the new stockings they found, while discarding the old ones. Apart from the nineteen actively involved in the rebellion, the other slaves remained calm and did not associate with the nineteen. As the *Creole* sailed closer to Nassau, Madison Washington took a pistol from one of the nineteen and said he did not want them to have any arms when they reached Nassau.

It is impossible to know the range of emotions on that ship during the night of the slave rebellion, while the *Creole* was hove to, but one can imagine that the nineteen slave mutineers were overjoyed that their audacious plan had been successful—at least so far—and that the crew and passengers were terrified, expecting the worst—brutal beatings and near decapitation (as happened to John Hewell), and perhaps the rape of Mrs. Ensor and her young niece. Apart from the nineteen, the remaining slaves were probably filled with a mix of emotions: amazement that a slave rebellion seemed to have worked, hope that this would lead to their freedom, but worry that the actions of the nineteen would bring dreaded retaliation to all of the slaves. For all, tension must have crackled in the air.

At daybreak on Tuesday, November 9, the *Creole* came in sight of Nassau. To reach the port of Nassau, a ship must enter a long, narrowing channel; on the port side was Hog Island, at the western end of which was a red-topped lighthouse.[12] Nassau itself was located on the starboard side, deep into the channel. Overlooking the entire harbor area was the huge Fort Charlotte, built at the end of the American Revolutionary War. Its forty-two heavy cannons protected the entrance to the channel south of the lighthouse.

The *Creole* arrived at about 8:00 a.m. and anchored in the westward end of the channel, about a mile from the heart of Nassau. It is customary for a "pilot," a local authorized guide very familiar with the currents and shallows of a harbor area, to come on board any visiting ship. Thus, a Bahamian ship pilot and his crew—all Negroes—came on board the *Creole*, mingled with the slaves, and told them "they were free men; that they could go on shore, and never be carried away from there."[13] The pilot brought the ship into the long, thin body of water separating Hog Island from the main island of New Providence, at the south end of which was the harbor of Nassau, where the ship anchored.

A Bahamian harbormaster[14] came alongside for the routine inspection of the ship. Since the captain was badly wounded, Gifford, the first mate, took charge and seized the opportunity to jump into the harbormaster's boat, and to explain that a mutiny had taken place. Gifford asked to be taken ashore, and pleaded that Bahamian officer then watch the vessel and allow no one to disembark. Gifford knew that if the slaves got off the ship and onto land in British Nassau, they would be free. The Bahamian quarantine officer's boat brought Gifford into the harbor at Nassau. Gifford jumped onto the land, and the quarantine officer conducted Gifford to the local representative of the US government, the American consul, John F. Bacon. Bacon was a native of Massachusetts, but had practiced law in Albany, New York, and had served as clerk of the New York Senate.

Once again, the emotions and tensions on board must have been at a high level: most of the slaves trying to understand their unsought good fortune, hoping that they would be able to step into freedom on the soil of the British colony; the nineteen mutineers also must have been hoping for freedom they felt they had earned, but undoubtedly they were also worried that the British might throw them in jail or, worse, return them to the United States to face a horrible fate. The fifteen remaining passengers and crew must have clung to the belief that their nightmare would now end, once British authorities took control of the vessel and ensured their safety and the punishment of those slave leaders who took Hewell's life, wounded others, and stole their possessions. But, clearly, none of the people on the *Creole* knew for certain what would unfold. They were in uncharted territory.

Let us now freeze that picture, before we discuss what happened next in Nassau. Let us now step back to understand the larger picture in which this event on the high seas took place.

I

The Context: Pre-November 1841

Chapter One

The United States

THE CONTEXT

In 1841, the flag of the United States had only twenty-six stars; Michigan was the most recent to be added, four years earlier. The country was compact: from the Atlantic coast to Missouri, Arkansas, and Louisiana in the west, and from Maine in the north to Georgia in the south. The population centers were concentrated on the Atlantic or the Gulf; only one of the top ten cities in 1840 was located in the inland "west," Cincinnati.[1] The perimeter of the nation was problematic: the Maine/Canada border was disputed, the Oregon country was under joint US-UK occupation, to the west of Louisiana was the newly independent Republic of Texas, and US territories—not yet states—included Iowa/Wisconsin,[2] Florida, and the vast unorganized territory stretching from the northern border of the Republic of Texas to Canada. In the Florida Territory, acquired from Spain exactly twenty years earlier, the second Seminole War had been under way since 1835.

The total US population was around 17 million (including 2.5 million slaves), about half the size of Russia, and 65 percent the size of Great Britain (at 27 million). Significant immigration was just beginning. There was very little immigration from 1770 to 1830, in part because of lingering doubts as to the viability of this new country; in 1830, about 98.5 percent of the population was native-born. But during the 1830s immigration more than quadrupled, led by the Irish and the Germans, and so by 1840, almost 5 percent of the population was composed of immigrants. The huge growth in immigration did not occur until much later in the 1840s due to the failed European revolutions of 1848, the dramatic expansion of the US frontier, and the promise of farms and jobs.

American writers in the 1820s finally won acclaim in Europe: Washington Irving's *Legend of Sleepy Hollow* and *Rip Van Winkle*, and James Fenimore Cooper's *Last of the Mohicans* were well known. In 1841, James Fenimore Cooper published the last of the series of the very popular Leatherstocking tales, *The Deerslayer.* Cooper focused on historical novels of the frontier and Native American life, which created a unique form of American literature. Also in 1841, Edgar Allan Poe wrote *The Murders in the Rue Morgue*, recognized as the first detective story, which led directly to Arthur Conan Doyle's Sherlock Holmes and Agatha Christie's Hercule Poirot. This new genre reflected the public's interest in crime, due to rapid urban development and the reports in the press about crime and trials. Poe was the first serious critic of Charles Dickens in the United States. Poe managed to guess the outcome of the murder plot in Dickens's 1841 serialized historical novel *Barnaby Rudge.* As a result Dickens eliminated the clues Poe had identified when Dickens later published it in book form.[3]

In the mid-1830s, the US economy expanded rapidly, and the price of land, cotton, and slaves rose sharply. Significant capital was invested in the United States from Great Britain. Anglo-American banking houses, such as Baring Brothers, served as the engine of much of the westward expansion, financing internal improvements (canals, roads, etc.) that permitted industrial growth. Railroads and canals spread, especially across the Northeast. By 1840, nearly three thousand miles of track had been laid in the United States, more than in all of Europe.[4] The development of the steam engine, first for vessels and then for railroad locomotives, changed transportation. The Mississippi River system involved more than 15,000 miles of navigable waterways; the arrival of steam-driven riverboats "emancipated the Mississippi Valley from its reliance on animal energy."[5] In 1829, Andrew Jackson came to Washington for his inaugural in a carriage pulled by horses, but when his two terms ended in March 1837, former president Jackson returned to his beloved Hermitage plantation near Nashville in a train pulled by a steam locomotive.[6]

But the classic "boom and bust" cycle kicked in, and in mid-1837, the United States fell into a deep recession, a financial meltdown known as "the Panic of 1837."[7] Banks collapsed, businesses failed, wages deflated, and the price of cotton plummeted. In mid-May 1837, all the banks in New York City stopped redeeming paper money in silver or gold.[8] All sections of the country felt the collapse of the economy, but the South probably felt it most, because of its overwhelming reliance on cotton. It was not coincidental that in 1837, just after he was admitted to the Illinois bar, a young attorney in Springfield, Illinois—Abraham Lincoln—spent most of his professional time on debt collection cases. Bank failures in upstate New York in 1837 propelled Joseph Smith Jr. to move his fledging Mormon flock westward.[9] It is not surprising that the first modern federal bankruptcy legislation was adopted in April 1841, the Bankruptcy Act of 1841.[10] That same year, eight states and the Territory of Florida defaulted on their debts; yields for state bonds rose to 12 percent in early 1841 and to nearly 30 percent by 1842.[11] The great recession continued through the entire Van Buren administration and was the outstanding political quandary of Van Buren's presidency.[12]

By 1820, the basic political division of the country was no longer large states versus small states; it had become North versus South. A new political compromise was fashioned to deal with the future of slavery, which had become complicated because of all the new lands acquired in the West. The Missouri Compromise of 1820 essentially divided the new lands evenly, according to the presence or absence of slavery; to keep the political balance, free Maine was admitted along with slave Missouri. Also in 1820, the American Colonization Society established the new settlement of Liberia on the African continent.[13] As one scholar noted, antislavery pressure "existed before the 1830's, but it was tepid and overly concerned with not upsetting the political status quo."[14]

The August 1831 Nat Turner slave rebellion in Virginia led to the deaths of more than fifty whites, most of them women and children.[15] In response, Virginian patrollers butchered about one hundred slaves; Turner and twenty-two other rebels were tried and hanged. This bloody rebellion terrified Southern slave owners. The 1833 decision of the British Parliament to abolish slavery gradually in its overseas possessions worried the Southern slave owners as much as it encouraged abolitionists in the North. As one scholar aptly put it, from "the mid-1830s . . . people on each side of the sectional line had reason to believe they suffered from aggressive action against their way of life, interests, rights and sovereignty."[16] At about that time, abolitionists began to mail their literature to prominent Southern whites who, they hoped, might be open to persuasion. Leaders of the New York Antislavery Society, influenced by the model of the British, mailed antislavery literature to Southern ministers, hoping to convince Southern Christians that slavery was wrong.[17] President Jackson stopped that practice, claiming that such mail might incite slave insurrection; with Jackson's support, Postmaster General Amos Kendall encouraged local postmasters to censor the mail.[18] Abolitionist literature in the South, therefore, stayed largely undelivered.[19]

For more than four decades, there had been a religious revival movement in the United States, commonly termed the Second Great Awakening, though it was ebbing. The Methodists and Baptists reflected the movement in a great increase in membership, at the relative expense of the traditional Episcopal and Congregational churches. The movement focused on man's spiritual equality and the duty of Christians to purify society. In the South, preachers converted slaveholders and slaves, and revivals inspired some slaves to insist on their freedom. The African Methodist Episcopal (AME) denomination was established in 1816.

For some, this religious revival movement, which espoused repairing social evils, flowed naturally into bolstering the ranks of the abolitionists. The American Anti-Slavery Society was formed in late 1833 in Philadelphia; it was a pacifist group demanding the immediate abolition of slavery. (On the other hand, ending slavery did not always equate to a demand for equality; the new Pennsylvania Constitution of 1837 provided for the disenfranchisement of nonwhite men. In March 1838, thousands of African Americans gathered in Philadelphia to protest this regression.)[20] William Lloyd Garrison was one of the early leaders of the American Anti-Slavery Society. By 1839, the society had some 250,000 members. A major break occurred in the society in late 1839, when the Liberty Party was formed by abolitionists who wanted to work within the political system, as opposed to Garrison's rejection of the political process. The Liberty Party held its first national convention in April 1840 and nominated a slate for the presidential elections of 1840. (Salmon P. Chase joined the party in 1841; he joined Lincoln's cabinet in 1861 and later became chief justice of the United States.) The party faded away by the mid-1850s, as its ideas were taken over by more mainstream parties.

The British foreign secretary, Lord Palmerston, had made the elimination of the African slave trade his personal cause, but the Portuguese and Spanish were being difficult, since they had great colonies in the Americas that needed a continuous influx of new slaves. So, in 1839, Lord Palmerston decided to try to enlist the help of Pope Gregory XVI. The papal representatives explained to the British that the pope could not help if it were to appear that he was acting at the request of a Protestant government. Patient diplomacy worked.[21] On December 6, 1839, the pope issued a document, which began with the words "At the Supreme Summit of the Apostolate" (in Latin, *In supremo Apostolatus fastigo*), published as a pamphlet. In it, the pope wrote to dissuade the faithful from "the inhuman trade in Blacks or any other kind of men." The slave trade was strictly prohibited.[22]

In the United States, the pope's *In supremo* was read aloud by abolitionists in Boston's Faneuil Hall, and Gregory XVI was cheered. During the 1840 presidential election campaign, Secretary of State Forsyth, a Democrat and slaveholder from Georgia, wrote to his former constituents in Georgia, trying to link the Whig candidate, Harrison, with the pope and abolitionism. Forsyth argued that the pope's statement condemned the sale of slaves within the United States, not only the international slave trade. Bishop John England of Charleston, South Carolina, the leading Catholic prelate in the United States, made the response. Bishop England wrote articles asserting that the Catholic Church had always accepted domestic slavery, which was "not incompatible with the natural law."[23]

The slave trade in America had changed dramatically since the early years. In the eighteenth century, most slaves sold in British North America were imported, from the Caribbean or directly from Africa. But, after the American Revolution, and dramatically more so after the import of foreign slaves was banned in 1808, the domestic slave trade blossomed. Most Southeastern states found they had a surplus of slaves, and the demand from the newly opened lands in the Southwest required a relatively massive redistribution of the slave population. The market value of a slave in Richmond now depended on what a buyer in New Orleans would pay.[24] The number of slaves in New Orleans in 1835 was larger than the entire population of the city in 1806.[25] The cotton gin led to the explosion of land devoted to cotton, and the new, easily available lands in Mississippi, Alabama, and Louisiana were ideal. Since growing and harvesting cotton was labor intensive, slaves were needed. The Chesapeake Bay region (Delaware, Maryland, and Virginia) became the main source of slaves for the domestic slave trade, and "professional" slave traders developed and spread. Not only was this domestic slave trade an outlet for surplus slaves in that region; it also provided a channel for slave owners to get rid of "troublesome" slaves.

New Orleans was America's third most populous city in 1840 and was a very cosmopolitan place. Its wharves groaned beneath the weight of "corn from Illinois, whiskey from Kentucky, cheese from Wisconsin, furs from the Canadian backcountry, and, of course, towering piles of the [Mississippi] Valley's monarch: King Cotton arrayed in bales that reached for the heavens."[26] In eleven months of 1835 alone, some 2,300 steamboats arrived in the port, and that did not include the thousands of river-bound flatboats and oceangoing vessels that competed for dock space.[27] New Orleans was originally an outback of the French Empire; Emperor Louis XV gave it to Spain in 1762. Judged by colonial standards, Spain's rule was relatively progressive. When Spain withdrew shortly before the Louisiana Purchase (1803), "no other Southern city had as many taverns that catered to slaves or as many free people of color."[28] Plantation owners' best and most liquid asset were their slaves; and in New Orleans even free people of color made up a sizable class of slave owners.[29]

The Panic of 1837 caused the price of cotton to sink dramatically, and so the price for slaves dropped correspondingly. By the early 1840s, however, the markets for both began to rebound. The domestic slave trade was somewhat seasonal. Most slaves in the upper Southeast were sold in the fall, after they had worked the harvest. The slaves were transported to the lower southeast or to the southwest for sale and distribution there in the winter and early spring, so that they would be available for work during the spring planting. Auctioneers played a major role in these transactions. In Richmond, several firms had a lucrative business, sometimes selling hundreds of slaves a day from their auction rooms.

Abolitionists identified the domestic slave trade as the key to the destruction of American slavery. If that interstate trade could be prohibited, slavery could no longer survive. By the 1830s this became a major abolitionist theme. The issue was whether it was constitutionally permissible. Clearly, the federal government had no authority to ban slavery in the states. However, Congress did have power over interstate commerce and the commerce on the high seas. Abolitionists argued, sensibly, that if Congress had the power to outlaw the international African slave trade, as it did in 1808, surely it had the legal power to ban the domestic interstate slave trade. The defenders of slavery, in turn, argued that Congress could not interfere with property rights, and that the power to regulate interstate commerce did not include the power to destroy it.[30] The Supreme Court never rendered an opinion on the question before it became moot by the addition of the Thirteenth Amendment in December 1865.

The abolitionists' arguments were brilliantly set forth in 1839 by William Jay, the son of the first chief justice of the United States, John Jay.[31] William Jay was a leading abolitionist and judge in New York; he had drafted the constitution for the American Anti-Slavery Society. William Jay's 1839 book was titled *A View of the Action of the Federal Government, in Behalf of Slavery*.[32] It was a broad attack on the moral bankruptcy of slavery, the excessive political power held by the South, and the political weakness of the Northern political figures. It was also a legal attack on the misconstruction of the Constitution, as he saw it.

Jay referred to the most recent (1836) presidential election campaign, where the candidates were Van Buren, White, Harrison, and Webster, under the heading "The Obsequiousness of the Presidential Candidates." Jay said Van Buren explained that he was "uncompromisingly" against any effort of the Congress to abolish slavery in the District of Columbia, Hugh White claimed that Congress had no power to do so, and General Harrison agreed. Only Daniel Webster, a failed Whig candidate, made no proslavery pledge, and he received no votes from any slave state. Jay attacked the Fugitive Slave Act for being a deviation from the Constitution. In a broad and biting comment, Jay charged that since the time of the adoption of the Constitution, the profits from cotton—and therefore slavery—had paralyzed "the conscience of the nation" and divested the nation "of the sense of shame."

Jay described the problems that occurred during the War of 1812, when many slaves took the opportunity of the presence of British armed vessels to escape from bondage, and how the 1814 Treaty of Ghent—which ended the war—dealt with that problem. Under the treaty, the British had to return property (slaves) originally captured in forts, but there was no reference to slaves who had voluntarily sought protection on British ships. Jay reported that British Admiral Cockburn[33] refused to surrender any fugitive slaves, since the treaty did not require it!

Though his book was published two years before the *Creole* affair began, Jay was prescient in describing the experience of American coastal slave

Figure 1.1. A broadside published by the American Anti-Slavery Society in 1836, condemning slavery in the District of Columbia. The images on the bottom level illustrate slaves in chains, a ship loading slaves, and a slave holding pen.

ships that were wrecked and their slaves freed in the British Caribbean colonies: the 1831 *Comet*, the 1833 *Encomium*, and the 1835 *Enterprise*. Jay attacked the use of American diplomacy to demand compensation from the British:

> Thus, for six successive years did the Cabinet at Washington keep sending despatches [*sic*] to their agents [American Envoys] in England, urging them to obtain payment from Great Britain for these *cargoes* of human flesh. . . . Mr. Stevenson [the American Minister] tried the virtue of a diplomatic hint that the United States would go to war for their slaves.[34]

In bitter language, Jay exposed the power of slave interests over the federal government, both the Congress and the Executive. He pointed out that if a murderer should escape from England and land in the United States, the United States would refuse to surrender him. In contrast, "when West India [*sic*] authorities refuse to deliver two hundred and eighty-seven innocent men, women, and children, thrown by the tempest under their protection, into hopeless interminable slavery," Congress pronounces it an outrage to the American flag! By so protecting the coastal slave trade, he claimed, the federal government was indeed protecting the slave trade, which all civilized nations outlaw.

Jay attacked a great variety of examples of what he termed the "Federal Government Slave Power": the congressional gag rule (ban on slavery petitions), the refusal to recognize the government of Haiti,[35] the effort to secure independent Texas as a slave state, and the censoring of the mails. Finally, Jay suggested that the day might well come when the South would make an effort to secede. Interestingly, Jay then presented some of the arguments as to why secession would not be in the South's best interests—including some used by Lincoln in his first inaugural address twenty-two years later.

THE PRESIDENT

When Martin Van Buren became president in March 1837, his timing could not have been worse. Up until then, he had compiled an extraordinary resume: he was attorney general of New York (1815–1819), US senator from New York (1821–1828), governor of New York (1829), secretary of state (1829–1831), and US minister to Britain (1831–1832). In Andrew Jackson's second term, Van Buren was the vice president (1833–1837). He was the Northern anchor of the Jacksonian Democrats. Van Buren was the first president who was not born a British subject. But that year also turned out to be the beginning of the worst recession America had known: the Panic of 1837 brought widespread bankruptcies and joblessness. It was no wonder, then, that Van Buren lost his bid for reelection in 1840, and the Democrats were damaged nationally.

The Whigs held their first national convention in Pennsylvania in early December 1839, almost a year before the next presidential election. The candidates were William Henry Harrison, a sixty-seven-year-old war hero from Ohio; Henry Clay of Kentucky, the Whig's congressional leader with almost solid Southern support; and General Winfield Scott. Scott was a hero of the War of 1812, and managed the Second Seminole War in 1836 and the removal of the Cherokee Nation in 1838. Scott had also successfully reduced tensions along the New York and Maine borders with Canada, in early 1838 and 1839, respectively. A young Whig from Illinois, Abraham Lincoln, came out for Harrison chiefly because he felt that old military heroes should be honored.[36]

Clay and Harrison were nearly tied on the first ballot, with Clay slightly ahead. Then, Scott seemed to have some momentum, but Thaddeus Stevens, a young Pennsylvania state legislator and abolitionist, passed a letter to the Virginia delegation that was purportedly from Scott to New York abolitionists expressing support. That letter was enough for the Virginia delegation to withdraw from Scott.[37] On the third ballot, Harrison clearly won. At bottom, suggests one scholar, the Whigs turned to Harrison because "he had a good war record, was personable and dignified, and had not held office long enough or recently enough to have much baggage."[38]

The Whigs decided that, for vice president, they needed a Southerner in order to balance Harrison and also to soothe the unhappy Clay supporters. Serious Clay men were too bitter at their loss to agree to run. Perhaps the party leaders were somewhat desperate when they finally chose John Tyler of Virginia. Daniel Webster, and virtually everyone else who might have been a "first choice," rejected the idea of accepting the vice presidential nomination—a post that traditionally was virtually meaningless. John Tyler had been a congressman, governor of Virginia, and a US senator when he was chosen as Harrison's vice president. He had not been close politically to the Whig leaders, but that had been deemed unimportant for the vice presidential position. No president had ever died in office.

The presidential contest of 1840 is considered the first "modern" election campaign. It had great theater: torchlight parades, catchy slogans, and campaign songs. Harrison had defeated the Shawnee Indians in the Battle of Tippecanoe in 1811, and hence the slogan: "Tippecanoe and Tyler too." One wag concluded that the ticket had "rhyme but no reason to it."[39] Tyler remained inactive during most of the campaign, at Harrison's request; his main contribution was his surname.[40]

President Martin Van Buren was a Democrat from Kinderhook, New York. Naturally, he became known as "Old Kinderhook." Thus, the phrase "OK" entered the general vocabulary. "OK Clubs" were formed to ridicule

Figure 1.2. General Winfield Scott, circa 1847.

Van Buren's opponent, Harrison. A Democratic newspaper ridiculed Harrison for being old and ineffectual, and suggested that he would be happier in a log cabin with a barrel of hard cider.[41] Harrison and the Whigs turned this slap into an emblem of frontier honesty and honor: Harrison adopted the log cabin and hard cider as his campaign symbols—connected to the common man, in the style of the popular Andrew Jackson. (In reality, Harrison lived in a twenty-two-room mansion with a large wine cellar in Indiana.) The "common man" style was in contrast to the lifestyle of the Van Buren White House, which

> sparkled with excellent food, fine wine, and witty conversation. [Van Buren] wrangled a sixty-thousand-dollar appropriation from Congress to refurbish the Executive Mansion and spent it on gold plate, goblets, marble mantles and Royal Wilton carpets. . . . Van Buren soon learned, however, that too great a love of luxury could be politically harmful.[42]

The election was a sweeping Whig victory. Harrison received 53 percent of the popular vote, and a landslide of 234 electoral votes to the Democrats' 60. The election stimulated the participation of 80.2 percent of the eligible voters, the greatest percentage ever.[43] Although Harrison captured nineteen of the twenty-six states, the voting pattern was not sectional: the Democrats (Van Buren) captured the lead in New Hampshire in the North; Virginia, South Carolina, and Alabama in the South; and Illinois, Missouri, and Arkansas in the West. Former president John Quincy Adams did not have a high opinion of Harrison. Adams had reluctantly appointed Harrison to be the US minister to Colombia in 1828, when Adams was president, but described Harrison as a "shallow mind, a political adventurer, not without talents, but self-sufficient, vain and indiscreet."[44] Adams declined an invitation to attend Harrison's inaugural.

After his election, Harrison's first task was to appoint the members of his cabinet. Quite unlike today's fifteen members of the presidential cabinet, there were only six cabinet positions for him to fill.[45] The first among equals in the cabinet was the secretary of state. Henry Clay and Daniel Webster were the powerful Whig leaders in Congress, and Harrison offered the position of secretary of state to Senator Clay, but Clay declined the offer. Clay recommended Webster, and Harrison agreed, as did Webster.[46]

Daniel Webster was probably America's most renowned lawyer. He was "one of the greatest advocates who has ever appeared before the Supreme Court," as judged by the late Chief Justice William Rehnquist.[47] Webster argued 171 cases before the US Supreme Court over thirty-seven years, a record never surpassed.[48] His cases include the landmark defense of his alma mater (Dartmouth) in 1819[49] and the famous case of *Gibbons v. Ogden*[50] in 1824, in which he supported a broad congressional commerce power. Webster's friend from Massachusetts, the brilliant Supreme Court Justice William Story, was the source of the statement that whenever Webster spoke in court, "a large circle of ladies, of the highest fashion, and taste, and intelligence, numerous lawyers, and gentlemen of both houses of Congress, and, toward the close, the foreign ministers, or at least two or three of them" crowded in to listen.[51]

Webster had twice served in the House (1812–1817 and 1823), and in the Senate (1827–1841), where he was perhaps the greatest orator of his day. Indeed, the record of Webster's dramatic debate encounter with South Carolina Senator Robert Y. Hayne on the nature of the Union in January 1830, at the opening of the 21st Congress, remains a basic document in American history.[52] The Webster-Hayne debate was a foreshadowing of the secession and Civil War thirty years later. It was in that debate that Webster's famous peroration concluded: "Liberty and Union, now and forever, one and inseparable!"[53] The Webster-Hayne debate continued for months, and involved twenty-one of the Senate's forty-eight members in sixty-five speeches.

Webster supported President Jackson's actions to suppress South Carolina's lurch toward nullification and secession, but, like Clay, opposed Jackson's economic policies, especially Jackson's campaign against the National Bank. Webster joined with Clay (and other former Federalists and National Republicans) to form the Whig Party in 1833. In 1836, Webster unsuccessfully sought the presidency. When the party nominated Harrison for president in 1840, Webster was offered the vice presidency, but declined.

Harrison filled out the rest of his cabinet with five Whigs, all lawyers, reflecting a geographic balance: Thomas Ewing, who had been a senator from Ohio, became the secretary of the treasury; on the advice of Webster, Harrison appointed John Bell, former speaker of the House from Tennessee, as secretary of war; Harrison appointed the senator from Kentucky, John Crittenden, as attorney general (John Quincy Adams had nominated Crittenden to the US Supreme Court in 1828, but the nomination failed); Francis Granger, a House member from New York was appointed postmaster general; and George E. Badger, a Whig political leader in North Carolina, was appointed secretary of the navy. None of Harrison's cabinet members had strong ties to Vice President Tyler. Harrison had not sought Tyler's advice on his cabinet appointments, and Tyler offered no advice. However, Tyler expressed to friends that Webster would not have been his first choice for secretary of state, because he feared that Webster's selection would touch off a factional struggle.[54]

At 11:00 a.m. on March 4, 1841, the Senate galleries were packed to capacity for hours. John Tyler entered the room accompanied by the justices of the Supreme Court and the diplomatic corps. The president pro tempore of the Senate, William R. King, then swore in Tyler as vice president, after which Tyler offered a three-minute address. Shortly after noon, the party rose from the Senate and moved to the Capitol's east portico, where a crowd of fifty thousand waited to witness the oath taking of President Harrison. Deter-

Figure 1.3. Secretary of State Daniel Webster, at the end of his first term of service as secretary, 1843.

mined to demonstrate his virility, Harrison did not wear a hat or an overcoat as Chief Justice Roger B. Taney administered the oath of office.

Webster had worked hard to edit Harrison's ninety-minute, 8,445 word inaugural speech, given in a snowstorm on March 4, 1841, the longest inaugural speech on record. The address was filled with Roman references and Greek philosophies. Harrison set out to present a "summary of the principles" that would govern him in the discharge of his duties. One of his principles was that there was great danger in the "accumulation" of power by any of the branches of government, and, specifically, he believed that the president should be limited to only one term. Until the Constitution could be so amended, Harrison said, he would renew the "pledge heretofore given that under no circumstances will I consent to serve a second term."

Harrison caught a cold, and it turned into pneumonia, which on March 27, the physicians deemed "not dangerous."[55] The doctors bled him and gave him a regimen of laudanum and brandy, and other medical care. On April 1, Webster sent word to Tyler at his plantation in Virginia that Harrison was gravely ill. It would have been unseemly for Tyler to rush to Harrison's bedside in anticipation of succeeding to the highest office.[56] Harrison suffered a relapse, and died early on April 4. He was sixty-eight years old. Webster sent his son, Fletcher,[57] and the Senate assistant doorkeeper, Robert Beale, to Tyler to report Harrison's death. Tyler was asleep when Fletcher Webster and Beale arrived on horseback at one o'clock in the morning.[58] After sunrise, Tyler journeyed by horseback and boat to get back to Washington at 4:00 a.m. the following day.[59]

Former president John Quincy Adams worried for the nation, because he thought so little of John Tyler:

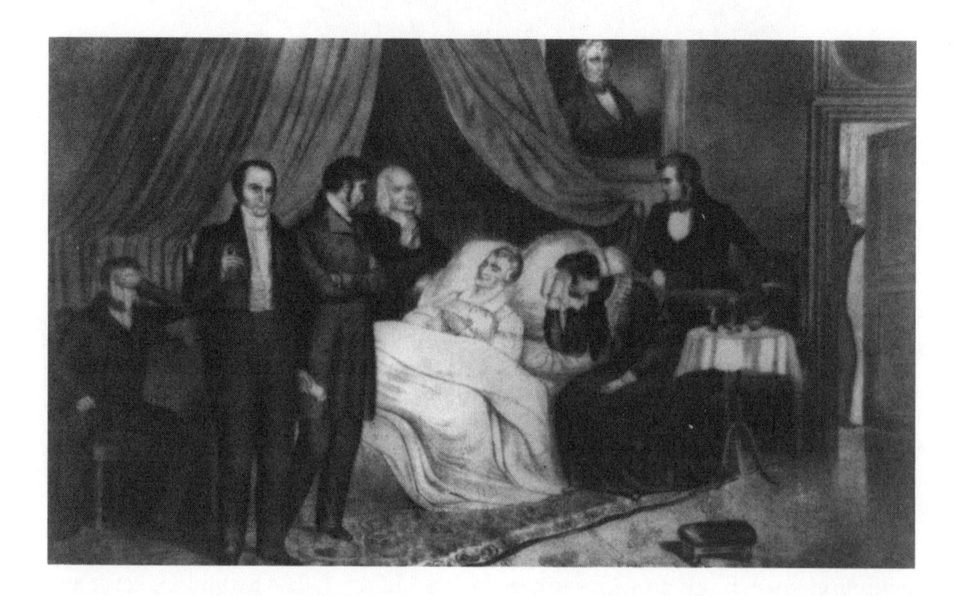

Figure 1.4. President Harrison on his deathbed, April 1841. Secretary of State Webster is standing, the second figure on the left. Postmaster General Francis Granger is standing in the doorway.

> Tyler is a political sectarian, of the slave-driving, Virginian, Jeffersonian school, . . . with all the interests and passions and vices of slavery rooted in his moral and political constitution—with talents not above mediocrity, and a spirit incapable of expansion to the dimensions of the station upon which he has been cast by the hand of Providence, unseen through the apparent agency of chance. No one ever thought of his being placed in the executive chair.[60]

Despite Adams's misgivings, John Tyler came with an impressive résumé of deep governmental experience: he had served in both houses of his state legislature, in both the US House and US Senate, and as governor of his state.

Until Amendment XXV to the Constitution in 1967, the Constitution provided in Article II, Section 1:

> In the case of the removal of the President from Office or of his death, resignation, or inability to discharge the powers and duties of the said Office, the same shall devolve on the Vice President.

It was unclear, based on only the text of that section, whether it was necessary or appropriate for a vice president to be considered president in order to execute the powers and duties of the president. Tyler, not surprisingly, took the position that his vice presidential oath covered the possibility of having to take over as chief executive, and so there was no need for him to take a separate presidential oath of office. Most of the cabinet and the informed public disagreed, and so Tyler yielded and decided to take the presidential oath.

On April 6, John Tyler took the oath of office, administered by William Cranch, the chief judge of the US Circuit Court. The event took place at Brown's Indian Queen Hotel ten blocks from the White House.[61] Harrison's body lay in state in the East Room of the White House in a coffin with a glass lid that allowed mourners to see the face of a president they barely knew.[62] In addition to the new president, the cabinet, members of Congress, and the diplomatic corps were in attendance, along with seventy-three-year-old John Quincy Adams—the former president and now congressman from Massachusetts. While Adams had thought little of President Harrison, he thought far less of the new President Tyler, whom he thought was "a political sectarian, of the slave-driving, Virginian, Jeffersonian school, principled against all improvement"; Adams even thought that Tyler should refer to himself as "Acting President."[63]

On April 7, 1841, Harrison's funeral procession led from the White House, with his horse, Whitey, trotting down the street riderless. Solomon Northup, a free black man who lived in Saratoga, New York, with his wife, Anne, and three children, was in Washington that day with two new friends. He wrote in his autobiography—which formed the basis for the film *Twelve*

Figure 1.5. John Tyler, the tenth president of the United States.

Years a Slave, the 2014 Oscar winner for best picture—his impressions of the funeral procession:

> [T]here was a great pageant in Washington. The roar of cannon and the tolling of bells filled the air, while many houses were shrouded with crape, and the

> streets were black with people. As the day advanced, the procession made its appearance, coming slowly through the Avenue, carriage after carriage, in long succession, while thousands upon thousands followed on foot—all moving to the sound of melancholy music. They were bearing the dead body of Harrison to the grave.[64]

On April 9, two days after Harrison's funeral, President Tyler issued a statement, which became known as "President Tyler's Address," and which was the functional equivalent of an inaugural address. In the foreign policy part of that address, and with the British-American tensions high, Tyler promised a policy that would do justice to all countries, while submitting to injustice from none. He also urged the creation of a stronger army and navy to ensure that "the honor of the country shall sustain no blemish."

There was some uncertainty about Tyler's exact status when President Harrison died. Some suggested that he should resign, but he stood firm, explaining: "My resignation would amount to a declaration to the world that our system of government has failed."[65] But was he now the "acting" president until the next regular election? Did he have the full powers of the office? His detractors called him "His Accidency," but he was determined to be fully in charge; he was not going to be a figurehead, a mere pawn of the Whig Party, and not a placeholder—he would not be merely a vice president acting as president. At Tyler's first cabinet meeting as president, Webster informed him that, under Harrison, the cabinet made decisions on the basis of majority vote. Tyler flatly rejected that approach, and sought only the advice and counsel of the cabinet.

Tyler had been a Democrat. But, he defected for the Whig Party in 1834, because of his discomfort with Jackson's pressures on South Carolina during the nullification crisis. Tyler was a longtime advocate of states' rights,[66] and he did not support the basic principles of the Whig Party: high tariffs, federal funding for infrastructure, and a strong Congress. So, it was quite natural that the congressional Whigs were—at best—uneasy about the new President Tyler. Henry Clay, the powerful Whig senator, was especially embittered; Clay became one of Tyler's enemies, especially during Tyler's first year.

The first session of the 27th Congress convened on May 31, 1841, and that prompted Tyler's first official message to Congress on June 1, 1841. Quite in contrast to his next message on December 7 (see appendix II), he stated that it was not "deemed necessary on this occasion" to have a detailed statement with respect to foreign relations, though he mentioned Secretary of State Webster's correspondence with the British minister in Washington concerning the status of Alexander McLeod. Tyler also explained the need for territorial expansion, beginning with the desire to annex Texas and to incorporate the Pacific coast.

On domestic economic matters, Tyler conflicted almost immediately with Clay and congressional Whigs, particularly over bank legislation. Many Whigs charged that he was a renegade Democrat without allegiance to Whig principles. While he was a senator (1831–1837), Treasury Secretary Thomas Ewing supported the rechartering of the Second Bank of the United States. As secretary, Ewing proposed plans for a new depository for the federal government's funds, including a new National Bank. The Senate's Whig leader, Henry Clay, was highly supportive, but President Tyler vetoed the national bank bill for the second time in early September 1841. In the Congress, Clay and most Whigs saw Tyler's veto as the last straw. Clay and the other leaders of the Whig party, in effect, expelled Tyler from the Whig Party. The pressure was on for the cabinet to walk out on Tyler.

Postmaster General Badger hosted a dinner on September 9 to which he invited the other members of Tyler's cabinet. Each explained his intention to resign, except for Webster; one of the reasons for the dinner was to put pressure on Webster to join the mass exodus.[67] The afternoon of Saturday, September 11, 1841, was eventful. During a five-hour period, the treasury secretary (Ewing), the war secretary (Bell), the navy secretary (Badger), the postmaster general (Granger) and the attorney general (Crittenden)—all Whigs—separately walked in to President Tyler's office.[68] Each handed Tyler a letter of resignation. The single exception was Daniel Webster. This mass exodus was part of a plan by Senator Henry Clay to force Tyler himself to resign.[69] Since there was no vice president, the president pro tempore of the Senate, New Jersey Senator Samuel L. Southard, a prominent Whig, would replace Tyler. Southard happened to be a protégé of Henry Clay.

Webster asked Tyler, in effect, whether the president wanted him to stay, or to go with the others. Tyler said it was up to Webster himself. Webster said: "If you leave it to me, Mr. President, I will stay where I am." Tyler was moved by Webster's decision to remain, and the two men shook hands on the arrangement. Tyler felt he needed Webster on his side for his ongoing battle with Clay-led Whigs in the Senate and also because Webster was working hard on resolving the growing conflicts with Great Britain.[70] Webster's reasons for remaining were more complicated: though he was not a great admirer of Tyler's abilities, he and Tyler concurred on foreign affairs issues, and if Webster left the cabinet, he felt it might force Tyler's resignation and create turmoil in the nation and threaten peace. Webster also was proud of the steps he was taking to reduce tensions with Great Britain, and of course, he loved being secretary of state.[71]

Tyler quickly assembled five new cabinet members over the weekend, and by Monday, September 11, he submitted his nominations to the Senate, where they were quickly approved. The new cabinet reflected a geographic balance: Walter Forward of Pennsylvania, who had been Harrison's comptroller of the currency, moved to treasury; John C. Spencer, a New York political figure, became secretary of war; Hugh S. Legare, a South Carolina lawyer and former House member, became attorney general; Charles A. Wickliffe, a former governor of Kentucky, and somewhat of an opponent of Clay, became postmaster general; and Virginia lawyer and states' rights advocate, Abel P. Upshur, became secretary of the navy.

Attorney General Hugh Swinton Legare would play an important role in the months ahead as events relating to the *Creole* unfolded. He was born and grew up in South Carolina. His interests quickly tended toward the scholarly, particularly his interest in Roman and continental civil law, which he developed while studying at Edinburgh University in Scotland. He was also a politician. Shortly after he returned from Scotland in 1819, Swinton entered state politics, serving in the South Carolina legislature and then, in 1830, he became the state's attorney general. He held that position at a critical time: the nullification crisis over which South Carolina threatened to secede. Legare spoke out in support of the Union. Perhaps as a reward, he was given a diplomatic post in Brussels. Upon his return to the United States, he was elected to the US House of Representatives, and then he practiced law. Finally, in 1840, he became a Whig and actively supported the Harrison/Tyler ticket.

Tyler was known as an Anglophobe. On Washington's birthday, February 22, 1841, president-elect Harrison and vice president-elect Tyler attended the "twisting the lion's tail" ceremony in Richmond, a ceremony involving a ceremonial sword honoring Virginia's sons who had fought heroically against the British in the War of 1812. In contrast to Tyler, Webster was an Anglophile. He had served for years as US legal counsel for the premier British financial institution, the House of Baring. Barings helped finance the Louisiana Purchase in 1803, and, indeed, Alexander Baring himself came to the United States to pick up the US government's bonds, bring them to London, and then bring the cash to Paris. (Napoleon used the money to support his war against Britain!) In 1839, Webster and his wife, Caroline, toured the British Isles, a trip that was in part funded by Baring, and they stayed at Alexander Baring's estate in England. Baring's title was the 1st Baron Ashburton. Webster's finances had been hurt in the Panic of 1837, because he had speculated heavily in western land, and he incurred personal debt from which he never recovered. But that did not restrict his propensity for living habitually beyond his means.

THE CONGRESS

The great French observer of early America, Alexis de Tocqueville, spent nine months in the United States in 1831, and then wrote his famous *Democ-*

racy in America. In the second volume, published in 1840, he had the following comment about the US House of Representatives and the US Senate:

> When you enter the House of Representatives in Washington, you feel yourself struck by the vulgar aspect of this great assembly. Often the eye seeks in vain for a celebrated man within it. Almost all its members are obscure persons. . . . They are, for the most part, village attorneys, those in trade, or even men belonging to the lowest class. . . .
>
> Two steps away is the chamber of the Senate, whose narrow precincts enclose a large portion of the celebrities of America. . . . They are eloquent attorneys, distinguished generals, skillful magistrates, or well-known statesmen. All the words that issue from this assembly would do honor to the greatest parliamentary debates of Europe.[72]

In the Congress, the issue of slavery, thought settled by the Missouri Compromise of 1820, was forcing its way to the surface. Abolitionist sentiment was growing stronger in the North and increasingly resented in the South. Hundreds of thousands of petitions bombarded the House demanding an end to slavery in the District of Coumbia and proposing other restrictions on slavery. On May 26, 1836, the Democratic-controlled House adopted (117–68) a "gag rule" that automatically tabled petitions relating to slavery.

Figure 1.6. Houses and buildings in Washington DC in 1839. In the background is the Capitol building with its original dome, completed in 1824. The current dome was constructed 1855-1866.

Congressman (and former president) John Quincy Adams had been a member of the House since 1831. He objected to the gag rule on constitutional grounds. The following year, at the next session of the same 24th Congress, the speaker ruled that all special rules adopted in the previous session had expired. So, on January 18, 1837, the House passed (129–69) once again, the same gag rule. Adams persisted in presenting slavery-related petitions, and so a South Carolina member moved to censure Adams—for being "guilty of a gross disrespect to this House" by attempting to introduce a petition from a slave. But the motion to censure easily failed.

The 25th Congress (March 1837 to March 1839) was again Democratic controlled. Near the beginning of the second session, on December 21, 1837, a new gag rule, expanded to cover slavery in the territories as well as the District and the states, passed in the House, 122 to 74. On December 11, 1838, during the third session of the 25th Congress, freshman Congressman Charles G. Atherton, a states'-rights Democrat from New Hampshire, introduced a gag Resolution whose logic was based on the principle that Congress had no constitutional power to legislate on slavery-related issues.

The Resolution provided:

> *Resolved, therefore*, That all attempts, on the part of Congress, to abolish slavery in the District of Columbia or the Territories, or to prohibit the removal of slaves from State to State, or to discriminate between the institutions of one portion of the country and another with the views aforesaid, are in violation of the Constitution, destructive of the fundamental principles on which the Union of these States rests, and beyond the jurisdiction of Congress; and that every petition, memorial, resolution, proposition, or paper, touching or relating in any way or to any extent whatever to slavery, as aforesaid, or the abolition thereof, shall, on the presentation thereof, without any further action thereon, be laid on the table without being debated, printed, or referred.

The "Atherton" Resolution passed the next day with a vote of 126–78. At that same session, a new member from Ohio, Joshua Reed Giddings, took his seat. He was elected as a Whig to fill the vacancy caused by the resignation of Congressman Whittlesey. Giddings, from Ashtabula in northeastern Ohio, was a strong opponent of slavery, and a very successful lawyer.

At the beginning of the 26th Congress (March 1839 to March 1841), a young Whig from Virginia, Henry A. Wise,[73] moved to change the formal Rules of the House to institute a permanent gag rule. On January 28, 1840, a permanent gag rule was adopted, which prohibited even the *reception* of slavery petitions (i.e., no longer a mere Resolution relevant to a session, but a permanent change in the House Rules):

> Resolved, That no petition, memorial, resolution or other paper praying the abolition of slavery in the District of Columbia, or any State or Territory, or

the slave trade between the States of Territories . . . shall be received by this House.

The Resolution passed (114–108), and Rule 21 was adopted. In December 1840, Adams tried to rescind Rule 21, but he was defeated (82–58). Joshua Reed Giddings assisted Adams in his opposition to the gag rule.

President Van Buren, a Democrat, supported the gag rule when he was a candidate running for reelection, but that didn't help him win the election in late 1840 against the Whig, Harrison. The 27th Congress (March 1841 to March 1843) was the first with a Whig majority in the House. Since the Whigs were generally less inclined to support the gag rule, Adams anticipated success in overturning the rule. But by mid-June 1841, the Whigs were tired of the politicking and controversy surrounding the gag rule, and were eager to begin work on their policy agenda. Nevertheless, Rule 21 remained, but by a very narrow vote of 119–103.

THE SUPREME COURT

The first Supreme Court in 1789 was composed of six justices, and the Judiciary Act of 1807 increased the number to seven, corresponding to the seven judicial circuits. But by 1837, nine new states had been admitted to the Union. As a practical matter, this meant that almost one-fourth of the nation

Figure 1.7. A 1839 lithograph presenting a satire on enforcement of the "gag rule" in the US House of Representatives.

did not enjoy easy access to a circuit court, which was the chief trial court of the federal judiciary. Over the years, there had been efforts to expand the number of circuits and justices, but Congress was reluctant to give a president the opportunity to fill new seats on the court. However, on President Jackson's last full day in office, Congress passed the Judiciary Act of 1837.[74] The act reorganized the Seventh Circuit, and formed the Eighth Circuit (Ohio, Kentucky, Tennessee, and Missouri) and the Ninth Circuit (Alabama, Arkansas, Louisiana, and Mississippi). As a result, two new justices were added to reflect the two new circuits. This brought the court's membership to nine justices. The new justices were John Catron of Tennessee, nominated by President Jackson on his last day, and John McKinley of Alabama, nominated by President Van Buren in September 1837.

President Jackson nominated the new chief justice, Roger B. Taney, in December 1835. Clay, Webster, and Calhoun opposed his nomination, but Taney was confirmed on March 15, 1836. Before then, Taney had served as Jackson's attorney general (1831–1833) and secretary of the treasury (1833–1834). As he presided over the court for the first time in January 1837, "Taney wore plain democratic trousers, not knee breeches, under his robe."[75] With Taney and the expansion of the circuits and the membership of the court, the Supreme Court entered a new era.

At the beginning of 1841, six of the nine justices sitting on the bench of the Supreme Court were appointed by President Andrew Jackson (Baldwin, Barbour, Catron, McLean, Taney, and Wayne), and one each by presidents Van Buren (McKinley), Madison (Story), and Monroe (Thompson). Justice Story had served the longest, since 1812, and Justice McKinley was the newest, serving only three years. On February 25, 1841, Justice Philip Barbour died; a week later, President Van Buren nominated Peter V. Daniel, and the Senate confirmed him on January 10, 1842. Both Barbour and Daniel were Virginians. Five of the nine judicial circuits were composed of slave states.

At that time, the justices only met in Washington for short periods, between January and March, while for the rest of the year, the justices served in their respective circuits for at least two sessions a year. In early 1841, the Supreme Court decided two important slavery-related cases.[76] Both cases were argued in February and decided in March. One was the dramatic and emotional maritime slavery controversy, the *Amistad*; the other was a relatively obscure case involving the interstate slave trade and Mississippi.

The *Amistad* case was not the first case involving the international slave trade that was brought before the court. The first case was the *Antelope*,[77] which, in 1825, presented the question of the legitimacy of the international slave trade. A privateer had captured the slave ship, the *Antelope*, and it was in turn seized by an American revenue cutter, USS *Dallas*, and brought to Savannah for trial in June 1820. President Monroe instructed Secretary of

State John Quincy Adams to advise the US district attorney that an African brought into US jurisdiction "must be free."[78] A jury acquitted the captain of the *Antelope*, John Smith, but then he entered the parallel civil proceedings in admiralty, seeking the return of the ship and cargo, competing with the captain of the *Dallas* and the Portuguese and Spanish original owners of the ship. The Sixth Circuit Court held that the US prohibition against the slave trade was not applicable to foreign vessels, and noted that the slave trade was not prohibited by the law of nations—thus, the ship and its cargo had to be returned to its original owners.

An appeal from the circuit court was docketed at the Supreme Court in 1822, but it was held over for argument until 1825. The question that reached the Supreme Court was what to do with hundreds of Africans found on board and claimed by both Portuguese and Spanish slavers. Attorney General William Wirt[79] and Francis Scott Key argued the US position in February 1825 that the case presented a conflict between a "claim to freedom" and a "claim to property." Wirt asserted that the slave trade violated international law, and therefore the Africans were free, and could not be considered merchandise. The arguments attracted overflow crowds.[80]

Chief Justice John Marshall wrote the Opinion for the Court. Marshall acknowledged that the slave trade was contrary to nature, but—however noxious—it "could not be pronounced repugnant to the law of nations."[81] Therefore, some thirty Spanish slaves were returned to their claimant/owners, but some 120 apparent Portuguese slaves were repatriated, since there was no evidence that they actually belonged to anyone. Marshall's decision clarified that American courts were not available for condemning foreign vessels engaged in the slave trade.[82]

In 1837, the Supreme Court decided a somewhat bizarre case involving the international slave trade prohibition. Slave owners from New Orleans visited France and took their slaves with them. When the slaves returned to New Orleans, zealous federal authorities tried to seize the ships that carried them from France, charging that seizure was proper, since the federal law prohibiting the importation of slaves into the United States was violated. Chief Justice Taney presided over the court for the first time and wrote the Opinion for the Court. In a voice that suggests frustration, Taney said that the law was "obviously pointed against the introduction of negroes or mulattoes who were inhabitants of foreign countries, and cannot properly be applied to persons of colour who are domiciled in the United States, and who are brought back to their place of residence, after a temporary absence."[83] No law was violated by the return of the slaves. (This idea—that a slave does not lose his slave status by virtue of a "temporary sojourn" in a location where there is no slave law—was presented again exactly twenty years later by Chief Justice Taney in the famous *Dred Scott* case.)

United States v. Amistad[84]

Even though Spanish law prohibited the slave trade from Africa to Spanish-ruled Cuba, the Spanish government officials looked the other way, because the great sugar plantations needed slave labor. Two planters bought Africans at a slave market in Havana and chartered space for fifty-three Africans on a Spanish schooner, the *Amistad*, which was sailing from Havana to the plantations along the north coast of Cuba in the Province of Puerto Principe. During the voyage in July 1839, a group of ethnic Mende from present-day Sierra Leone in west Africa revolted, killed the captain and the ship's cook, and self-emancipated themselves.[85] They coerced the Spanish to sail eastward to Africa, but the captive crew deceived the slaves and directed the schooner in a northerly direction along the American east coast. In late August, the *Amistad* was seized, along with its "cargo" of forty-two surviving African Mende, off the coast of Long Island by commander Lieutenant Thomas Gedney on the revenue cutter the *Washington.* The *Amistad* was towed to New London, Connecticut, and there, Lieutenant Gedney submitted a written statement (technically, a libel) claiming the rights to the salvage of the schooner and its cargo. Under traditional marine law, compensation is permitted to persons who save a ship and its cargo from impending loss. The fact that Lieutenant Gedney was acting in his official capacity was irrelevant at that time to his claim for salvage rights.[86]

There ensued an extremely complex set of judicial proceedings.

On August 29, 1839, Judge Judson of the US District Court for Connecticut convened a special session to set a date to hear the claim for a salvage award. In addition, the US attorney announced that he would bring criminal charges against the leaders of the revolt; they were indicted for murder and piracy. A committee of abolitionists, led by Lewis Tappan, raised funds and assembled a team of lawyers to defend the Africans. Roger Sherman Baldwin[87] of New Haven (grandson of the Revolutionary War figure, Roger Sherman), and Seth Staples and Theodore Sedgewick, both New York lawyers, came to their defense, technically serving as "proctors." The Van Buren administration stationed a navy schooner in New London's harbor to await the verdict, ready to sail the Africans back to Cuba.[88] The US Circuit Court for the District of Connecticut convened on September 17 and impaneled a grand jury, but the presiding judge (Supreme Court Justice Thompson, sitting as a circuit judge) ruled that the court had no jurisdiction over an alleged crime that took place on the high seas in a non-US vessel. On the other hand, Thompson decided that he could not release the Africans, since they were also the subjects of property claims in the admiralty case before the district court.

On January 7, 1840, Judge Judson opened the maritime trial in the district court. After a five-day trial, the judge announced that the Africans were not slaves, and so he could not order their return to Cuba. Judge Judson also awarded Lieutenant Gedney and his crew one-third of the value of the vessel and its nonslave cargo, as a salvage award. On April 29, the US Circuit Court heard the appeal of Judge Judson's decision. Justice Thompson quickly upheld the Judson decision, and the case moved quickly to the US Supreme Court on appeal by the US attorney.

From the beginning, the British government brought diplomatic pressure on the Van Buren administration to release the Africans. The British minister in Washington, Henry S. Fox, leaned hard on Secretary of State Forsyth, arguing that the United States had treaty obligations under international law to suppress the slave trade. Forsyth responded by explaining—yet again—that, under the US Constitution, the courts must decide these matters of the applicability of laws without interference by the Executive.

The Spanish government was furious and insisted that the United States had no right to try a case involving harm to Spanish subjects arising from events on a Spanish ship in international waters. The Spanish demanded the immediate return to Cuba of the African slaves. Making a nice point, the Spanish pointed out that domestic slavery was permitted in the United States and in Cuba, and the courts in Cuba were the proper venue to determine the status of these slaves, just as a court in Charleston might similarly determine the status of a slave in South Carolina.

President Van Buren agreed with the Spanish. That decision was motivated, at least in part, by the fact that his reelection campaign was only a year away, and he wanted to demonstrate his administration's abhorrence of slave uprisings in order to be acceptable to the South.[89] But he hoped the Court would take the issue out of his hands.

The abolitionists' funding for the defense lawyers ran out, and only two lawyers remained on the case pro bono, including Roger Sherman Baldwin. They asked John Quincy Adams to join them in the appeal to the Supreme Court, and Adams agreed.[90] When he agreed, Adams was not expecting to make a personal court appearance; he had never had much confidence in himself as a lawyer.[91] Adams traveled to Connecticut to meet with the Mende Africans, who remained in federal custody. Adams also requested all the relevant papers from the State Department, and concluded that Secretary of State Forsyth (a Georgia slave owner) was prejudiced against the captives in his correspondence with the Spanish. Adams was interested in the precedential value of the *Antelope* case, which had been argued by Francis Scott Key, and so Adams consulted Key about the case.[92]

On Washington's birthday, February 22, 1841—at the same time that president-elect Harrison and vice president-elect Tyler were twisting the lion's tail in Richmond—the arguments began in the Supreme Court. US Attorney General Henry Gilpin, a Quaker who was born in England, presented the case for the administration. He argued that the United States had treaty obligations to return slave property to the Spanish planters in Cuba. Baldwin began the rebuttal arguments. On February 24, John Quincy Adams made his fifth, and last, appearance before the court. (The last time Adams had appeared before the court to argue a case was in 1809,[93] when Jefferson was leaving the White House.) For more than eight hours, the seventy-three-year-old Adams passionately defended the Africans' freedom on legal and moral grounds. Adams condemned the Van Buren administration for its efforts to send the Mende Africans back to Cuba. Adams also attacked the Spanish claim that the Africans were robbers and pirates:

> According to the construction of the Spanish minister, the merchandise were the robbers and the robbers were the merchandise. The merchandise was rescued out of its own hands, and the robbers were rescued out of the hands of the robbers.[94]

The fact that the former president—and current House abolitionist—played such a prominent and public role certainly infuriated Southern slaveholders.

Supreme Court Justice Philip P. Barbour died in his sleep on February 25, and so the court took a recess in his honor. During the break, Adams sought help from Above. In his diary, he prayed: "I implore the mercy of Almighty God so to control my temper, to enlighten my soul, and to give me utterance, that I may prove myself in every respect equal to the task."[95] The oral arguments resumed on March 1. Adams concluded his argument and bade farewell to the court. Justice Joseph Story wrote to his wife that the old, former president's argument was "extraordinary . . . for its power, for its bitter sarcasm, and its dealings with topics beyond the record and points of discussion."[96]

Five days after the inaugural of President Harrison, on March 9, 1841, Justice Joseph Story, the court's senior member by ten years, delivered the Opinion of the Court. Six justices joined Story, including Justice Thompson, who had heard the circuit court case in Connecticut. Story said that the Africans had never been slaves, and ordered them freed. Justice Henry Baldwin dissented but wrote no opinion. In seizing the *Amistad*, wrote Story, the Africans had exercised the "ultimate right of all human beings in extreme cases to resist oppression and to apply force against ruinous injustice." Story made no rhetorical excess comments about slavery—perhaps to draw his Southern colleagues to his side—and construed the legal issues narrowly to accommodate both moderate antislavery and proslavery interests.[97]

Adams asked his friend from Massachusetts, the new secretary of state, Daniel Webster, to talk with the navy secretary, Upshur, to arrange transport of the Africans on a US ship. But Secretary Upshur was uninterested. By early November 1841, abolitionists had raised enough money to provision a

Figure 1.8. Joseph Story, US Supreme Court justice (1811-1845), friend of Daniel Webster and drafter of the Court's Opinion in the *Amistad* case. Daguerreotype of Story by Mathew B. Brady, 1844–1845.

ship (the *Gentleman*), and on November 27—just two weeks after the *Creole* entered the harbor at Nassau—the thirty-five surviving Africans, along with one of their interpreters and five white missionaries and teachers, sailed from New York for Sierra Leone on the west coast of Africa.[98]

Although the subjects of the case were not American slaves, and therefore it was not immediately or directly relevant to American slaveholders and American abolitionists, the *Amistad* affair widened Northern antislavery sympathies and aggravated North-South enmities. It also reinforced Adams's determination to continue his crusade against slavery. And, of course, it also made Adams even more of a congressional lightning rod on the slavery question. America's relations with Spain were severely strained, since the ship and its cargo were Spanish, and Spain demanded reparations.[99]

The other major slavery case of 1841 was argued in the Supreme Court over six days in mid-February, and decided five to two on March 10, 1841: *Groves v. Slaughter*, 40 US 449 (1841). It touched on the explosive issue of the interstate slave trade and the conflict between the power of the federal government over interstate trade, on the one hand, and the power of the states over their internal police authority.

In 1832, Mississippi adopted a constitution that provided that, after May 1833, the introduction of slaves into the state—as merchandise or for sale—was prohibited, although importation of slaves by new settlers in Mississippi was permitted. The goal of this provision was not remotely antislavery. Rather, the goal was to protect the state's domestic slave regime: the price of local slaves was being depressed by commercial imports; commercial slave traders who had brought slaves into the state often misrepresented their health or character.[100] Despite this Mississippi state constitutional prohibition, a commercial slave trader, Robert Slaughter, sold some slaves in Natchez, Mississippi, in 1835–1836. The buyer gave Slaughter some promissory notes in partial payment for the slaves. The purchaser, Moses Groves, later refused to pay on the notes when they came due; Groves argued that the State's constitution made the entire transaction void. On the other hand, the seller, Robert Slaughter, claimed that the Mississippi constitution's provision was void, because it conflicted with the federal power over interstate commerce.

The case made its way to the US Supreme Court. The opening arguments were made on February 12, 1841, and continued for a full week. The court's decision, written by Justice Smith Thompson of New York, who had been appointed by President Monroe, skirted the potential federal/state conflict issue, by finding that the Mississippi constitutional provision was not self-executing: "[T]his article [of the Mississippi Constitution] does not *per se* operate as a prohibition to the introduction of slaves as merchandise, but required legislative action to bring it into complete operation."[101] Four justices—Joseph Story, Smith Thompson, James M. Wayne, and John McKinley—concurred with the court's narrow Opinion that the US Constitution did not interfere with the regulation of slaves by the Mississippi Constitution. Justice Catron was sick and did not sit on this case, and Justice Barbour died before the case was decided.

Therefore, Groves had to pay on the notes, and the court avoided getting into the question of whether a state could ban the introduction of slaves into that state for any reason. But not quite.

Justice John McLean of Ohio, appointed by President Jackson in 1829, was not a sympathizer with slavery, and he wrote a concurring Opinion. He wanted to present his belief that a state could indeed ban the interstate slave trade without violating the federal commerce clause, even though he acknowledged that Congress has the exclusive power to regulate foreign and interstate commerce. McLean explained that the US Constitution treats slaves as persons, while by the laws of certain states, "slaves are treated as property."[102] Thus, the Constitution would not permit his home state of Ohio to prohibit the introduction of Southern cotton or Northern manufactures, but the Constitution will permit a state to prohibit slavery or to regulate it. In sum, McLean asserted "Each State has a right to protect itself against the avarice and intrusion of the slave dealer, to guard its citizens against the inconveniences and dangers of a slave population."[103]

Chief Justice Roger B. Taney of Maryland had been appointed to the court by President Jackson only five years earlier, when he was Jackson's attorney general. Taney had not planned to write a separate concurring Opinion, but he felt moved to do so because of Justice McLean's comments. Taney made absolutely clear that the issue of the "power of Congress to regulate the traffic in slaves between the different States" simply was not before the court, and so McLean's comments on that topic were *dicta* (i.e., expressions in a court's Opinion that go beyond the facts before the court and so are the individual views of the author of the Opinion, and not binding in subsequent cases).[104] To counter the McLean view, Taney flatly stated his opinion that "the power over this subject [to regulate the traffic in slaves between the different states] is *exclusively* [emphasis added] with the several States . . . and the action of the several States upon this subject cannot be controlled by Congress."[105]

Taney went on to explain that he was not arguing the point, but rather he stated his opinion "on account of the interest which a large portion of the Union naturally feel on this matter" and his concern that his silence might be "misconstrued." In short, Taney was signaling to the southern slaveholding states that the chief justice felt strongly that Congress did *not* have the power to prohibit the interstate traffic in slaves. One could almost hear a sigh of relief from the slave owners and traders in Taney's Maryland or in Virginia, when they learned Taney's view that Congress had no power to block their export of surplus Chesapeake Bay–area slaves to the slave markets in New Orleans.

Another member of the court could not restrain himself from speaking out. President Jackson appointed Justice Henry Baldwin, a Pennsylvania lawyer and Yale Law School graduate, in January 1830. (He was the only dissenter in the *Amistad* case.) He too was "not willing to remain silent, lest it may be inferred that [his] opinion coincides with that of the judges who have now expressed theirs."[106] In direct contrast to McLean, Baldwin noted that though he "may stand alone among the members of this Court," he felt bound to make it clear that, in his opinion, slaves are property by the law of the states before the Constitution was adopted, and, therefore, this "right of property exists independently of the Constitution." Slaves were articles of commerce among the several states, "as property capable of being transferred from hand to hand as chattels." In short, whether slaves or bales of goods, transit of property is lawful commerce among the several states, and the Constitution protects that transit. Thus, Baldwin's comments must have warmed the hearts of Southern slaveholders concerned about protecting their right to sell slaves in the interstate trade.

Those slaveholders could take some comfort in knowing that at least two members of the court—Taney and Baldwin—believed that Congress could not prohibit the interstate trade in slaves. Moreover, the court had a five-to-four majority of justices from slaveholding states.

The issue of runaway slaves was of enormous importance to Southern slaveholders. A case—*Prigg v. Pennsylvania*—involving the obligation of Pennsylvania to permit the return of slaves to Maryland was at the doorstep of the Supreme Court in 1841.[107]

During the Constitutional Convention of 1787, South Carolina's Pierce Butler successfully proposed a provision to Article IV to require fugitive slaves to be returned.[108] The 1793 Fugitive Slave Act implemented this constitutional provision. The act allowed slave owners (or their agents) to capture fugitive slaves in the North, to bring them to any federal or state magistrate in that Northern state to obtain a "certificate of removal," and then to take the runaway back to the slave state. Northern states over the years enacted laws to protect their free black populations from kidnapping or mistaken seizure. For example, in 1840, New York State adopted a law to empower the governor to appoint and compensate agents to establish proof and take legal proceedings to restore a kidnapped free citizen held in slavery.[109] The constitutionality of such state laws, and the 1793 Federal Fugitive Slave law itself, had never been tested. But as the *Creole* entered the harbor in Nassau, a heartrending case was set for argument at the Supreme Court. The Southern slaveholders—especially those in the Upper South with borders adjacent to the free states—and the Northern abolitionists were awaiting the oral arguments, and the court's decision in early 1842.

The case began in 1837 when a "professional" slave catcher from Maryland, Edward Prigg, seized Margaret Morgan, a runaway slave living in Pennsylvania.[110] Prigg applied to a local justice of the peace for a certificate of removal under the 1793 Fugitive Slave Act and the Pennsylvania personal liberty law (protecting free blacks) of 1826. The justice of the peace refused. Nevertheless, Prigg took Margaret Morgan back to the slave state of Maryland; Pennsylvania then indicted Prigg for kidnapping under its 1826 law.

The two states entered into protracted negotiations in an effort to find the best way to reach a resolution. They finally agreed.

Maryland agreed to extradite Prigg to Pennsylvania for trial (March 7, 1838), and then Pennsylvania passed a law (May 28, 1839) that permitted the case to be expedited through the Pennsylvania Supreme Court, and from there a writ of error would take the case to the US Supreme Court to determine the power of the states to legislate on the rendition of fugitive slaves.[111] In essence, Maryland took the position that Prigg was merely executing a constitutional right and that Pennsylvania was obstructing it.[112] Pennsylvania, on the other hand, asserted that it had an obligation to protect its residents from being kidnapped.

The case heading to the Supreme Court, *Prigg v. Pennsylvania*, was the first fugitive slave case to arrive before the US Supreme Court.[113]

The issue of the rendition of fugitive slaves was critical for the slave states. It was no coincidence that in December 1860, when South Carolina seceded, it asserted that the central cause was the failure of the Northern states to comply with the Constitution's obligation to return fugitive slaves. When it seceded, South Carolina issued a "Declaration of the Immediate Causes which Induce and Justify the Secession of South Carolina from the Federal Union." After listing the ways in which the Northern states had "rendered useless" the right of slave rendition, the declaration concluded: "Thus the constitutional compact has been deliberately broken and disregarded by the non-slaveholding States, and the consequence follows that South Carolina is released from her obligation." So, in late 1841, many Southerners were waiting for the Supreme Court's decision, which was expected in early 1842.

Slave-related tensions were not limited to a federal-to-state context. A fugitive slave conflict, involving state-to-state "diplomacy," occurred between New York State and Virginia; it began in late 1839 but dragged on for years. New York was a center for abolitionist sentiment, and Virginia was the largest border slave state. A Virginia slave escaped to New York on a ship that sailed from Norfolk, Virginia. Virginia authorities charged three free black sailors (all New York State citizens) with aiding the slave's escape. Officers from Virginia traveled to New York, recovered the escaped slave, and had the three sailors jailed in New York under a Virginia warrant. Virginia sought to have the three New Yorkers extradited from New York, but New York governor William Seward refused. Seward asserted that neither the law of New York, nor international law, recognized slavery. In February 1841, the Virginia Assembly retaliated by ordering the inspection of all New York ships leaving ports of Virginia.[114]

Therefore, in late 1841, when the *Creole* entered the harbor at Nassau, major slavery issues, including the rendition of escaped slaves and the authority of the federal government to regulate (and, potentially, to eliminate) interstate transportation of slaves, were before the US Supreme Court. And the court had just dealt with a dramatic slave revolt on the high seas.

Chapter Two

US-British Relations—At the Brink

After Napoleon's defeat at Waterloo in 1815, Britain became the preeminent superpower. In 1841, Britain dominated the world well out of proportion to the size of its population, 18.5 million. (The US population was 17 million, and France's was 34 million.)[1] The Royal Navy controlled the seas. It had almost 100 ships of the line, in contrast to about fifty each for Russia and France. The US Navy consisted of only about fifteen such warships. In November 1840, Britain achieved a brilliant naval victory over Egyptian forces occupying the Syrian coast (now northern Israel) that awed military strategists everywhere: this was the first time that steam warships had been successfully used in a coordinated sea and land campaign.

Britain was The Superpower, "involved" all over the world. The Empire was a sprawling affair, a conglomeration of many parts: white colonial settlements (North America, Australia, New Zealand), the Indian Raj, and a collection of naval bases (Malta and Gibraltar), trading centers (Hong Kong and Singapore), and slave colonies in the Caribbean. The Monroe Doctrine of 1823,[2] designed to stop European colonization in the Western Hemisphere, did not stop the British from occupying the Falkland Islands in 1835. Beginning as a dispute over British sales to China of opium from India, the Anglo-Chinese Opium War erupted in November 1839, when the British blockaded the mouth of the Pearl River. By 1841, the British forces controlled Canton and Shanghai, and occupied Hong Kong.

On the other hand, the British were not always successful. The relevant blemish on its enormous power related to Afghanistan. That centered on the rivalry between Britain and Russia for influence in central Asia, known in Britain as the "Great Game" and in Russia as the "Tournament of Shadows." Britain invaded Afghanistan in 1839, because it thought that Russia was about to get there first, and Britain was worried about access to, and control of, India. The British (and Indian) force that invaded Afghanistan was massive. It included thirty thousand camels to carry baggage, three hundred of which were earmarked to carry the military's wine cellar.[3]

Only later did the British realize that they had misjudged the war's cost. By early 1841 there was serious resistance to the British.[4] By the fall, Afghan religious leaders began calling for jihad against the British. In November 1841—at about the time that the *Creole* entered the harbor in Nassau—an insurrection broke out in Kabul, and a British diplomat, Sir Alexander Burns, was murdered. It was clear that the British had to leave, and within a couple of months, the British retreated from Kabul. The retreat became a massacre, a humiliation for the British: "the retreating army of [8,000] British officers, Indian soldiers and a multitude of camp followers was slaughtered almost to a man as it struggled back through the Khyber Pass in January 1842."[5] The British force "battled through biting cold, knee-deep snow and apoplectic tribesmen. Some died from the extreme cold. But most died at the hands of Afghan sharpshooters, who picked apart the force from behind rocks, on horseback, and through daring ambushes and raids."[6] This disaster alone, one might imagine, probably was a factor in the desire of the British government to settle the outstanding controversies it had with the Americans—to cut some deal with the Americans—rather than face another distant military conflict.

The British had other worries, as they consolidated their influence and rule in south Asia, from the Middle East to China. The Ottoman Empire was Britain's chief barrier against Russia's southern expansion, but the Ottoman Empire seemed to be on the verge of collapse from within. At about the same time, Persia had entered into an alliance with Russia, seeking to recover parts of Afghanistan; this arrangement would also give Russia a road to British India.

Ever since the independence of the Republic of Texas in 1836 (recognized by the United States in March 1837), Britain had been negotiating British diplomatic recognition of the new and large republic. The two governments would have much to gain: Texas was interested in Britain as a potential protector against a threatened counterattack by Mexico; the British were interested in Texas cotton in order to break the American cotton monopoly, and an independent Texas would balance American power and lessen the threat of attack by the United States against British Canada. From the American perspective, Southerners were worried about the possibility of Britain allying with Texas as part of Britain's perceived interest in emancipating Texas's slaves. Thus, it was not surprising that in October 1841, President Tyler, the Virginia slaveholder, asked his secretary of state about the possibility of acquiring Texas by treaty, and whether the Northern states would tolerate that. Secretary Webster let it be known that the North would not reconcile itself to the concept of more land for the slave power.[7]

During the War of 1812, the British encouraged American slaves to escape from their masters and to cross over into British hands; thousands of slaves in Virginia alone crossed British lines. As one historian noted: "Slaveholding Virginians loathed the British for encouraging the runaways, which was not only potentially economically ruinous but also perceived as a direct attack on their homes and way of life. Whites lived in a constant 'cocoon of dread' of slave revolt."[8] A generation later, and viewed from the American South, London was the center of evil, or at least misguided, abolitionism, which was a part of sinister British Imperial designs. By getting the Americans to abolish slavery, the British would undercut Southern production of staples, destroy the US economy, and expand British domination of world commerce and manufacturing. Southerners were sure that the British were plotting revolution among the slaves of Cuba, and planning to incite the Mexicans and Indians against the United States. One distinguished scholar summed up the situation this way:

> Many Southerners became so alarmed by the consequences of British emancipation in the Caribbean that they pictured a British seizure of Cuba as well as the British use of black troops in an invasion of Florida and the Gulf states—all part of an overreaching plan to destroy the slave societies with which the impoverished British colonies could no longer compete.[9]

More broadly, the view of Britain held by many Americans was not helped by "contemptuous anti-American essays in British periodicals, and by unflattering descriptions by English travelers that were widely reprinted in the United States."[10] Irish immigrants in America, not surprisingly, viewed England as their eternal enemy. Some Americans even blamed the United Kingdom for the severe economic depression beginning in the late 1830s.

Queen Victoria acceded to the throne in June 1837, at age eighteen, and she married Prince Albert of Saxe in February 1840. Four months later, the Queen experienced the first assassination attempt, during her routine carriage ride in Hyde Park.[11] She used her brush with mortality to affirm her popular legitimacy with her subjects, by commanding her driver to "drive on" almost as soon as the would-be assassin's pistol was discharged.[12] Prince Albert soon became the president of the Society for the Extinction of Slavery.

England itself was free of slavery,[13] though slaves brought into England and then returned to a British colony did not become emancipated by virtue of the stay in England.[14] Britain had ended its participation in the international slave trade in 1807, though it did not stop British investment in the slave trade or the building of slave ships in British dockyards. Pressured in part by the slave revolt in the colony of Jamaica in 1831–1832, put down by the British Army,[15] Parliament provided for gradual abolition of slavery in its colonies, as of September 1834.[16] All slaves under six years old were freed immediately, and all others were freed over five years. Britain compensated the slave owners in its Caribbean colonies; the government borrowed an amount equal to about 40 percent of its budget to meet the 47,000 claims for the loss of human property.[17]

Upper-class Americans, especially in the North, admired British accomplishments, were aware of the strong US-UK economic relationships, and respected British power. On the other hand, Anglophobia coexisted with this respect. Most Americans still viewed Britain as *the* major threat to their security and prosperity. Lack of trust between the two nations was palpable. As one great scholar of the period noted: "each nation feared the other's motives and made contingency preparations for a war neither side wanted."[18]

The War of 1812 and the burning of Washington by the British had taken place only one generation earlier. Many people had heard firsthand stories from their parents and grandparents about the awful British. British Canada was the place from which Americans expected an attack.

There were two separate British colonies in Canada, prior to 1841: Lower Canada, the former French colony stretching from Montreal northeastward toward Newfoundland, along the lower portion of the St. Lawrence River; and Upper Canada, comprising what is today Ontario, along the upper portion of the St. Lawrence River. The British Parliament, in July 1840, passed the Act of Union,[19] which, as of February 1841, abolished the legislatures of Lower Canada and Upper Canada, and established a new single political entity, the Province of Canada, to replace them. The new, merged colony had its seat of government in Kingston.

Three serious disturbances along the US border with British Canada cast long and dark shadows over US-British relations.

THE *CAROLINE* AFFAIR

In November 1837, a rebellion began in Lower Canada against the British colonial government, and it spread to Upper Canada. During these rebellions, sympathetic militias were formed in the United States. They fomented anti-British sentiment and helped the insurgents in Upper Canada, despite the efforts of the US government to maintain order and to restrain cooperation with the rebels. US law provided penalties against any Americans who aided "expeditions or enterprises" directed against any country at peace with the United States. In December 1837, some of the rebel leaders tried to raise forces in Buffalo, New York. The rebels set up a headquarters on Navy Island, which was on British territory just across the Niagara River from Schlosser, New York. Hundreds of Americans crossed by steamer to Navy Island to help the rebels.

On December 29, 1837, forty-five men, under the command of a British naval officer, left Upper Canada, rowed across the Niagara River, and stormed the US merchant ship the *Caroline*, which was docked at Schlosser, New York. The forty-six-ton ship had been hired by the American insurgents to transport supplies and men to Navy Island. The British officer ordered that the ship should be set on fire and be allowed to drift toward Niagara Falls. The ship sank, wreckage dropped over the falls, and an American citizen was killed. This incident led to a famous international law formulation setting out the limits of when a nation might resort to force.[20] One scholar noted that the *Caroline* case changed self-defense "from a political excuse to a legal doctrine."[21]

This British action provoked outrage in the United States, especially in New York State. Some called for a declaration of war against the United Kingdom. President Van Buren learned of the *Caroline* affair on January 4, 1838, just before a dinner he was hosting. General Winfield Scott and Kentucky Senator Henry Clay waited some time for the dinner to begin, but they

Figure 2.1. The American steamer *Caroline*, set on fire by British forces in December 1837, and sent adrift over Niagara Falls. This incident led to the US formulation on the limits of when a nation might resort to force.

were told that the president was in a cabinet meeting. Finally, Van Buren, "drawn and pale,"[22] entered the room and ordered Scott to go the Niagara border to establish calm. Secretary of War Poinsett was writing Scott's instructions at the same time. The president, a New Yorker himself, knew that war would be a disaster. Scott had been a hero of the War of 1812, and led the capture of the British Fort George at the Niagara River in Ontario in 1813. By mid-January, Scott was successful in persuading the American militias to abandon Navy Island, and some local calm was restored. Nevertheless, the British increased their fleet on the Great Lakes, and many Americans remained outraged at the British.

President Van Buren sent a message to Congress on January 5, 1838, asking for full powers to restrain unauthorized American actions. On the same day, Secretary of State John Forsyth sent a note to the British minister in Washington, Henry S. Fox, complaining about the outrage and suggesting redress. Fox's reply justified the attack on the *Caroline* on the basis of "self-defense." On May 22, 1838, US Minister Stevenson in London delivered to the British Foreign Secretary, Lord Palmerston, a formal US diplomatic claim for redress for the burning of the *Caroline*. Stevenson's note was in essence a legal brief based on international law. Lord Palmerston replied in early June, promising a substantive reply soon. In fact, the foreign secretary did not respond in full until more than three years later.

The local population in Buffalo remained inclined toward retaliation, and further conflict remained possible. Indeed, in late 1840, a congressman from the Buffalo area, Millard Fillmore, demanded redress from the British and sought funds to enhance the US Navy, especially in the Great Lakes.[23] The British government had already been bringing up militia and increasing the number of regular soldiers, but when news of the *Caroline* reached London, the British added further regiments. By 1840, almost 12,000 British regulars were in Canada. While aimed primarily at ending the rebellion and calming the border, this military presence also reflected a growing apprehension of war with the United States.

THE MCLEOD AFFAIR

Lewiston, New York, is a small town on the Niagara River, about halfway between Lake Ontario and Niagara Falls. On November 12, 1840, Alexander McLeod, a deputy sheriff from Upper Canada, while passing through Lewiston, New York, foolishly boasted of his part in the burning of the *Caroline*. Not surprisingly, he was promptly arrested by New York State authorities on murder and arson charges. At that point, the Van Buren administration just had been repudiated at the polls, and Van Buren himself was reluctant to upset his relations with his fellow New Yorkers. And so, as one scholar put it, better "to leave the unholy mess in the hands of this Whig successor, William Henry Harrison."[24]

The British minister in Washington, Henry Fox, wrote to Secretary of State Forsyth on December 13, 1840, demanding that McLeod be released. Fox took the position that everyone knew that McLeod had not been involved in the attack on the *Caroline*, but that, even if he had been, his involvement was as a part of an official action of the British government, and so should have no individual liability. This was not unlike a criminal defense plea: "I didn't shoot him, but if I had, it was in self-defense." In response, Forsyth took a position reflecting the federal nature of the American system: this was not a federal matter. McLeod was free to assert any defense he desired in a New York court, including that he was immune under international law.

In February 1841, a New York grand jury indicted McLeod on seventeen counts. The British foreign secretary, Lord Palmerston, told US Minister Stevenson in London that "if McLeod is executed, there must be war." Also in February, the chairman of the House Foreign Affairs Committee (Francis Pickens of South Carolina) publicly aired a report expressing concern about Britain's power, focused on the *Caroline* and the McLeod affairs. He declared Britain a global menace.

Daniel Webster became President Harrison's secretary of state on March 6, 1841. Former secretary of state Forsyth must have been delighted to pass off to Webster the international hot potato of the McLeod affair. Just six days after the new secretary took office, British Minister Fox wrote to Webster. Fox once again asserted that McLeod should be released, because he could have no personal responsibility for having engaged in actions taken by the British government. Fox pointed out in his March 12 letter that it was absurd for the US government to claim that it had no power to interfere with New York State on this matter. If that were the case, Fox asserted,

> such a doctrine . . . would go at once to a dissolution of the Union as far as its relations with foreign Powers are concerned; and that foreign Powers, in such a case, instead of accrediting diplomatic agents to the Federal Government, would send such agents not to that Government, but to the Government of each separate State.[25]

Webster's reply letter to Fox was delayed by the enormous intervening event of the death of President Harrison on April 4.

In the meantime, political pressures mounted in both countries. The US Minister in London since 1836, Andrew Stevenson—a holdover from the Van Buren administration—wrote to Webster on March 18, 1841, reporting that the British press and the people had the "strongest feelings of indignation" toward the United States because of the *Caroline* and the McLeod affair. Both the United States and the United Kingdom began military preparations. That same month, Russian Czar Nicholas offered to mediate the dispute, since he decided that a US-UK war would be harmful to Russian trade and alliances. His offer was not accepted.

Webster finally replied to Fox, the British minister in Washington, on April 24, 1841. Webster dealt with both the McLeod affair and with the *Caroline* issue. His letter contained what has become known as the famous "*Caroline* Rule" in international law. In a legally correct and politically brilliant step, Webster agreed with the British position that, under international law, McLeod could not be held personally liable for any acts ordered by the British government. Threading the needle, however, Webster explained—as had Forsyth—that under the US federal system, Washington could not order the release of someone held by New York State legal authorities.[26] After thus extending a nod to the British understanding of international law, Webster presented the now famous position that the British attack on the *Caroline* itself violated international law: international law required a proper assertion of "self-defense," and, in order to justify an attack, a nation must demonstrate the "necessity of self-defense, instant, overwhelming, leaving no choice of means, and no moment for deliberation."[27]

Webster then focused on the local legal situation in New York. He asked US Attorney General John Crittenden to meet with Governor Seward of New York to figure out some way to release McLeod. But Seward refused. Then, Webster decided that McLeod's local lawyers were not up to the task, and he pressured Crittenden to make sure that McLeod had a first-class lawyer. Quickly, a highly respected lawyer, Joshua A. Spencer, appeared as McLeod's counsel and—with amazing "coincidence"—Spencer also was named a US district attorney. McLeod's lawyers filed for a writ of habeas corpus in the New York State Supreme Court, which sat in New York City. Once again, with amazing coincidence, Webster showed up in New York City to meet personally with McLeod's lawyers. Despite these enormous efforts, McLeod's petition was rejected, 3 to 0, on July 12, 1841. Webster was furious.

In July 1841, President Tyler proposed legislation to strengthen the nation's land and sea defenses. On September 4, 1841, Congress passed a fortifications bill that was three times the average annual military appropriations during the previous decade. The next day, the British minister in Washington, Henry Fox, wrote to Webster and raised the prospect of the "heavy calamity of War." One scholar summed up the situation:

> It was widely anticipated in both Europe and the United States that the execution of McLeod would lead Britain to recall its minister from Washington, sever diplomatic relations, and declare war on the American republic. To avert such a predictable scenario, John Tyler told the British minister Henry S. Fox

> that if McLeod were to be executed the president intended to refuse Fox his passport and forcible [*sic*] keep him in the United States under virtual house arrest.[28]

McLeod's trial in upstate New York began on October 4, 1841, and lasted for eight days. His defense, argued by his new lawyer, Spencer, was comprehensive, and the jury deliberated less than thirty minutes before returning a verdict of not guilty. McLeod was promptly released. The sighs of relief were nearly audible across the Atlantic Ocean, and down to Washington. In his message to the Congress at the beginning of the second session of the 27th Congress on December 7, 1841, Tyler explained that Alexander McLeod "has been acquitted by the verdict of an impartial and intelligent jury, and has . . . been regularly discharged." Tyler took the occasion to propose to Congress that, in the light of the difficulty surrounding the McLeod juridical problems, Congress should consider legislation to provide for the removal of such cases in the future from the state to the federal judiciary.

But US-UK relations remained precarious even though the McLeod issue was resolved. President Tyler, in his December 7, 1841, message to Congress, made clear that the larger *Caroline* affair remained unsettled. Tyler continued to "indulge the hope" that the British would see "the propriety of renouncing, as a rule of future action, the precedent which had been set" over the *Caroline.*

THE AROOSTOOK "WAR"

At the same time that there were severe tensions along the New York State border with Upper Canada, the Maine border area was also under stress. During the War of 1812, the British occupied most of eastern Maine (then part of Massachusetts) and, after the war, the boundary line was disputed. Maine became a separate state in 1820, but the border with Lower Canada remained unclear. Problems flared between the United States and New Brunswick authorities in the late 1830s over lumbering and other property issues. In late 1838, Canadian lumberjacks from the province of New Brunswick cut timber in the disputed area of the Aroostook River, and it seemed that a military showdown was imminent.[29] By February 1839, the Maine legislature authorized militia to defend its positions on the Aroostook River. Maine was not alone: the "legislatures of Alabama, Virginia, Maryland, Massachusetts, Pennsylvania, Ohio, Indiana, and Kentucky all promised aid. The brigadier general of the Illinois militia offered military assistance."[30]

Perhaps there was too much excitement, and less substance. One scholar noted: "The so-called Aroostook War amounted to little more than a barroom brawl, the major casualties bloody noses and broken arms. But territorial dispute continued to threaten the peace."[31] Yet, the risk of this situation spinning out of control was sufficiently high for President Van Buren to assign General Winfield Scott to Maine in early 1839. Troubleshooter Scott had been successful almost exactly one year earlier in cooling the passions in upper New York State arising out of the *Caroline* incident. Once again, General Scott calmed the waters. Scott was able to persuade Maine to recall its militia, but tensions along the disputed border remained high for the next two years with occasional skirmishes. These local brawls made the United States realize how unprepared it was for a military conflict with Britain.[32]

SHIPPING SLAVES (*COMET, ENCOMIUM, ENTERPRISE, HERMOSA*)

A significant portion of the transfer of slaves from the slaveholding states in the east to the slave territories in the southwest took place by ship. Typically, a ship was loaded with slaves, other cargo, and some passengers in Baltimore or Richmond or elsewhere along the shore in the eastern slave states, and then the ship sailed to New Orleans, which had become the great capital of the American slave trade—and had become tied with Baltimore for being the second largest city in America, after New York. The voyage required passing relatively near some of the British possessions in the Caribbean. Sometimes the currents and winds brought a vessel dangerously close to rocky islets. Sometimes shipwrecks happened. Four such shipwrecks had caused problems in US-UK relations before the *Creole* left Richmond in the late fall of 1841.

The islands of the Bahamas were particularly suited to produce wreckage to the benefit of the local salvage business; the islands had shallow seas and thousands of barely concealed reefs. An increasing number of wrecks there brought seamen from Bermuda to the Bahamas where local shipyards started to build vessels specifically for the wrecking business.[33] Fast boats were needed, since there was a large area to patrol, and there were advantages to being the first boat on the scene of a wreck. By law, all salvaged goods were to be brought to the capital, Nassau. The wreckers were permitted to claim 40–60 percent of the value, the government claimed 15 percent for customs duties, and the warehouses and shipyards took their commissions too. Thus, all local parties thrived on salvage. Some outside the Bahamas considered the wreckers to be semi-pirates.

The *Comet* and the *Encomium*

The *Comet* sailed from the District of Columbia in 1830, heading to New Orleans with a cargo of 164 slaves. She became stranded on one of the keys off Abaco Island in the northern Bahamas. Wreckers took the crew and all persons on board to Nassau, where the British authorities liberated the slaves.

Similarly, the *Encomium* sailed from Charleston, South Carolina, in January 1834, heading for New Orleans with a cargo of forty-five slaves. She too was stranded at the same place, and the wreckers also took the cargo, crew, and slaves to Nassau, where local authorities liberated the slaves. One scholar summed up the combined impact of the *Comet* and *Encomium* affairs:

> Coming at a time of deepening southern fear over the security of the slave-holding system, the two incidents seemed to be part of an ominous international pattern that included the Nat Turner uprising, the Garrisonian escalation of antislavery vehemence, and the triumph of abolition in the British colonies.[34]

The US government made a claim against the British government for compensation for the value of the lost slaves. In May 1839, the Van Buren administration reached an agreement with the United Kingdom for compensation. The British agreed to pay about $115,000, including interest and expenses, for the 179 slaves who were freed.[35] The State Department then distributed the funds, about 80 percent of which went to insurance companies that had already reimbursed most of the slave owners who had the foresight to have purchased insurance for their "property." As the Van Buren administration was about to leave office in early 1842, Secretary of State Forsyth transferred the British funds to the US treasurer. By 1842, other claimants surfaced, but the treasurer refused to pay them unless authorized by Congress. A bill was introduced in the House providing that authorization. On February 13, 1843, Congressman Joshua Giddings of Ohio—an outspoken abolitionist—objected. He argued that the slaves were not "property," as the United States had claimed to the United Kingdom, and so the funds the British paid had been extorted from the people of England by fraudulent pretenses. As a result, he said, he could not involve his Ohio constituents in this fraud by voting for such a bill. The bill passed, despite Giddings's passionate argument. Thus, the claimants received a proportional distribution of some $7,695 remaining in the fund.

The *Enterprise* and the *Hermosa*

The brig *Enterprise* sailed from the port of Alexandria, the District of Columbia,[36] on January 22, 1835, bound for Charleston, South Carolina. She carried merchandise, seventy-eight slaves, and their owners. A hurricane pushed the *Enterprise* well off course, and she began to leak, and so on February 11, she put in to Port Hamilton in Bermuda for supplies and to refit. She remained at anchor in the harbor, rather than alongside at the wharf, as the vessel took on the needed supplies and the sails were repaired. During this time, no one from shore was permitted to communicate with the slaves. When it was time to leave, on February 19, the captain went to the customs house to clear the brig for its departure. That's when a problem surfaced: the captain was told that there was a delay in getting the papers, but that he could return the next morning when they would likely be available. The captain protested the detention of the ship's papers and explained his fear that "the colored people of Hamilton would come on board his vessel at night and rescue the slaves, as they had threatened to do."[37] The port authorities assured the captain that the "colored people would do nothing without the advice of the whites."

At almost six o'clock that same evening, the chief justice of Bermuda sent a writ of habeas corpus on board requiring the slaves to be brought to his court. (Known as the Great Writ, the full Latin name is *habeas corpus ad subjiciendum* [we command that you bring the body]; it requires that a person being detained be brought to a court by the custodian and the reason for the detention be explained.)[38] A "file of black soldiers armed" then came on board and ordered the captain to bring all the slaves to the court. The chief justice interviewed each of the slaves well into the night, asking whether they wanted to remain free in Bermuda or to return to the United States as slaves. Seventy-two declared that they would remain on the shore; a woman and her five children decided to remain on board when the *Enterprise* sailed the next day.

The US minister in London, Martin Van Buren, was instructed to demand compensation for the liberated slaves, but the British secretary of state for foreign affairs, Lord Palmerston, refused. The United Kingdom rejected the claim, because at the time of the *Enterprise* slavery had been abolished in Bermuda, unlike the situation prevailing at the time of the other two earlier vessels, the *Comet* and the *Encomium*. Senator John C. Calhoun of South Carolina chided Minister Van Buren "for merely 'tapping gently' at Lord Palmerston's door for the compensation due to slaveholders."[39]

Senator Calhoun—a former vice president and secretary of war, and a future secretary of state—led the congressional assault against the British actions, calling the freeing of the slaves on the *Enterprise* "one of the greatest outrages ever committed on the rights of individuals by a civilized nation."[40] In March 1840, Calhoun, angered by the British position, introduced a series of Senate Resolutions asserting the rights of slaveholders under international law. The Resolutions offered a statement of international law that, when a ship is forced by weather or otherwise into a port of another nation, she and the people and cargo are placed under the protection of that nation. In its final paragraph, the Resolution applied that principle to the *Enterprise*:

> that the seizure and detention of the negroes on board by the local authority of the island, was an act in violation of the law of nations, and highly unjust to our own citizens to whom they belong.

Calhoun supported his proposals in a speech on March 13, 1840, in which he viciously attacked the British antislavery position, which he cleverly contrasted with the harsh British treatment of the Irish, Indians, and Chinese. Calhoun asserted that the British had to adopt one of two untenable propositions: either British municipal laws were superior to international law, or slavery itself was a violation of international law. The first proposition would lead to war, and the second was without foundation.[41] Calhoun's speech was reprinted as a pamphlet and also appeared in newspapers from Baltimore to South Carolina.[42] The Senate easily adopted Calhoun's Resolutions.

The schooner *Hermosa* sailed from Richmond heading toward New Orleans with thirty-eight slaves on board. On October 19, 1840, she was wrecked on a key at Abaco, the Bahamas. Bahamian wreckers came alongside and took off the captain, crew, and passengers, along with the slaves. The captain of the *Hermosa* asked the salvage leader to take them to a port in the United States. However, the wrecker refused and carried them all to Nassau. Upon arrival in Nassau, on October 22, the captain of the *Hermosa* was careful to ensure that the slaves were not put ashore and also that they had no communication with anyone on shore. The vessel remained in the harbor at anchor, a distance from the wharves. The captain got to shore and called on the US consul, John F. Bacon. Fifty-one-year-old Bacon had arrived at his post in Nassau only seven months earlier, having practiced law in New York State and also having served as clerk of the New York Senate. The captain enlisted Bacon's assistance in procuring another vessel to take the crew, passengers, and slaves to a port in the United States.

At that point, uniformed magistrates, supported by British West Indian soldiers carrying muskets and bayonets, took possession of the vessel and arranged to transport the slaves to the shore. From there, a guard of soldiers marched the slaves to the office of the magistrate, where, after some judicial proceedings, they were set free. This was done in the face of the urgent remonstrances of the *Hermosa*'s captain and of the American consul.

On December 1, the governor general of the Bahamas, Sir Francis Cockburn, wrote to the British secretary of state for war and the colonies, Lord John Russell, concerning the *Hermosa.* Cockburn explained that the ship would have been lost, but for the "gallant exertions of the boatmen" who saved the crew and passengers from "a watery grave." Cockburn was careful to point out that he decided not to "afford [the thirty-eight slaves] the use of the Government Building at Roslyn . . . which is appropriate to the use of captured Africans, lest it should have the appearance of [Cockburn's] taking any possession of them."[43] Cockburn also lamented the fact that the boatmen who salvaged the goods and personnel received no remuneration from the ungrateful Americans.

In short, during the decade preceding the *Creole* affair, there were four instances of American vessels arriving in British Caribbean ports with slave "cargo." All of them were caused by acts of nature; none was caused by violent revolt and murder on the part of the slaves. In all of them, the slaves were freed. In all of them, the US government protested vigorously to the British authorities, and in some the British paid compensation.

AFRICAN SLAVE TRADE INTERDICTION

In 1808, the United States outlawed the importation of slaves. In Article 10 of the Treaty of Ghent,[44] which ended the US-UK War of 1812, both countries expressed moral condemnation of the African slave trade and implied that both countries would take action against it. (John Quincy Adams was one of the American negotiators in that Belgian city in late 1814.) But it was only the British Navy that was strong enough to be relatively effective in suppressing the slavers. Increasingly, slave traders from third countries found it smart to hoist an American flag on their vessels, knowing that the American government opposed any action by the British Navy to board and search American ships. While secretary of state (1817–1825), John Quincy Adams suggested an agreement with the British for a joint cruising plan based on an understanding that the slave trade was considered piracy under international law. The Senate, however, refused to consent. Similarly, in 1834, the British proposed to Secretary of State Forsyth that the United States join with the United Kingdom and France to stop the slave trade, but the Americans again decided that it would deal with the slave trade by its own naval patrols.

The 27th Congress began its extra session[45] on May 31, 1841, and President Tyler sent his first Presidential Message. Near the end of the message, Tyler addressed the issue of the African slave trade. He suggested there was reason to believe that it was on the increase, but that it was pointless to attempt to understand why. Nevertheless, Tyler said that the "highest considerations of public honor, as well as the strongest promptings of humanity, require a resort to the most vigorous efforts to suppress the trade."

In June 1841, the House of Representatives passed a Resolution seeking information with respect to the seizure of American vessels by British armed cruisers "under the pretense that they [the American ships] were engaged in the slave trade," to which Tyler responded with a report from Secretary Webster listing all the efforts made by diplomatic notes since 1837 on that subject. There had been more than twenty diplomatic exchanges on this topic so far just in 1841. For example, Minister Stevenson sent a note on April 16, 1841, to Lord Palmerston concerning the "continued seizure and detention of American vessels by British cruisers on the high seas," about which Stevenson expressed "painful surprise" that the "repeated representations on the subject" had "failed to receive the attention which their importance merited."

In that same note, Stevenson added yet another list of four American vessels that had been boarded by British naval officers. Stevenson concluded that "these continued aggressions upon the vessels and commerce of the United States cannot longer be permitted." Webster wrote to Stevenson on June 18, 1841, explaining that President Tyler had read with interest the accounts of his exchanges with Lord Palmerston on this subject and was "strongly impressed." He added that the United States was "determined to protect its flag."

In September 1841, Lord Aberdeen replaced Lord Palmerston as British foreign secretary. Minister Stevenson lost no time in sending a note to Lord Aberdeen, on September 10, complaining about the problem of the African slave trade. On October 13, Lord Aberdeen responded with the fullest statement of the British position: yes, the flag of a vessel is prima facie evidence of the nationality of a vessel, but it is "sufficiently notorious that the flags of all nations are liable to be assumed" by those who have no right, and the American flag "has been employed for the purpose of covering this nefarious traffic." Indeed, the fact that the slave trade is "extensively carried on under the fraudulent use of the American flag" justifies the British action, since there are reasonable grounds of suspicion; this "abuse creates the right of inquiry." Of course, if the British cruiser had "a knowledge of the American character of any vessel, his visitation of such a vessel would be entirely unjustified."

The second session of the 27th Congress began on December 7, 1841, and Tyler sent another message (see appendix II). This time, the section dealing with the African slave trade was sharply focused on the British practice of interdicting American flagged vessels off the African coast. He explained that however much the United States would like to see the end of the African slave trade, the United States could not accept the claim of the United Kingdom to have a right to "visit and detain vessels sailing under the American flag, and engaged in prosecuting lawful commerce in the African seas." He also promised to urge upon Great Britain "full and ample remuneration for all losses, whether arising from detention or otherwise, to which American citizens have heretofore been subjected, by the exercise of rights which this Government cannot recognize as legitimate and proper."

NEW FACES

The year 1841 saw a near total change in the people dealing with US-UK relations:

On the British side, the prime minister, William Lamb (the Viscount Melbourne) left office on August 30, and his foreign secretary, John Temple (the Viscount Palmerston), left his office on September 2. The new prime minister, Sir Robert Peel, took office on August 30, and his new foreign secretary, George Hamilton Gordon (the Earl of Aberdeen), took over in September. The secretary of state for war and the colonies had been Lord John Russell until August 30, but Lord Stanley succeeded him on September 3.

On the American side, President Van Buren left office in March and was succeed by President Harrison; Tyler became president on April 4. Secretary of State Webster succeeded Forsyth on March 6, and the US minister in London, Andrew Stevenson, resigned on October 21 and was replaced on December 16 by Edward Everett.

The only person who remained in place during this period was the British minister in Washington, Henry S. Fox, who was at his post from 1836 until 1843. Fox was not a political heavyweight. He was a professional diplomat, having served previously in Italy, France, and Brazil. Fox was unhappy with his posting in Washington and became somewhat of a recluse. Another professional diplomat, Richard Pakenham, did not replace Fox until December 1843.

This enormous change in personnel in a single year would be unsettling to the bilateral relations of any two countries at any time. But to have this taking place at a time—1841—when US-UK relations were severely strained was unprecedented. The absence of close personal relationships and habits of dealing with each other carried dangers. On the other hand, with new faces on both sides of the Atlantic, there was the opportunity to begin a fresh approach in the US-UK relationship and perhaps to reduce the tensions.

In contrast to the British approach, the American envoys were political figures of some weight. The US minister to Britain from 1836 until October 21, 1841—formally known as the "Envoy Extraordinary and Minister Plenipotentiary to the Court of St. James"—was Andrew Stevenson.[46] He had been a Democratic congressman from Virginia who had served as the 15th Speaker of the US House of Representatives, from December 1827 to June 1834. The new president, John Tyler, had previously represented the same first congressional district of Virginia that Stevenson had earlier represented. Stevenson's tenure in London, however, was made difficult because he was a slave owner, a position that was seen as an irritant to the growing abolitionist sentiment in the United Kingdom. In 1838, an Irish leader denounced Stevenson in public as a "slave breeder." The outraged Stevenson responded by taking steps to challenge his British accuser to a duel. In the end, however Stevenson let the issue drop.[47] This embarrassment did not help Stevenson in his task of defending America's interests with respect to the United Kingdom. In late 1841, Stevenson returned to Virginia, where he was celebrated as a national hero for having defended American interests in the case of the *Enterprise* and other slave shipping interests.[48]

Secretary of State Webster decided that his old friend from Massachusetts, Edward Everett, would make an excellent replacement for Stevenson. Everett was close to John Quincy Adams and Henry Clay, and was a Whig. His term as governor of Massachusetts had ended in 1840, after which he traveled extensively in Europe. He also had the virtue of being available for this new assignment. Webster had little trouble in persuading President Tyler to appoint Everett to the London post. On November 20, 1841, even before Webster was advised that Everett had arrived at his new post, Webster wrote to Everett to instruct him that the two subjects of the "most commanding interest and highest importance" were the *Caroline* problem and the British search of American vessels off the African coast. Webster had not yet received any information about the *Creole* event.

Figure 2.2. Edward Everett, American minister to Great Britain during the *Creole* affair, former governor of Massachusetts, and orator remembered for his two-hour Gettysburg Address preceding Lincoln's two-minute Address.

In contrast to the very tense US-UK political-military relations, at the cultural level Americans in all regions were captivated by at least one young Englishman: Charles Dickens. Americans devoured pirated editions of *The Pickwick Papers* (1836–1837), *Oliver Twist* (1837–1839), *Nicholas Nickleby* (1838–1839), and *The Old Curiosity Shop* (1840–1841).[49] In September 1841, just two months before the *Creole* affair erupted, twenty-nine-year-old

Dickens wrote to his publisher: “It would be a good thing, wouldn’t it, if I ran over to America about the end of February, and came back, after four or five months, with a One Volume book?”[50] Dickens planned his visit for early 1842.

Chapter Three

The British Bahamas

The islands of the Bahamas were the site of Christopher Columbus's landfall in the New World in 1492, but the native people of the Bahamas disappeared within twenty years. English Puritans arrived in the mid-1650s. In the early 1700s, law and order collapsed, and Blackbeard—Edward Teach, a former British privateer—and other pirates made Nassau their base of operations in the Caribbean.

The Bahamas became a British Crown Colony in 1718. Not surprisingly, given the geographic proximity, there were many ties between America and the Bahamas. England acquired east Florida from Spain in 1763, under the terms of the Treaty of Paris, which ended the Seven Years' War (the French and Indian War), and the Spanish withdrew from their brief occupation of the Bahamian islands. East Florida remained an English colony until 1783, at which time it was ceded back to Spain.

At the time of the American War of Independence, British Loyalists were virtually driven out of what is now the United States. Several thousand of them—mostly from Georgia and South Carolina—came to east Florida with their slaves. At the time of the retrocession of east Florida to Spain in 1783, the English colonists were given eighteen months to remove themselves and their property (i.e., their slaves). While some returned to Georgia and South Carolina, most were taken by British transport to the Bahamas. Those Loyalists received grants of Crown land in the Bahamas.[1] The influx from the United States of these Loyalists and their slaves "probably doubled the population of the colony, tripled the slave population, and increased the percentage of blacks in the population to about two-thirds."[2] The "Loyalist invasion" from the United States brought talented people to the Bahamas, such as Joseph Eve of Pennsylvania, who invented a cotton gin, which helped the

Bahamas become an exporter of cotton.[3] These Loyalists constructed public buildings, churches, and libraries.

During the War of 1812, the Bahamas played a minor role. Nassau was a resupply location for British warships—the naval station in Nassau was under the jurisdiction of the West Indies station headquartered in Jamaica—and the Bahamas depended upon imported food from the United States brought by neutral ships. The Bahamas did play a significant role as a prisoner of war depot for American POWs, most of whom were brought from captured merchant vessels and a few privateers. A total of 836 American POWs were received and held during the period August 1, 1812, to March 13, 1815.[4]

On March 25, 1807, the British Parliament made the transatlantic slave trade illegal, effective in January of 1808.[5] In time, this had a profound impact on the population and society of the Bahamas. After 1807, many slavers took a gamble on not being caught, since "a slave purchased for $20 in Africa could be sold in Cuba for $350 [and many] slavers would first drop off their cargo of slaves on an isolated Bahamian cay until they could smuggle them into Cuba to sell."[6] To suppress the illegal slave trade, British ships were stationed along trade routes, and they seized slave ships and brought them to the nearest British port, where they were condemned as prizes.[7] The Africans on those confiscated ships were to be protected and provided for by the British, specifically the local collector of customs. The Bahamas were located just north of Cuba, and so many slave ships were confiscated at Nassau, the main port and seat of the government of the Bahamas. Thousands of liberated Africans were settled in the Bahamas. The duty of the collector of customs was to bind the Africans to suitable masters so they could learn a trade; apart from serving as apprentice domestics or laborers, some enlisted in the navy and in the Second West India Regiment stationed in the Bahamas.[8]

On February 8, 1841, the British governor general of the Bahamas faced a dilemma when two or three hundred Africans were brought into Nassau, originally bound for Cuba. Governor Cockburn wrote to London on that date, explaining that atrocities had taken place on the slave ship, including the murder of at least one African. Cockburn was uncertain whether his Admiralty Court in Nassau had jurisdiction to try those responsible, since a foreigner committed the murder on board a foreign ship engaged in the African slave trade. In his letter of that date to the attorney general, Cockburn reported that the "inclination of my mind . . . is so strongly in favor of the existence of the jurisdiction"[9] that he would not hesitate to indict such a murderer.

By the beginning of the nineteenth century, the influx of liberated Africans increased apprehension among prominent whites. Slave owners were particularly unhappy, because there were now significant numbers of free Africans who would compete with their slaves and depress their "property" value. Previously, most of the slaves in the Bahamas had been born in the Americas, and they did not have strong or direct ties to Africa and to African culture. But after the termination of the slave trade in 1808, the liberated Africans who arrived in the Bahamas, especially those who settled on the island of New Providence on which Nassau is located, maintained strong African connections. Their Africanness impacted Bahamian society and culture in language, religion, music, and food. The numbers of Africans liberated in the Bahamas grew during the 1830s, especially on the island of New Providence and around its port of Nassau. Villages of freed Africans were created outside Nassau: Grant's Town (1820s), Carmichael (1832), Adelaide (1831), and Gambier (1830s).[10] The Africans divided themselves into ethnic groups, such as the Yoruba, Congoes, Eboes, Mandingos, Fullalis, and Hausas, and retained many of their tribal distinctions and languages.

Although slavery remained legal in the Bahamas into the 1830s, the government took a series of steps in the period from 1823 to 1833 to ameliorate the conditions of the slaves. Even before that, however, the conditions of slaves in the Bahamas, especially in New Providence and its capital, Nassau, were generally better than elsewhere in the British West Indies, because a significantly smaller percentage of slaves there were field hands.[11] These steps comprised a trilogy of statutes, beginning with the Amelioration Act, passed in January 1824. It legalized slaves' marriages and prohibited the breakup of slave families. The second statute, passed in 1826, allowed slaves to give evidence in civil and criminal cases[12] and it permitted slaves to inherit and to own real estate and personal property. The third act was passed in 1830 and clarified the rights of the slaves.

At the same time that these "humanizing" acts were being introduced into the Bahamas, slavery was largely eliminated in the American North. However, in 1820, New York State had about the same number of slaves as Missouri. Slavery remained legal in New York until 1827 and in Connecticut until 1848. Tougher restrictions on slaves were enforced in the American South, following the 1822 Denmark Vesey slave conspiracy in South Carolina and the bloody Nat Turner slave revolt in Virginia in 1831. Thus, the condition of slaves in the Bahamas occupied sort of a middle ground between abolitionist developments in the American North and the harsher developments in the American South.

The next and most significant slave-related event to impact Bahamian society took place on August 28, 1833, when the Royal Assent was given to the act adopted by the British Parliament that abolished slavery throughout most of the Empire.[13] The effective date was August 1, 1834. In practice, however, only slaves younger than six were freed immediately; those over six were redesignated as "apprentices" (subdivided into three classes), in which status they could remain until August 1, 1840. However, the apprentice system proved impossible to administer, and all the slaves were freed on

August 1, 1838. The view from the United States was far from positive; as one scholar has noted: "the dominant portrayal of the freed West Indies [not confined to the Bahamas] in the American political press was overwhelmingly negative . . . [the mainstream press] emphasized the rebelliousness and laziness of former slaves."[14]

Some of the descendants of the original British Loyalists decided to leave the Bahamas, because they believed that without slavery, the last hope of a viable agricultural economy was destroyed. Many colonial plantations shut down as slave labor vanished, a point noted by the slave owners in the American South. Emancipation achieved little of practical value for the freed blacks, since white planters still controlled the economy and the social order. For example, enfranchisement laws placed the property qualifications so high that the former slaves were in fact excluded.[15] In November 1841, when the *Creole* arrived in the harbor of Nassau, the last local slave had been freed only three years earlier.

At that time, Nassau had a population of about 7,000 inhabitants, a mix of Afro-Bahamians and Anglo-Bahamians. Emancipation had caused many of the former American Loyalists and their slaves to leave Nassau, but this was somewhat offset by an influx of former slaves from Africa, mainly from Nigeria and Congo. While visitors described Nassau itself as pretty, pleasant, and well ordered, Afro-Bahamians lived separately in poverty.[16] American commercial visitors bought and sold goods with British sterling, Bahamian pounds, and Mexican and Spanish currency. "Newspapers brought from North and South America, from Europe and America . . . international news, local gossip and advertisements that announced the latest arrival of goods."[17]

When the *Creole* entered the harbor at Nassau on November 9, 1841, it would have been difficult to create a scenario more bleak and fraught with danger:

- There were severe US-British tensions, especially along the northeast border dividing the United States and the Province of Canada, and serious concerns in the United States about the prospect of a third war with Britain. Southerners in particular were very upset with the British, because slaves being shipped from the Southeast to New Orleans in the past decade had been freed in the British West Indies. Years later, after he left office, Tyler wrote from his plantation on the James River his reflection that, in the first five or six months of his presidency, a devastating conflict with Britain appeared imminent, and "the peace of the country had been suspended by a thread."[18] This deep presidential worry was at a time just *before* the *Creole* sailed into Nassau.
- America had its third president in that single calendar year: Van Buren, Harrison, and Tyler. President Tyler was a slave owner who had awful

relations with the Whig-dominated Congress. The entire cabinet had resigned only a couple of months earlier, except for Secretary of State Daniel Webster. Across the Atlantic, a new British government had just taken power, but the British drive for universal abolition remained intense.

- In the Congress, attention was focused on slavery, especially in the House, where the former president John Quincy Adams spearheaded the abolitionist cause.
- An emotional maritime slave issue (the *Amistad*) had just been dealt with by the Supreme Court, along with the issue of whether the interstate slave trade could be regulated (and perhaps eliminated) by the federal or state governments (*Groves v. Slaughter*). The explosive fugitive slave issue (*Prigg v. Pennsylvania*), centering on the Southern demands to be able to retrieve their runaway slaves, was scheduled for argument just a few months away.
- The population around Nassau was composed substantially of free Africans and newly freed former slaves, including many whose freedom had been obtained as recently as three years earlier. The white population was numerically very small.

The last thing that anyone in the United States, or in the United Kingdom, would want at this time was a conflict between the two governments over a slavery issue. This was the "perfect storm" into which the *Creole* sailed as it entered the harbor of Nassau.

Let us now return to the scene in Nassau harbor on November 9, 1841.

II

Forward: November 1841

Chapter Four

In Nassau

The office of the American consulate in Nassau was about a mile from where the *Creole* anchored that morning, November 9, 1841. The first mate, Gifford, was the acting senior officer, in light of the severe wounds that Captain Ensor had suffered. Gifford quickly made his way to the consulate, with the help of the Bahamian quarantine official, and, luckily, was immediately able to meet with John F. Bacon, the US consul. As US consul, Bacon frequently received American mariners, usually to deal with relatively technical maritime and trade questions.

Bacon had been new in his job when, almost exactly a year earlier, he had had to deal with the problem of the *Hermosa.* That was the ship, sailing from Richmond to New Orleans with fewer than forty slaves, that was wrecked on one of the Bahamian islands. The wreckers brought the crew and slaves to Nassau, where British authorities freed all the slaves. Therefore, as Gifford began to explain the situation of the *Creole*, Bacon undoubtedly thought that he faced a problem similar to that with the *Hermosa*—though with three times the number of slaves—and Bacon probably assumed that he would deal with it in a similar fashion. However, Bacon must have been taken aback by the dreadful story that Gifford told him: the horrors that had taken place on board the *Creole*, involving mutiny, mayhem, and murder. One could easily imagine the blood draining from Bacon's face, and his stomach tightening as he took in the fact that the *Creole* problem—now in his lap—was fundamentally more difficult than was the *Hermosa* incident.

The initial concern of both men was that the American slaves might get off the ship and come ashore. Bacon and Gifford knew that, once on British colonial soil, the slaves would be untouchable by US authorities. Bacon must have remembered the messy problem he had had with the British colonial authorities during the *Hermosa* episode. On that occasion, British soldiers took the slaves from the wreckers' vessel and marched them to the magistrate, who then freed the slaves. Bacon's protests to Governor Sir Francis Cockburn at that time had no impact.

Bacon knew that it would be essential to attempt to obtain the help of the British authorities immediately to prevent the slaves from disembarking, and generally to prevent this situation from spinning out of control. He also wanted to ensure that those slaves who led the revolt, and who murdered John Hewell and severely wounded Captain Ensor, were held on board so they could be returned to the United States to face trial or other measures.

The senior British government official in the colony was the governor general, Sir Francis Cockburn. As a young captain in the army serving in Upper Canada, Cockburn had fought against the Americans in the War of 1812. After the war, he remained in Upper Canada as an administrator. Prior to coming to the Bahamas in 1837, Cockburn had been the superintendent of British Honduras for seven years. Cockburn was knighted two months earlier in 1841. The next day, November 10, 1841, would be Sir Francis's sixty-first birthday.

Sir Francis's older brother, Sir George Cockburn, had also fought the Americans in the War of 1812. It was Sir George, an ambitious rear admiral, who led a squadron of ships up the Chesapeake Bay, enthusiastically plundering along the way. And it was Sir George who had organized the burning of the public buildings in Washington, DC, in August 1814. The story was that Cockburn stood on the chair of the speaker of the House and asked rhetorically: "Shall this harbor of Yankee democracy be burned?"[1] He became the most hated man in America; Americans compared him to Attila the Hun.[2] Two months before the *Creole* came into Nassau, Sir George was elected to the British Parliament and became First Naval Lord. One must assume that the Cockburn brothers did not have an instinctive deep affection for the United States.

Bacon took Gifford to Government House, the impressive Georgian colonial building on the ridge that overlooked the harbor of Nassau. In front of the imposing coral-colored building stood a large statue of Christopher Columbus, which had been erected a decade earlier. Fortunately, the governor general was available. Consul Bacon introduced Gifford, who must have looked shaken, and who bore a visible wound where the slave's bullet had grazed his head. Together, Gifford and Bacon explained the dire situation, and the problem floating at anchor in Nassau's harbor just down the hill.

Consul Bacon asked the governor to take measures to prevent the slaves from coming onshore and escaping inland, and to secure the murderers. Cockburn was somewhat reluctant to become so involved, because he doubted whether he was authorized to interfere at all. Nevertheless, in the end, the governor agreed in principle, but he pointed out that he did not have full information. He questioned Gifford directly and insisted that Bacon put his request in writing. Bacon then told Gifford to return to the *Creole* to ensure that the American colors were still flying and to tend to the wounded.

Bacon quickly wrote and sent to the governor "a written application," as the governor requested. In it, Bacon requested: "that your Excellency will be pleased not to suffer any of the slaves on board to land until further investigations can be made." Almost immediately, the governor's secretary responded with a note acknowledging Bacon's written request, explaining that the governor had "ordered a military party on board of the said brig. There will be, however, no impediment to any of the white persons on board landing here."

Shortly after that, Bacon himself went on board. At about noon, twenty West Indian soldiers and a West Indian sergeant and corporal, commanded by a white British officer, soon joined Bacon on board. Bacon introduced the senior officer to Gifford as the mate in charge, and then Bacon returned to shore, bringing the severely wounded Captain Ensor with the assistance of two crewmen. As soon as he landed, Bacon was told that the governor requested that he meet immediately with the governor and council then in session. At that meeting, the governor read from a document informing the US consul that:

1. courts in the Bahamas had no jurisdiction over alleged crimes committed on the high seas;
2. in light of the "grave charge" alleged it would be "expedient that the parties implicated" should not be allowed to go at large, and that an investigation under oath should be made; and, finally, if it appeared that Bacon's information was correct, all the parties implicated in such a crime "should be detained here [in Nassau] until reference should be made to the Secretary of State [for War and the Colonies]" to determine whether those detained should be delivered over to the US authorities; and, finally,
3. all persons on board not implicated in the alleged offenses "must be released from further restraint." (One might speculate whether Cockburn underlined the use of the word "persons," rather than "slaves" or the ship's "cargo.")[3] The statement concluded by noting that a report on this matter would be sent to the British minister in Washington.

After reading from this statement, the governor asked Bacon if he was satisfied. Nonplussed, Bacon responded that he was indeed satisfied with respect to sending troops on board, and launching an investigation, but he declined to provide a further answer at that time.

The governor and council ordered two magistrates to go on board the *Creole* to begin their examination. Bacon went on board at the same time.

"Reliable persons" had told Bacon that an attempt would be made to liberate the slaves by force. The consul observed "a large collection of boats near the brig" and there was a "great concourse of people collected on the shore opposite" where the *Creole* was anchored. Bacon returned to his office and found Gifford waiting for him. Gifford advised Bacon of the "threatening nature" of the situation and that the "crew were greatly intimidated."

The magistrates' examination continued on Tuesday and Wednesday, was suspended on Thursday, but on Friday, November 12, it was abruptly terminated. At noon on that Friday, Consul Bacon sent another note to the governor. He explained that, as he was proceeding to board the *Creole* that morning, he saw a large collection of people on shore near the vessel and was advised that, as soon as the soldiers left the vessel, an attempt would be made to board her by force. Bacon sought protection for the vessel and her cargo. Cockburn's response was immediate. One could imagine Cockburn's nose in the air as he stated in his reply note: "I beg to state that I cannot think it possible that any of Her Majesty's subjects would act so improperly as to attempt to board by force." Nevertheless, should such an attempt be made, Cockburn said that he "shall be quite ready to use every authorized means for preventing it." Bacon was also requested to attend the council in session again that day.

At the council session, the governor told Bacon that the council had directed that the attorney general, along with the provost marshal and police, go to the brig, have the troops and prisoners removed to the shore, see that no violence was committed by the assembled people, and also that "no impediment be given on board the vessel to the passengers [slaves] should they desire to leave."

At that time, it happened that there were two other American ships in the harbor at Nassau: the bark *Louisa* and the brig *Congress.* On that Friday morning, November 12, Consul Bacon asked the master of the *Louisa*, William Woodside of Maine, to go on board the *Creole.* This was part of a rescue plan that Bacon proposed: as many of Woodside's crew as he could spare, along with four sailors from the *Congress*, should board the *Creole* and assist her to sail to Indian Key (about four hundred miles away) where there was a US warship. Thus, that morning, Captain Woodside and his men rowed out to the *Creole* with muskets and cutlasses—obtained from the *Congress*—wrapped in an American flag and concealed in the bottom of the boat. In a dramatic scene, the British officer on the deck of the *Creole*, along with his twenty-four soldiers with loaded muskets and fixed bayonets, yelled that Woodside's boat should stand off or be fired on. Woodside withdrew.[4]

Later, Woodside returned without the men and arms, and boarded. Soon, two Episcopal clergymen (Reverend Poole, the chaplain at Fort Charlotte, and Reverend Aldridge, from one of the Anglican churches in Nassau) came on board also. Woodside got the impression that the two clergymen seemed to be giving instructions to the slaves. Just before 11:00 a.m., two magistrates came on board to identify the alleged criminals. Almost immediately, a sloop, a large lighter, and other boats came to the starboard side of the *Creole* and anchored about thirty feet away. At the same time a great number of small boats surrounded the *Creole*, all filled with black men. Woodside saw clubs being passed from the sloop and the lighter to the smaller boats. At noon, another boat arrived with five white men on board, and Woodside explained to the British authorities that they had been sent by Bacon to relieve the crew members, but the British officer ordered the American boat to move away.

Early that same Friday afternoon, Woodside came on shore and met with Bacon, who reported on the results of his session with the governor and council that morning (i.e., that the troops would be removed, that the alleged criminals would be brought ashore, and that all the slaves would be free to leave the *Creole*). Bacon asked Woodside and Gifford to return to the ship and to protest any actions of the attorney general that might result in liberating the slaves. Both the attorney general's party and the boat carrying Woodside and Gifford arrived at the *Creole* at about the same time.

The attorney general came alongside the large launch filled with local men and ordered the men to throw away their clubs, explaining that as soon as the soldiers left, they could come alongside and take away any of the former slaves who wanted to leave. The attorney general informed the nineteen slaves, whom the British authorities in their investigation had identified, that they were charged with mutiny and murder, and would be held in custody. The attorney general then turned to the other slaves and told them they were free. The word was then given to the surrounding boats to approach and make fast to the *Creole* so they could remove the freed slaves. Gifford and the crew members were threatened with violence if any attempt was made to interfere.[5]

The slaves rushed to get on board the boats, except for five slaves—three women, a boy, and a girl—who decided to remain on the *Creole* and concealed themselves.[6] (Gifford later claimed that many of the male slaves and nearly all of the female slaves would have remained on board were it not for the intimidation and pressure they felt from other slaves and the local authorities.) There was a great celebration as the former slaves reached land. Local Bahamians gave five cheers that echoed across the harbor. Some two thousand Bahamians accompanied the former slaves on a march through the streets of Nassau and brought them to the superintendent of police, where they registered as temporary residents of the Bahamas.[7]

Gifford asked the attorney general for protection for himself and the crew, because he feared that those in the boats might return and engage in violence. Without responding, the attorney general left the vessel at the same time the slaves were climbing over the rails with the assistance of two people in the attorney general's party. About thirty minutes after the slaves left, a launch came alongside and took off the nineteen prisoners and the soldiers.[8] The prisoners were put in the Nassau jail; one of them died the next day from wounds suffered during the mutiny.

On Monday, November 15, the attorney general wrote to Captain Ensor formally, advising him that the "passengers" [the freed slaves] had applied to him for assistance in obtaining their baggage from the *Creole.* He instructed Ensor to assist in getting their baggage ashore. Gifford replied—with Bacon's assistance—that he considered the slaves to be cargo, the property of their owners, and so their masters owned any such slave baggage. Perhaps insulted by Gifford's response, the attorney general sent a customs officer and his men on board, and they removed apparel, blankets, and other items.

The relationship between the Americans and the local British authorities continued to deteriorate. The next step in the downward spiral took place the following day, when the captain proposed to sell some of the surplus supplies of meat and bread from the ship, since they would not be needed for the short voyage ahead. The funds were needed to pay for the expenses of the *Creole* during her stay in Nassau. However, the local collector of customs refused formally to "enter" those provisions unless the now-freed slaves were also formally entered as "passengers." The captain, not surprisingly, refused.

On that same Monday, November 15, Consul Bacon wrote to Governor Cockburn formally to enter his "solemn protest" concerning the manner in which the slaves were put ashore and the part played by the British authorities. Those slaves, Bacon asserted, "were as much a portion of the cargo of the said brig, as the tobacco and other articles on board . . . while they were under the American flag." Finally, the American consul explained that he expected that the *Creole* would soon be able to sail away, and so he requested that the nineteen slaves being held by the British should be transferred to the *Creole* for transport to the United States, in order that they might be tried there. Bacon pointed out that it might take time for London to decide whether to bring the nineteen to trial in Nassau or to permit them to be tried in the United States, but at that late point the witnesses probably would be disbursed and unavailable to trial. This dilemma would be solved, argued Bacon, by letting the *Creole* take the nineteen slaves to the United States now.

Sir Francis replied immediately. The message was rather personal. The governor reported that he felt "somewhat disappointed" by Bacon's letter, because he thought Bacon had not objected to any of Cockburn's actions and, indeed, had acquiesced in all of them. He then stated that the attorney general's official report dated November 14—a copy of which Cockburn enclosed—made it clear that none of the authorities had anything to do with the slaves leaving the ship, other than the nineteen being held in custody. As far as the request to permit the nineteen to leave the Bahamas on the *Creole*, Cockburn stated, in effect: I already told you that we were seeking instructions from London, to which you acquiesced. The official report of the attorney general, G. C. Anderson, indeed, flatly contradicted much in the depositions of all the Americans. For example, Anderson reported that Gifford had "cheerfully" complied with the request to bring the slaves on deck so that Anderson could tell them that they were free, and that they had Gifford's "free permission to quit" the vessel. In like fashion, Merritt also addressed the slaves, according to the attorney general's report, and told them that they "were at perfect liberty to go on shore if they pleased." Similarly, Gifford told the attorney general directly "his perfect acquiescence" in these events.

There is, of course, no way of knowing which characterization of these events was closer to the truth. However, it might seem difficult to imagine Gifford being "cheerful" about the Bahamian actions, or that Merritt—who was serving as a guard for some of the slaves—would have been so passive at the idea of his slaves leaving the vessel. On the other hand, we will learn later (see chapter 7) that the British witnesses claimed that Gifford and Merritt were, in fact, delighted to get rid of the slaves, since they were terrified of sailing home with them on board and so risking another bloody mutiny. Nevertheless, this fundamental factual conflict between the American and British versions of events seems not to have been a subject of heated conflict at the higher levels of the US-UK dialogue.

Bacon later learned that, on November 18, about fifty of the former American slaves were sent from Nassau to Jamaica—another British colony in the Caribbean—and that another shipload was planned.[9] It is possible that the British sent the *Creole*'s former slaves to Jamaica to protect them from recapture. It is also possible that they did so to prevent the destruction of Nassau—with only its inadequate Fort Charlotte for defense—by American warships.[10] The British authorities may have been eager to move the newly freed slaves far from Nassau, perhaps so they would not be available if the Americans came looking to retrieve them.

There is no record of what happened to the freed American slaves. Many may indeed have ended up in Jamaica or some other nearby British colony. Whether in Nassau or elsewhere, they probably had little difficulty fitting in with the local population, and certainly they had to have been welcomed by the locals. Because they spoke native [American] English, they may even have had an advantage over some locals whose English was more recently acquired. Without leaving a trace, however, these former American slaves simply melded into the local scene and otherwise vanished.

The governor and council may have felt that they would have faced a potential internal threat if they had not cleared the way for the American slaves to gain their freedom. The ratio of blacks to whites in the Nassau vicinity was at least four to one: some 12,000 backs and only 3,000 whites.[11] A great many of the local blacks were former slaves who had a natural and overwhelming sympathy for the slaves on board the *Creole*. Despite a general respect for British authority, Nassau's black population might well have acted on its own to secure the liberation of the slaves on the ship.[12] Moreover, for a British governor to be seen protecting the American "property" and preventing the slaves from climbing off the vessel to their freedom might have been dangerous. The memories of the great slave revolt in the British colony of Jamaica, less than ten years earlier, probably remained in the minds of the Bahamian colonial authorities.

The worry the local British authorities had about their safety was not confined to internal unrest. Would the Americans send a warship or two to vent their anger over the British handling of the *Creole*? The huge Fort Charlotte—complete with moat, ramparts, and dungeons—was more than half a century old; it had been named after the wife of King George III. While it held a commanding position about a mile west of the center of Nassau, overlooking the harbor, it had not been adequately maintained or provisioned. On November 24, Sir Francis wrote again to Lord Stanley in London about the "insufficient state" of the garrison: "both as concerns the number of troops stationed here and the dilapidated state of the works." Cockburn explained that the fort was so "dilapidated" that one American warship could easily make the situation of the colony "desperate."[13] Stanley was the secretary for war as well as the secretary for the colonies.

On November 17, Cockburn wrote to Lord Stanley to report the events and the actions he had taken. Cockburn began his letter, "I have been placed in a situation of some difficulty and delicacy" by the *Creole* events. He attached copies of the written exchanges, including Consul Bacon's formal protest. Consul Bacon also wrote to Secretary of State Webster on November 17, and again on November 30, and provided a full report, including copies of his exchanges with the governor along with the affidavits he had taken of the crew, passengers, and captain of the *Louisa*; he also included the reports of the Bahamian attorney general.

On November 19, the *Creole* sailed from the harbor at Nassau and headed to New Orleans. Gifford remained in charge as the acting master, but the severely wounded Captain Ensor was too ill to travel. He was left in Nassau.[14]

Given the great distance from Government House in Nassau to Downing Street in London, Governor Cockburn's dispatch of November 17, with all its attachments, did not reach London until early January. On January 7, 1842, Lord Stanley replied to Cockburn. Stanley was "happy to be able to convey [Sir Francis Stanley's] approval of the course which [Cockburn] had pursued."[15] Stanley explained that, while he would have liked to furnish Cockburn with definite instructions for future guidance, "in a question of such international importance," he rather "thought it right to call upon the Law Officers of the Crown . . . for their Opinion." He hoped to have the results by mid-March so as to relieve Cockburn of the "anxiety which [he] must naturally feel in a case of so novel and embarrassing a nature."

Within only three weeks, on January 29, 1842, three members[16] of Doctors' Commons sent to Lord Stanley their twenty-eight-page handwritten Opinion on the "Case of the *Creole* . . . General Question of Giving up fugitives to a Foreign Power." The Doctors' Commons was a body established in the 1500s to advise on great legal issues, particularly ecclesiastical and admiralty. It was housed in a building near St. Paul's churchyard. Its members had to be doctors of law from either Oxford or Cambridge.[17] The Crown Legal Advisers at the Doctors' Commons answered the six questions that Lord Stanley had asked:

1. None of the nineteen persons alleged to have committed crimes on board the *Creole* is amenable to the courts of the Bahamas. Their actions do not amount to the crime of piracy, either under international law [the "general Law of Nations"] or under British law, and therefore are not cognizable by any English Tribunal. The intent and object of the slaves was not that of plunder; their sole object was their freedom. They may be chargeable with the crime of murder, but, since they are not British Subjects and the crime was not committed on board a British vessel, they cannot be tried by a British Tribunal for that offense.
2. Since the offense was committed by persons subject to American law, on an American ship, against American citizens, the offense is "exclusively cognizable" by the criminal tribunals of the United States.
3. There is no general state practice of delivering up persons charged with crimes who have taken refuge elsewhere, and there is no rule of international law [the Law of Nations] so requiring. Yes, the mutual surrender of criminals is sometimes provided by treaty, but the United Kingdom does not have such an extradition treaty with the United States.
4. The conduct of Governor Cockburn was not in any respect at variance with the law and practice of civilized nations, or with the municipal law of the Kingdom.
5. The letter of Consul Bacon of November 14, 1841, was based on a "misapprehension of the facts." The correct understanding of the facts is that the "slaves were not liberated by the British Authorities, nor does it appear that any control was exercised by them . . . over the crew of the ship."
6. The customs officers of the Bahamas might lawfully grant clearance for the *Creole* to return to the United States, and they did not have a duty to ascertain whether the slaves were returning to the United States of their own free will.

The Crown legal advisers then raised an issue of their own: if the British government decided that it would be "just and proper" to comply with an American request to deliver those in custody for trial in the United States, does the municipal law of England pose an obstacle? The Crown lawyers acknowledged that, on this question, they "felt very considerable difficulty." Interestingly, the first citation offered by the Crown lawyers was to *Conflicts of Laws*, published in 1834 by US Associate Supreme Court Justice Joseph Story—Daniel Webster's friend. The Crown lawyers reported that they gave this question "a most minute investigation." They concluded, "the British Government cannot legally direct the delivery up of the persons now in custody in the Bahamas to the Authorities of the United States."

Two days later, Lord Stanley, writing from Downing Street to Governor Cockburn, enclosed the text of the full Opinion of the Crown lawyers.

Stanley's cover letter—marked "Confidential"—explained that the law officers opined that a charge of piracy would not apply to the "Negroes" who took over the *Creole*. Therefore the offense—not amounting to piracy—"being committed by Foreigners on board of a Foreign vessel, cannot be tried" in the Bahamas, or any other British colony. Rather, "whatever be the offense charged against the Negroes . . . the Courts of Justice of the United States have exclusive jurisdiction in the matter."

Moving on, Stanley noted that Cockburn had reported that the American consul had formally "protested against the liberation . . . of those Negroes . . . not charged as having taken any part in the acts of violence which were committed, but who have availed themselves of British Law within a British Port to assert their freedom." On that point, Lord Stanley was quick to respond: "Her Majesty's Government could not hesitate for a moment." The slaves were not liberated by any act of British Authority:

> being within the limits of British Territory, within which limits the condition of Slavery is not recognized by law, & being charged with no crime, they voluntarily quitted the vessel on board of which there was no legal power to detain them.

Lord Stanley then turned to the second point: Bacon's demand that the mutineers be returned to the United States for trial. He acknowledged that the decision "is one of the highest importance" and so he had sought the Opinion of the Crown's law officers whether the government was required to surrender the slaves, or whether it had discretion to surrender them, on the demand of the United States. Stanley quoted from the Opinion that "the British government cannot legally direct the delivery up of the persons now in custody in the Bahamas to the Authorities of the United States." Stanley noted that he really did not know whether such a demand had been made by the United

States, or whether the US government would affirm any part of the claim made by Consul Bacon.

The secretary of state for war and colonies then formally instructed Cockburn, "Her Majesty's government cannot legally surrender these persons to take their trial in the United States." Lord Stanley then acknowledged that, as a consequence, "upon the charge of murder there is no power vested anywhere for bringing these persons or any of them to trial." Stanley then instructed Cockburn to advise Consul Bacon that, even though the law officers of the Crown are "strongly" of the opinion that a charge of piracy cannot be sustained, since that is the only charge upon which this case can be judicially investigated, Cockburn is to afford every facility for such an investigation, if Bacon wants to make that charge in the commissioners' court in Nassau. If the consul declines to institute any such prosecution, the matter can be discharged "according to the regular course of law." Lord Stanley closed his letter by once again stating that Her Majesty's Government "entirely approve" the course which Cockburn took in "difficult circumstances."

In light of the position taken by the Crown lawyers and Lord Stanley, Lord Aberdeen, the foreign secretary, announced in the House of Lords on February 14 that the American slaves held in custody in Nassau would be freed.

On March 29, 1842, Sir Francis wrote to Lord Stanley, acknowledging his letter of instruction of January 31 and expressing appreciation that London had approved his handling of the *Creole* matter. But then Cockburn said he still sought "further and more detailed instructions for future guidance." Lord Stanley replied on April 30, reproaching Cockburn for failing to be specific in his request for guidance: "It would have been more convenient if you had recapitulated the specific questions on which you felt yourself to be still insufficiently instructed." Stanley, nevertheless, provided guidance for the future: when a vessel arrives in port, and if you have "credible testimony" that persons on board were "illegally detained against their will . . . it would be your duty to verify the fact and to afford to persons so circumstanced the protection of the British Law."

On April 5, Governor Cockburn wrote to Lord Stanley to advise him of the measures he had taken to comply with Stanley's confidential letter of instructions of January 31 concerning the Americans who had been kept in custody in Nassau. The special session of the admiralty court in Nassau was ordered to assemble on April 16. While claiming to have had no conversation with anyone on the topic, Cockburn said that it was "very doubtful whether the grand jury will find a Bill against the accused, or whether the Judges will agree to any postponement of the trial." In other words, Cockburn was signaling that he had arranged for the matter to be handled according to "the regular course of law," as Stanley had desired.

On April 17, Cockburn reported to Stanley on the implementation of the plan. The special session of the admiralty court had indeed assembled on April 16, and the Americans in custody were brought into the court by the provost marshal. The attorney general moved on behalf of the new American consul—Timothy Darling, who had been formally recognized by Cockburn on April 6—that the Americans should be committed for trial for piracy at the next general session, since there was not sufficient evidence for an indictment on that charge at this time. The court had before it all the depositions made by all the various participants in the events. In addition, Consul Darling submitted a statement explaining that, if the motion by the attorney general were granted, he would ask his government to make arrangements to bring from the United States those witnesses relevant to the piracy charge.

The court retired and discussed the matter privately for an hour, and, upon their return, the chief justice delivered the unanimous decision of the admiralty court: there was nothing in any of the depositions that would in any way warrant support that an act of piracy had been committed, and therefore the motion was denied and those Americans who had been detained "were discharged accordingly."

The seventeen former slaves—two of whom had died while in custody—left the court on the same day, April 16, 1842, and were free. They quickly melted into Bahamian society.[18]

Therefore, by mid-April 1842, events in Nassau moved to a secondary level. The *Creole* was long gone, and the remaining former American slaves were free. There was no longer a dramatic and emotional conflict to be discussed between Governor Cockburn and the new American consul. The focus turned sharply to Washington, where the *Creole* affair merged with long-standing, unresolved, and contentious British-American issues.

Chapter Five

In the United States

IN WASHINGTON

The second session of the 27th Congress opened on December 6, 1841. The next day, President Tyler sent the traditional Presidential Message that was the functional equivalent of today's State of the Union Address. News of the *Creole* events had not yet reached Washington, and so Tyler made no mention of them.

Relations with Britain dominated the message, which presented a lengthy catalog of unsolved problems with Great Britain. While the message was presented in the first person ("I invite your attention"), the hand of Secretary of State Webster was undoubtedly at work. Tyler noted that, in New York, McLeod had been acquitted by a jury, but he reminded Congress of the continuing issue that arose from the 1837 burning by the British of the *Caroline*: "No such atonement as was due for the public wrong done to the United States by this invasion of her territory . . . has yet been made." Tyler complained about the British practice of detaining and "visiting" American vessels off the African coast. For this, Tyler demanded of Britain "full and ample remuneration for all losses, whether from detention or otherwise, to which American citizens have heretofore been or may hereafter be subjected." Tyler also reported on the efforts to survey the boundary line between Canada and Maine/New Hampshire, and noted that the dispute over the boundary line was causing continued problems with the British.

Near the end of his message,[1] Tyler urged substantial appropriations for an expansion of the navy: not for "foreign conquests" or to compete "with any other nation for supremacy on the ocean" but, rather, to ensure that "no nation should be permitted to invade our waters at pleasure and subject our towns and villages to conflagration or pillage." Thus, the president underlined the fact that the US-British relationship was in trouble.[2] While the message was addressed to the US Congress, Tyler and Webster understood that the undisclosed addressee was the British government. And this was *before* the *Creole* affair had reared its head in Washington. (Because of the importance, and comprehensive character of this statement of US-UK relations, the relevant portions of the president's message are set out at appendix II.)

The *Creole* arrived in New Orleans on December 2.[3] The customs collector at the port wrote immediately to Secretary of the Treasury Walter Forward about the reported rebellion. President Tyler had appointed Forward treasury secretary only three months earlier; previously, he had been the comptroller of the currency and a lawyer in Pittsburgh. The *New Orleans Bee* of December 3 charged that the refusal of the British authorities to give up the mutineers for trial in the United States added to the "dark catalogue of outrages" the British had committed against American slaveholders.[4] On the other hand, the positive news—that the slaves had achieved their freedom—spread like a contagion throughout the slave quarters of the American South; the message was that freedom awaited anyone who reached British soil.

By mid-December, New Orleans was virtually in flames over the *Creole* affair. On December 18, the customs collector sent a formal protest detailing minutely the events of the mutiny and the activity in Nassau. Gifford, the acting master, and all the crew members of the *Creole* signed and swore to the protest; the passengers Merritt, McCargo, and Leidner formally attested to the truth of the facts presented by Gifford and his crew. (In maritime law, a protest is a "written statement by the master of a vessel, attested by a proper judicial officer or a notary, to the effect that damage suffered by the ship on her voyage was caused by storms or other perils of the sea, without any negligence or misconduct on his own part.")[5] The protest concluded: "if there had been no interference on the part of the legal authorities of Nassau, the slaves might have been safely brought to New Orleans." The protest recorded Bacon's proposal to permit the nineteen slaves who led the revolt to be sent to the United States on the *Creole* for trial and the British rejection of that proposition. The protest was widely reprinted in newspapers, especially in the South.[6]

On December 22, 1841, Senator Alexander Barrow of Louisiana rose in the US Senate to report that he had received a memorial from the New Orleans Insurance Company concerning the *Creole*. Barrow charged that this " subject involved the question of peace or war between this country and Great Britain, and [that] it was important . . . to [settle] whether the British Government had a right to do what they who lived in the South denied to their own Government—and that was, the right of suppressing the slave trade between the States."[7] Alabama Senator William King followed Barrow and opined that "the time was not far off when the question of war must inevitably arise." Perhaps in an effort to calm tensions, Senator William Preston of South Carolina said that although "he knew that the temper of the nation was exasperated," he would not allow himself to believe that an enlightened Great Britain could not be reconciled. Similarly, Virginia Senator William Cabell Rives urged some caution, but at the same time, "to make preparations for the country's defense."

South Carolina Senator John C. Calhoun followed Rives and turned up the rhetoric. He asserted that the British action with respect to the *Creole* was "the most atrocious outrage ever perpetrated on the American people."[8] Louisiana Senator Barrow rounded out the discussion, charging that the British government:

> knew that the transfer of slaves from one Southern state to another was an every day's occurrence; and if these contemptible British subjects at Nassau were permitted to seize by force of arms, the slaves belonging to American citizens and liberating them, the South would be compelled to fit our armaments and destroy Nassau, and also the towns which trampled under foot the laws of nations and the rights of American citizens.[9]

Thus, even before the year was over, senators from Virginia to Louisiana were expressing outrage over the *Creole* affair, and calls for a violent response were made—although there was a clear message of hope that the British would understand the importance of the coastal slave trade and somehow ensure that such events would cease.

Despite the great tension over the *Creole* affair, one Washington tradition continued unabated: the president's levee, a sort of "open house" on New Year's Day at the mansion. The East Room was glittering, and the diplomatic corps was present. According to one report, "the most conspicuous [guest] . . . was the Russian Minister, whose coat was one entire sheet of silver. A member of the late Cabinet had the beautiful wife of the Russian on his arm . . . the whole Democratic portion of the Senate were present . . . but few Whigs."[10] The one sad note was the figure of Secretary of State Daniel Webster, who was seen "to stalk grand, gloomy and peculiar, with a clouded brow, over to his own house." Undoubtedly, Webster's gloom was caused by the recent events in Nassau and the prospects for a very difficult time with Great Britain.

In the Senate, on January 10, 1842, Senator Calhoun introduced a Resolution:

> *Resolved*, That the President be requested to communicate to the Senate, a copy of the Protest of the officers and crew of the brig *Creole*, on her late passage from Richmond to New Orleans, should any such have been received; or any authenticated account which may have been received, of the murder of a passenger on board, and the wounding of the captain, and others, by the

> slaves on board the same; and also, to inform the Senate, if, in his opinion, it can be done consistently with the public interest, what step has been taken by the Executive, in reference to the transaction, having for its object the punishment of the guilty, the redress of the wrong done to our citizens, and the indignity offered to the American flag.[11]

The next day, the Senate adopted Calhoun's Resolution. On January 18, 1842, Secretary of State Webster sent the requested report to the president, who then transmitted it to the Senate on January 19. Webster explained that neither the owners of the slaves, nor the insurance underwriters had yet requested the assistance of the State Department. Webster also reported that he was preparing a dispatch to the American minister in London, Edward Everett.

Near the end of January, the Royal Mail Steamer reached the United States carrying English newspapers. The *Times* of London printed the announcement of the appointment of Lord Ashburton as special minister to the United States, charged with resolving all bilateral issues. The *Times* opined that his appointment was wise, because any further delay "might render an amicable adjustment unattainable, and involve both countries in all the horrors of war."[12] American newspapers reported that his appointment was favorably received in American commercial circles, because of his property holdings in the United States, his American wife, and his knowledge of the American Constitution.

On January 29, 1842, Secretary of State Webster sent the promised lengthy dispatch to his friend Minister Everett, who had been at his post in London less than two months. The dispatch laid out the American position with respect to British actions in Nassau. Webster began by characterizing the matter as "a very serious occurrence . . . one calling loudly for redress . . . [and] a clear case for indemnification."

Webster explained that the ship had been on a perfectly lawful voyage with slaves, which are "recognized as property by the Constitution of the United States in those States where slavery exists." The *Creole*'s arrival in Nassau was not voluntary, and it was the "plain and obvious duty of the authorities at Nassau" to assist the American consul to enable the vessel to resume its voyage and to take the murderers to the United States to answer for their crimes. But, on the contrary, not only did the local authorities fail to assist, they actually interfered to free the slaves. In political terms, Webster noted that this situation "cannot but cause deep feelings" in the United States. Webster knew already that Lord Ashburton was planning to come to the United States for negotiations, and perhaps Ashburton's authority would include this subject, but he urged Minister Everett to "lose no time" in bringing it to Lord Aberdeen's attention. Lord Aberdeen was the Peel government's foreign secretary, to whom Lord Ashburton reported.

As an extremely prominent lawyer, Webster could not resist arguing the American case. He questioned the right of the Nassau authorities to even inquire about the cargo, since there was no intention to import anything into the Bahamas. Perhaps to give the British a hint that the face-saving way out of the problem was to blame the local authorities in Nassau for exceeding their writ, Webster commented that the local authorities in Nassau had put London in "a very awkward position" with respect to the nineteen slaves being held in jail. Even if they were eventually sent to the United States for trial, the witnesses might be "scattered over half the globe," and so it is likely that they would end up "altogether unpunished." Moving into hypotheticals, Webster proposed that, if the British law provided that all blacks were slaves, and a free American black was forced by weather into Nassau, would the authorities in Nassau be authorized to enslave that man? Or, if the United States considered opium as poison, but opium was legal in London, would the United States be justified in destroying a cargo of opium on an English vessel that was forced into a US port?

Finally, Webster addressed the central issue: this problem has "dangerous importance to the peace between the two countries." He claimed that the United States and the United Kingdom were the two greatest commercial nations in the world. The fundamental international doctrine of noninterference in the domestic concerns of others was essential for peace to be maintained. The Bahamas lie almost directly on the track of the American coastal traffic, and it has seas full of reefs and sandbars and other dangers to navigation. Wrecks are not unlikely. Therefore, it is "quite essential" that we have full and clear knowledge of how such vessels, their crew, and their "cargo" are to be treated. In short, this problem has gotten worse over the years, and we really have to fix it, and set a peaceful course for the future, or "the peace of the world will always be in danger."

The secretary's message to Everett was reprinted widely in American newspapers.[13] A few days after Webster's dispatch to London, the legislature of Louisiana adopted a Resolution, forwarded to Congress, complaining of "repeated outrages" by Britain against American property arising out of coastal shipping and looking to the federal government for "vindication of the national honor." Over the next two months, the legislatures of Virginia and Mississippi adopted similar Resolutions. The Mississippi Resolution charged that without monetary restitution and the return of the slaves to their owners, "the slaveholding States would have most just cause to apprehend that the American flag is powerless to protect American property" and that their rights are in "imminent danger." The Virginia General Assembly resolved:

> That the Government of the U.S. owes the parties interested, whether as owners or insurers, indemnity through the British Government for all loss which

> has been or may be sustained in the consequence of the liberation by the authorities of Nassau of the slaves which were a part of the cargo of the *Creole*. [and further]
>
> Resolved, That this General Assembly has full confidence that the Government of the U.S. is keenly alive to the aggression committed on our rights, and appreciates the obligation to vindicate our honor as well as to protect the prosperity of our citizens.[14]

Many Americans believed that war was likely. The voice of an outspoken and ill-tempered slaveholder and states' righter could be heard when a former South Carolina congressman, James Henry Hammond, wrote that the nation was ready for war, with "such a stupid imbecile as Tyler at the head of Affairs, and such an unprincipled and cowardly Sect of State as Webster," the situation could hardly be worse. Hammond then charged that Webster was "in the pay of the great English Bankers, the Barings."[15] (At the end of 1842, Hammond became the governor of South Carolina, and in 1857, he became a US senator.)

IN CONGRESS

In the House of Representatives, the issue of slavery, as reflected in the controversy over the "gag rule," continued to hurtle toward a conclusion. In December 1841, Adams's attempt to repeal the "permanent Gag Rule" failed again, but this time by only three votes. The rule had endured since May 1836, despite Adams's crusade to rescind it. Yet public opinion was turning against it, and support for the gag by Northern congressmen steadily ebbed. Even Adams's enemies respected his intellectual and oratorical powers. Congressman Henry Wise of Virginia described him as the "acutest, the astutest, the archest enemy of Southern slavery that ever existed."[16] The inevitable collision over the gag rule—a direct attack on Adams—took place in January 1842 at the opening session of Congress.

Perhaps Adams expected that his Supreme Court victory in the *Amistad* case would provide some protection.[17] On January 21, 1842, Adams introduced new slavery petitions, just as he had for the previous six years, and all of them were tabled without being officially received, since the rule had been extended once again.[18] One of the petitions called for censuring the conduct of the American consul at Nassau "in relation to the mutineers of the *Creole*, and requesting his recall."[19] Undeterred, Adams began reading a petition from the Pennsylvania Anti-Slavery Society stating that a US war with England to uphold slavery would be more unjust than England's war in 1776 to keep America in bondage. The Speaker declared Adams out of order, but Adams continued. The next day, the Speaker again pronounced Adams out of order and instructed him to take his seat. Finally, on January 24, Adams presented a petition from the citizens of Haverhill, Massachusetts, calling for the dissolution of the Union, because of sectional favoritism. That night, Southern Whigs drafted a resolution of censure, to stop Adams from splitting the party along sectional lines.[20]

The visitors' galleries were full on January 25, when the Resolution of Censure was presented. Congressman Henry A. Wise, a Whig of Virginia, asserted that Adams was acting in concert with a sinister English plot, whose aim was to overthrow the US government, to free its slaves, and to establish a monarchy that would turn white Americans into virtual slaves. At the very least, Wise claimed, Adams had fallen under the sway of British abolitionists. Ohio's Congressman Joshua Giddings and others came to Adams's defense. The debate was fiery and continued for days, with Adams on the attack. Finally, on February 7, John Botts, another Virginia Whig, moved to lay the censure resolution on the table (i.e., to not discuss it). The motion carried, 106–93. The House then voted to table the Massachusetts "dissolve the union" petition that Adams originally tried to introduce, 166–40. The battle was over. The attack on Adams, the former president and son of a president, had ended. Adams had won.

But the Whig leadership found another target, a newer and much easier target: Representative Joshua Reed Giddings, one of Adams's most dedicated lieutenants. Giddings had been a member of the House only for three years. On March 21, 1842, Giddings focused on the *Creole* affair and introduced nine Resolutions upholding the right of the slaves to go free. The first three Resolutions were so well supported that all parties (abolitionist and slave owner) could accept them. Southern leaders always repeated that slavery was an issue exclusively within the jurisdiction of the states, and, cleverly, Giddings's opening resolutions accepted their position:

(1) prior to the Constitution, the states had full jurisdiction over slavery within their territory;
(2) by adopting the Constitution, none of those powers were delegated to the federal government, but were reserved by the states;
(3) the Constitution (Article I, Section 8 ["The Congress shall have Power To regulate Commerce with foreign Nations, and among the several States"]) provides that the states surrendered jurisdiction over commerce and navigation on the high seas;

The fourth Resolution began to slip into territory that slaveholders might find offensive, although it reflected the approach that English and American courts had taken since the 1772 decision of Lord Mansfield, the chief justice of the King's Bench, in *Somerset v. Stewart*:

(4) slavery, being an abridgement of the natural rights of man, can exist only by force of positive municipal law;

By the time Southern congressmen read Giddings's fifth Resolution, they could see where he was heading, and they could not have been pleased:

> (5) when a ship belonging to citizens of a state leaves the territory and waters of that state, and enters upon the high seas, the persons on board cease to be subject to the slave laws of that state, and are governed by the law of the United States;

From a Southern perspective, this Resolution was a disaster, since it would effectively end the interstate coastal transport of slaves from the east coast to the large plantations of the Mississippi region. With his sixth Resolution, Giddings sought to apply these principles to the specific situation of the *Creole*:

> (6) when the *Creole* left the territorial jurisdiction of Virginia, the slave laws of Virginia ceased to have jurisdiction over the persons on board, and they became amenable only to the laws of the United States;

Having laid out these six principles, Giddings then related them to the actions of Madison Washington and his fellow mutineers. Not surprisingly, he absolved them:

> (7) the persons on board the *Creole*, in resuming their natural rights of personal liberty, violated no law of the United States, incurred no legal responsibility, and are justly liable to no punishment;

Since Giddings's seventh Resolution held the rebellious slaves innocent of any wrongdoing, and since they were only obtaining their "natural rights of personal liberty," it would follow naturally that the United States was honor-bound not to attempt to return them to a condition of slavery. Thus, US consul in Nassau should step back from any pressure on the Bahamian authorities, and Secretary of State Webster should stop pushing the British government over this incident.

> (8) all attempts to re-enslave those persons are unauthorized by the Constitution, and are incompatible with our national honor; and

Giddings put these first eight Resolutions into the broadest possible setting, well beyond the specific case of the *Creole*, and took the sharpest aim at his ultimate target: the coastal interstate trade in slaves:

> (9) all attempts to exert our national influence in favor of the coastwise slave trade, or to place the nation in the attitude of maintaining a "commerce in human beings" are subversive of the rights and injurious to the feelings of the free states, are unauthorized by the Constitution, and are prejudicial to our national character.

In this fashion, the politician-lawyer from Ashtabula, Ohio, laid out a brilliant brief supporting the proposition that there was no legal basis for the coastwise slave trade, and that efforts by the slave states to continue that practice "hurt the feelings" of the northern states and diminished Americans' national standing. Specifically, he argued that Virginia's slave law governed the slaves on board the *Creole*, but only until the vessel left Virginia's territorial waters; once in the Atlantic Ocean on the high seas, there was no law enslaving them, and so they were free.

Giddings's legal position was virtually identical to that of the British authorities, except for the domestic US constitutional issues. Angry Southerners, together with many Northern Democrats, tabled the Giddings Resolutions, which they termed "incendiary." Southerners were angry over the slavery issue, and northern Whigs were angry at Giddings's actions, because they threatened to cut the threads holding together the Northern and Southern wings of the party.[21] The House refused to vote on the resolutions. Instead, Congressman John M. Botts, a Whig from Virginia, moved instantly to introduce a resolution to censure Giddings. Botts's accusation was that Giddings had justified mutiny and murder, and that Giddings was creating "excitement, dissatisfaction, and division"[22] among the people at a time when the United Kingdom and United States were in negotiations on that subject that might result in war.[23] Importantly, and in contrast to the prior attack on Adams, Giddings's opponents refused to give Giddings any chance to defend himself. This time, their aim was on target: the vote, on March 22, 1842, to censure Giddings was 125 to 69.

"Censure" is a formal vote by a majority of the members present disapproving of a member's conduct.[24] There were then—and still are—no House rules laying out consequences after a member has been censured, but the political ignominy of being formally and publicly admonished by one's colleagues usually leads to resignation. Giddings was the second member of the House ever to be censured; there have been only twenty other members censured in the 172 years since then.[25] Giddings promptly walked over to the stunned Adams and shook his hand. Giddings, always a gentleman, then took leave of the House with a formal farewell to the Speaker and officers, and with a formal bow, left the chamber. He left Washington that same evening. His formal letter of resignation from the House was dated March 22.[26] But that was not the end of the Giddings story.

On April 2, 1842, the *Ashtabula Sentinel* carried this article:

> The Hon. J. Giddings late member of Congress from this District, having been censured by the House of Representatives, for presenting to that body resolutions expressive of his views in relation to the case of the *Creole*, resolutions which were constitutional, and honorable to the head and heart of an American legislator, and which will be so considered by the better portion of the citizens

Figure 5.1. Congressman Joshua Reed Giddings of Ohio (1838–1859). This image was made about fifteen years after the *Creole* affair.

> of this country, and the world, is again in the midst of his constituents. He arrived at his residence in Jefferson on Thursday last.[27]

On May 5, 1842, Giddings's northeastern Ohio constituents reelected him overwhelmingly (7,469 to 393) to the congressional seat he had just vacated. By late May, Giddings was back at his desk in the House of Representatives. Southern members were far from pleased that Giddings was back, and they tried unsuccessfully to prevent him from regaining his chairmanship of the committee on claims. At that time, it was common for slaveholders to bring claims for slaves that were lost. Shortly after Giddings's return, such a claim was brought concerning slaves lost during the Florida war with the Seminoles. Giddings gave an Adams-like speech on the floor opposing the slave claim, but the claim prevailed.

The Mississippi legislature adopted a Resolution relating to the *Creole*, and on May 10, 1842, the Resolution was referred to the Foreign Affairs Committee of the US House of Representatives. It provided in Section 3:

> *Resolved*, That the Legislature of the State, in view of the late murderous insurrection of the slaves on board the *Creole*, their reception in a British port, the absolute connivance at their crimes, manifest in the protection extended to them by the British authorities, most solemnly declare their firm conviction that, if the conduct of those authorities be submitted to . . . or atoned for in any mode except by the surrender of the actual criminals to the Federal Government . . . the slaveholding States would have just cause to apprehend that the American flag is powerless to protect American property."[28]

This was strong stuff, but it reflected the political pressure on Webster and Tyler by the Southern states to defend their interests. And that was while the British authorities in Nassau were still holding the slaves who had participated in the "murderous insurrection" on board the *Creole*. However, by early May 1842, word reached Washington that the British authorities in Nassau had released the remaining seventeen American slaves who had been held in custody since the previous November. Senator John C. Calhoun of South Carolina—the former vice president, under Jackson—was so furious at the release of the slaves that he said it was "the most atrocious outrage ever perpetrated on the American people."[29]

At the time Giddings returned to Washington, Congress was considering a resolution to reduce the size of the army. Those members opposed to the resolution argued that the *Creole* issue was a matter of national honor, and the defense of that honor might unfold into a war with Great Britain, and so this was exactly not the time to reduce the army's strength. Cleverly, Giddings saw this topic as an opportunity. On June 4, 1842, Giddings rose in the Committee of the Whole and asserted:

> we cannot *honorably* lend any encouragement or support to "that exorable commerce in human flesh." Every principle of morality, of national honor, forbids that we should lend any aid or assistance to those engaged in a traffic in the bodies of men, of women, and of children. . . . Sir, I would not retain a single soldier in service to maintain this slave-trade; on the contrary, I should rejoice if every slave shipped from our slave-breeding States could regain his liberty, either by the strength of his own arms, or by landing on some British island.

Giddings then proceeded to review many of the arguments that had resulted in his censure less than two months earlier: once the *Creole* had left Virginia waters and that slave state's jurisdiction, the slaves on the brig were freed. He acknowledged that he was "aware that the expression of these views is not agreeable to the feelings of those around" him, and that they were "also in direct conflict with the letter of instructions from the Secretary of State to our Minister at London." Nevertheless, he said bitterly that the "people whom I represent are unwilling to be made parties to this purchase and sale of men." He further explained that his constituents have "no intention to shed their blood in defense of this slave-trade." Giddings claimed that the logical conclusion of the legal fact that the slaves had been in law free on the high seas, was that the slave owners—in shipping them to New Orleans—had committed the act of piracy! The United States had laws that demanded hanging for those engaged in piracy, and those laws should be enforced. Then, in a nice turn, Giddings asked rhetorically why Secretary Webster had demanded payment from the British "for the bodies of these freemen":

> Neither the British Government, nor the people of England had gained any pecuniary benefit by the freedom of these persons. The Negroes secured their own liberty, and were the only persons benefited. Why then should this nation demand from the people of England compensation for their liberty? . . . the President and Secretary of State have overstepped the limits of their Constitutional authority; that the character of the nation has suffered from this unauthorized attempt to extort money from the people of England to compensate these slave-merchants for the loss of their "human chattels."

Finally, Giddings pointed directly at Webster, whom he acknowledged was "an eminent lawyer," and scolded him for calling the *Creole* slaves mutineers and murderers. This was wrong as a matter of law and of morals, since these men were merely asserting their freedom. Rather, they were heroes! Casting his rhetorical eye directly at Webster, Giddings asked: "Would he [Webster], with a craven heart and a dastardly soul, have quietly submitted to be carried to the barracoons of New Orleans, and sold like a beast of burden?" Many in the House on that June 4 must have been considering yet another censure for that outspoken member, beloved of his constituents.

A BRITISH VISITOR

It is often helpful, when trying to understand political climate and public pressures, to have the view of an outsider, even if that view is generally critical. The most popular writer in the English-speaking world, Charles Dickens, provided that perspective. His visit to the United States highlighted the anti-British sentiment in the United States, especially in the South, and the impact of the *Creole* affair.

Exactly one month after the *Creole* docked in New Orleans, and three weeks before the attack on Adams in the House, Charles Dickens and his wife, Catherine, boarded the steamer *Britannia* in Liverpool, and set sail for America. They arrived in Boston on January 22, 1842, and were met by adoring crowds. Bostonians warmly referred to the city as "Boz-town." ("Boz" was the pseudonym used by Dickens since his earliest writings.) Henry Wadsworth Longfellow and Charles Sumner—then a Boston lawyer and Harvard Law School lecturer—took Dickens for a ten-mile walk around the city. Boston held grand dinners in Dickens's honor, led in part by Oliver Wendell Holmes and Richard Henry Dana, who had published his popular *Two Years Before the Mast* two years earlier. Dickens then made his way down the coast to New York City, where, on February 20, he attended St. John's Church with former president Van Buren.

From New York, Dickens visited Philadelphia, arriving late on March 6. Two weeks before his visit, he arranged for a notice in the *Philadelphia Gazette* explaining that he "declines all dinners, parades, shows, junketings and things of that sort, preferring to meet such private unostentatious hospitalities as a courteous people should extend."[30] One of those private meetings was with Edgar Allan Poe. It is not unlikely that they discussed Poe's critique of Dickens's *Barnaby Rudge*, but it is unlikely that they discussed the character of Grip, the raven in *Barnaby Rudge*—which may have inspired Poe's most successful poem in 1845, "The Raven." Dickens stayed on Chestnut Street and described the building across the street as "a handsome building of white marble, which had a mournful ghost-like aspect dreary to behold."[31] That "mournful" building—with its eight severe Doric columns in the Greek Revival style—happened to be the infamous and spectacularly failed second Bank of the United States, a casualty of the panic of 1837. When its charter failed to be renewed in 1836, it became a private corporation and was liquidated the year before Dickens viewed it.

Dickens arrived in Washington on March 9. The morning after his arrival, he visited the president. Dickens described that event positively:

Figure 5.2. Charles Dickens in London reading his novel *Little Dombey*, which was published in monthly installments from October 1846 to April 1848.

> [A]t a business-like table covered with papers, sat the President himself. He looked somewhat worn and anxious, and well he might; being at war with everybody—but the expression of his face was mild and pleasant, and his manner was remarkably unaffected, gentlemanly and agreeable. I thought that in his whole carriage and demeanor, he became his station singularly well.[32]

Dignitaries called on Dickens at Fuller's Hotel (later the famous Willard Hotel),[33] including Secretary Webster and Senator Calhoun.[34] (Webster and Dickens had met each other in London a few years earlier.) On March 10, he was formally introduced on the floor of the House of Representatives and was presented to John Quincy Adams. On Sunday, March 12, the Dickenses had dinner at the invitation of Adams, and later that same evening Dickens also had dinner with a State Department friend of Washington Irving's, Robert Greenhow. Despite all the attention he was receiving, Dickens was not taken with Washington, which he thought should be known as "the City of Magnificent Intentions." He decided it was an unhealthy place and that "Few people would live in Washington, I take it, who were not obliged to reside there."[35]

On March 15, Dickens attended President Tyler's levee—sort of an open house—the last levee of that season. Twenty-six-year-old Priscilla Cooper Tyler, the president's daughter-in-law, served as the hostess, since the president's wife was seriously ill and confined to her bedroom.[36] Priscilla had become a charming and effective social mistress for the president; as a former professional Shakespearean actress, she was quite comfortable in the spotlight.

Dickens's friend and fellow literary celebrity, Washington Irving, was also at the levee, and was the co-honoree. (Tyler would shortly appoint Irving as US minister to Spain.) But Dickens was the star. As one press report put it: "[Dickens was] the greatest lion at the White House. The crowd oppressed him with kindness and thronged him wherever he moved."[37] Another report noted that, when he arrived,

> the fifteen hundred or two thousand people present went in pursuit of him like hounds, horses and riders in pursuit of a fox in the chase. . . . The people gazed, stared . . . stretched their necks. This fever was kept up for some thirty or forty minutes, until Boz turned upon his heels to get rid of his two thousand good-natured American friends who had taken the place by storm.[38]

Appalled by slavery, Dickens listened to Southern congressmen objecting to petitions to end the slave trade in the District and threatening abolitionists who might dare to come south. He also was repelled by the "abundance of drooling and spittle" in the House of Representatives, noting that American politicians "did not take good aim into their spittoons."[39] While in Washington, Dickens delivered petitions, signed by British and American literary luminaries (including James Fenimore Cooper and Washington Irving), pleading and demanding an international copyright law to protect stolen works from getting into print. His crusade for copyright did not result in any immediate action from the US government.

Dickens left Washington on March 16 for Richmond, where slavery, and the unseasonable heat, repelled him. He wrote to Lord Brougham about his time in Richmond: "the sight of Slavery, and mere fact of living in a town where it exists being positive misery to me."[40] The *Creole* affair had caused virulent anti-British rhetoric in the press and in political discourse. Charles Dickens later wrote to his brother, Fred Dickens, about his time in Richmond, the "southern people are perfectly frantic about the *Creole* business," and the British are excoriated for their handling of the mutineers. Dickens also wrote to his close friend, the actor and dramaturge William C. Macready, "The sight of slavery in Virginia; the hatred of British feeling upon that subject; and the miserable hints of impotent indignation of the South have pained me very much."[41] Whether the topic was intellectual property rights, prison conditions, or copyright protection, Dickens had to be very careful, because of the general "hostility to any British criticism of American social or political practices."[42]

At a Richmond dinner in his honor, Dickens addressed the audience: "the best flag of truce between two nations having the same common origin and speaking the same language is a fair sheet of white paper inscribed with the literature of each." In the same theme, one of the hosts offered a toast: "England and America. . . . May their future contests be in literature and not in arms."[43] These themes of military arms and the need for peace between the United States and United Kingdom were not as present in toasts offered earlier in Boston or New York.

Originally, Dickens planned to travel farther south to Charleston, South Carolina, but he was advised by Senator Henry Clay to change course and avoid the South. So he left Richmond on March 20 for Baltimore, where, on March 24, he left for western Pennsylvania and then traveled as far west as St. Louis.

Within months after sailing from the United States on June 7, Dickens began writing his next book, a travelogue and critique of the United States, *American Notes for General Circulation*, which was published in October 1842. Much of the material in the book was taken from letters he had written during his travels; most of those letters were written while he was in Baltimore, having just returned from Richmond. At that point in his journey, he seemed to have decided that he knew all there was to know about America.[44] In the book, he takes aim at Washington for being "the head-quarters of tobacco-tinctured saliva," which is "most offensive and sickening." Dickens imposed a rule on himself that he would not mention individual names in this book. But, in two passages he refers—but not by name—to John Quincy

Adams and Joshua Giddings, in the context of his description of the House of Representatives:

> an aged, grey-haired man [Adams], a lasting honour to the land that gave him birth . . . had stood for days upon his trial before this very body, charged with having dared to assert the infamy of that traffic, which has for its accursed merchandise men and women, and their unborn children. . . .
>
> There was but a week to come, and another of that body [Giddings], for doing his duty to those who sent him there; for claiming in a Republic the Liberty and Freedom of expressing their sentiments, and making known their prayer; would be tried, found guilty, and have strong censure passed upon him by the rest.[45]

Dickens was so concerned about slavery in the United States that in *American Notes* he added a chapter dealing exclusively with slavery. In it, Dickens reproduced dozens of clippings from American newspapers that reported on slave beatings, slave escapes, and so forth, designed to reveal how American "public opinion" is formed by the media. One of the most prominent newspaper reports that he included in his book was one headlined "Interesting Law-Case." It reported on the *Prigg* case—the fugitive slave case between Maryland and Pennsylvania—which was decided by the Supreme Court just a week before Dickens arrived in Washington.

AT THE SUPREME COURT

On the morning of February 8, 1842, lawyers representing Maryland and Pennsylvania in the case of *Prigg v. Pennsylvania* arrived at the Supreme Court to begin three days of argument in this case, which dealt for the first time with the scope of the fraught fugitive slave law. Each state sent two attorneys, including the attorney general of Pennsylvania and his deputy. The Supreme Court did not have its own building at that time.[46] Rather, the court met in a chamber directly below the floor of the Senate; after the British burned the Capitol during the War of 1812, the chamber was rebuilt in 1819. It was a relatively dark room, with three windows at the back of the justices' bench. In front of the bench and before the visitors' section, there was the place where the lawyers would argue.

The *Prigg* case brought the thorny political problem of fugitive slaves directly to the court.[47] The issue was how to permit legitimate slave rendition, while at the same time ensuring that kidnapping of free blacks would be prevented. Southern slaveholders watched anxiously in the hope that the court would protect their right to retrieve their slave property from Northern states to which slaves might have fled on the Underground Railroad. At the other end of the political spectrum, Northern abolitionists looked to the court to protect the rights of free blacks from capture by villainous slave catchers. Almost exactly a year before, the court had decided two slave cases (*Amistad* and *Groves*), but neither went to the core interests of the North or South, although there were hints in *Groves* that some justices might in the future decide that Congress had the power to ban the interstate slave trade.

Chief Justice Taney assigned the task of drafting the Opinion of the court to Justice Joseph Story, who had written the Opinion in the *Amistad* case the year before. Joseph Story of Massachusetts was a friend and mentor of Secretary of State Daniel Webster. Story was very highly regarded, perhaps best known for his treatise *Commentaries on the Constitution of the United States*, which dominated nineteenth-century jurisprudence. Story was the youngest justice ever appointed to the Supreme Court, at age thirty-two (by President Madison in 1811). It is possible that Taney selected Story because it would be politically wise to have a Northerner deliver the Opinion, which was likely to be seen as pro-slavery, and perhaps also because Story had successfully pulled together a variety of interests in *Amistad.*[48]

The heartrending facts of the case can be summarized as follows: A Maryland slave owner allowed his slaves to live almost freely, but he did not formally emancipate them. One of them (Margaret) married a free black, had children, and later moved to Pennsylvania, with the apparent agreement of the heirs of her original owner. Margaret bore additional children in that free state. The heirs of her original owner eventually decided to claim Margaret and her children, and they sent a slave catcher, Prigg, into Pennsylvania, from which he dragged them back to Maryland. Pennsylvania had enacted a law in 1826 that prohibited the removal of blacks out of the state for purpose of enslaving them. Under this law, Pennsylvania convicted Prigg of a horrible kidnapping. Maryland claimed that the 1826 Pennsylvania law violated the fugitive slave provision in Article IV, Section 2, of the Constitution.

On March 1, 1842, Justice Joseph Story read the Opinion of the Court in that basement-like chamber under the Senate in the Capitol building. At the outset, Story pointed out that the Fugitive Slave Clause in the Constitution was so essential to Southern interests at the time of its formation that, without it, the Constitution would not have been adopted. Moving from this fundamental historical position, Story announced that Pennsylvania's Personal Liberty law of 1826 was unconstitutional, because it denied the right of slaveholders to recover their slaves under Article IV of the Constitution and the Federal Fugitive Slave Law of 1793, which overrode Pennsylvania's law, in accordance with the Supremacy Clause. Prigg's conviction was reversed.

Story explained that slaveholders had the right and the power to seize fugitive slaves wherever they were found, as long as they committed no breach of the peace or engaged in no illegal violence, since the police powers of the states had not been surrendered to the federal government. Thus, Pennsylvania could not interfere with the rendition of fugitive slaves, but it—

and other states—could pass laws under their police powers that were broadly fashioned. Seven other justices agreed with Story that the Pennsylvania law must fall, but six justices could not quite agree on the reasoning. The chief justice thought that states could pass laws dealing with fugitive slaves but that those laws could not impair the right of rendition. Justice Daniel of Virginia also disagreed with Story's view of federal exclusivity, noting that states have concurrent authority to enact laws in aid of slave rendition.

Justice McLean of Ohio was the sole dissenter, though he agreed with Story that Congress had the exclusive power to enact laws enforcing the Fugitive Slave Clause. McLean focused on the practical problem of kidnapping, and he concluded that there were proper exercises of the state's police power that might interfere with the slave-owner's right of rendition, if, for example, the slave owner was mistaken. Abolitionists, while pleased with McLean's dissent, could not have been overjoyed, since his position was relatively narrow.

The evening that the court rendered its decision in *Prigg v. Pennsylvania*, John Quincy Adams read the Opinion, its concurrences, and the dissent. He was not happy. He wrote in his diary that the justices came to one terrible but overarching conclusion: "the transcendent omnipotence of slavery in these United States."[49] Adams's friend in the House of Representatives, Joshua Reed Giddings of Ohio, wrote, under the pen name of "Pacificus, a Whig from Ohio," that if, according to the *Prigg* decision, state officials should never interfere with a slave rendition, then, if a slave defends himself by killing his master, then the state should not care.[50] It is not clear whether Giddings had the *Creole* killing in mind when fashioning that assertion.

Interestingly, none of the nine justices dealt with the fact that Margaret had given birth to at least one child while she was in the free state of Pennsylvania. The status of that child—a rather fundamental issue, one would have thought—was simply not addressed. Underneath lay the broader question of whether all children of a slave become slaves themselves, or whether the place of birth determines one's status as a slave. In the context of the *Creole* story, the same issue was present: whether the location of those slaves in free Nassau meant that they were free, or whether their status as slaves, at the time they left Virginia, remained with them wherever they were.

Many severely disappointed abolitionists now realized that the Constitution was accepted by the Supreme Court as inalterably pro-slavery, and that the only ultimate remedy was disunion. As one great constitutional scholar noted, if this kidnapping action by Prigg in Pennsylvania, against Margaret and her children, was now constitutionally protected behavior, as the court held, "it was open season on free blacks everywhere in America."[51]

Most slaveholders were relieved and pleased by the court's decision, though others remained suspicious, because of the confused sets of reasoning among the eight justices. Nevertheless, Southerners took the *Prigg* decision as evidence that at least the court was with them, that their hold on their "peculiar institution" remained firm. One can imagine that Secretary of State Webster was elated that the South felt placated—at least on the explosive issue of fugitive slaves—and so perhaps the South would be relatively less upset and demanding with respect to the slave issues arising out of the *Creole* affair. This certainly would make Webster's negotiations with Lord Ashburton a bit easier when he arrived in Washington the following month.

Chapter Six

Enter Diplomacy; Crisis Averted

Governor Cockburn's dispatch of November 17, 1841, to Lord Stanley arrived in London in mid-December. It is likely that Cockburn's alarming dispatch of November 24—expressing worry that American warships would descend on a virtually defenseless Nassau—also reached London shortly thereafter. One can imagine that Lord Stanley, responsible for war and the colonies, quickly met with Foreign Secretary (and former secretary for war and the colonies), Lord Aberdeen, since it was obvious that this *Creole* incident could well be a tipping point toward war. Relations between Britain and America had been tense for a decade, and the *Creole* incident contained incendiary elements—slavery, murder, and mutiny—especially for the new slaveholding American President Tyler. There could be no doubt that, unless some dramatic step was taken to defuse this issue, and, ideally, to reset the general relationship with the Americans—from the Canadian border problems to the antislavery squadrons of the coast of west Africa—war could ensue. There could be little doubt that, while the US-Canadian border issue was the most long-standing and important, this new *Creole* problem could create a volcano of emotion in both countries. Emotion in diplomacy was dangerous.

Therefore, on Christmas Eve 1841, after consulting his two senior secretaries, Prime Minister Peel solemnly informed Queen Victoria that a third war with America was on the horizon. He proposed a special mission to Washington to resolve the host of problems between the two countries and so to preserve the peace. Queen Victoria quickly approved this proposal. This diplomatic technique—a special mission, rather than relying on existing representatives—made sense in this instance, because the British minister in Washington, Henry Fox, had not distinguished himself since he arrived in Washington in 1836, and was not well regarded. (The American minister in

London, Everett, had the advantage of being close to Secretary of State Webster, but he was too fresh in his post to be an ideal channel and negotiating partner.) A special British mission, however, carried the risk that failure could be more difficult to shield from the press.

Aberdeen suggested that Alexander Baring, the 1st Baron Ashburton, be appointed a special envoy with full powers to settle all matters in dispute. Lord Ashburton, born just before the American Revolution, now sixty-seven, was a wealthy banker and head of Baring Brothers & Co., one of the greatest financial houses in the world. It was said that there were six great powers in Europe: Britain, France, Austro-Hungry, Russia, Prussia, and Baring Brothers. He had served in Parliament from 1806 until 1835, and had served as Master of the Mint. Lord Aberdeen had negotiated the financing of the Louisiana Purchase.[1] He owned large land holdings in the United States—including one million acres of land in Maine—and he had married an American woman, Anne Louisa Bingham, daughter of Senator William Bingham of Pennsylvania. She received a large inheritance that helped Alexander acquire his partnership in Baring Brothers.

During the summer of 1839, Senator Webster and his wife, Caroline, had been presented to Queen Victoria at a ball, during the Websters' visit to London. They had had dinner earlier with Alexander Baring; Webster had served as legal counsel to the financial firm of Baring Brothers since 1831. The foreign secretary at that time, Lord Palmerston, suggested that the Queen invite the Websters to the ball, along with the American minister, Andrew Stevenson. Stevenson was gracious to Webster, even though Webster had voted against his confirmation in 1836. This relaxation of court etiquette was considered by Palmerston to be a wise long-term investment in the prominent Daniel Webster.[2] Webster spent a small fortune outfitting himself (and his wife) in appropriate court dress: he wore white silk stockings, diamond knee and shoe buckles, a coat lined with white silk, and lace frills over his hands.[3] In late September, while still in London, the Websters attended the marriage of their twenty-one-year-old daughter, Julia, to Samuel Appleton.

On December 27, 1841, Foreign Secretary Aberdeen informed the US minister, Everett, of the queen's approval of this special mission. For Everett, this must have created very mixed emotions: on the one hand, having a special mission, especially one led by such a distinguished man as Lord Ashburton, was a mark of respect for the United States; on the other hand, it had to be clear to Everett that the main task of improving US-UK relations would move from his office in London to Ashburton's mission in Washington. On New Year's Eve, the London press announced the appointment, and Everett wrote to Webster with the news. Ashburton wrote officially to Webster a couple of days later about the appointment.

In Washington, Tyler and Webster welcomed the news with a sigh of relief. The idea of sending a special mission to the United States was general-

Figure 6.1. Alexander Baring, 1st Baron Ashburton and Anne Louisa Bingham (the daughter of Senator Bingham of Pennsylvania) were married in 1798. This image was created around that time. Courtesy of the Fort Kent, Maine, Historical Society.

ly welcome to Americans, since it was a somewhat unusual step, especially for the mighty British. Lord Ashburton's selection was considered proof of "a genuine desire on the part of England to negotiate upon a sincere and friendly basis."[4] Webster, in particular, welcomed his friend Alexander Bar-

Figure 6.2. Anne Louisa Bingham. Courtesy of the Fort Kent, Maine, Historical Society.

ing. These were the perfect men to negotiate the resolution of the serious problems between the two countries. Since the mass cabinet resignations six months earlier, Tyler and Webster had grown closer. Tyler saw Webster as the head of the cabinet, and Webster had earned his complete confidence. Tyler and Webster "saw each other every day, dined together often, and kept each other informed of their thoughts and expectations."[5]

Foreign Secretary Aberdeen drafted instructions on February 8, 1842, for Ashburton to take with him to Washington. While these instructions gave a rather free hand to Ashburton, they did present issues in the order of importance to Aberdeen: the Canadian boundary (including Oregon and the northwest border),[6] the *Caroline* problem, and the right to search—or to visit, as the British preferred say—American vessels off the African coast. Oddly, Aberdeen had told Everett on December 31 that he thought a solution to the right of search would be the most important issue.[7]

In a rush to get started on his new mission, Ashburton left Britain in mid-February. He arrived on April 2, 1842 in Annapolis, Maryland, on the British frigate, the *Warspite*, with fifty-four guns and a crew of five hundred. Aberdeen wanted Ashburton's arrival to be fittingly ceremonial and impressive. It was. Despite its size, the frigate had been blown off course from the scheduled arrival in New York, and so ended up in Annapolis.

To assist him in dealing with the difficulties he would face in Washington, Ashburton brought with him three secretaries, five servants, three horses and a carriage, and a great quantity of luggage.[8] Ashburton arrived in Washington on April 4, and two days later he called on President Tyler and presented his credentials. Tyler, in turn, expressed his satisfaction that Britain wanted to preserve good understanding between the two nations. After those formalities, Webster and Ashburton left the White House to visit the Congress and the Library of Congress.[9]

Presidents do not get the luxury of spending their time exclusively on international affairs or on domestic affairs, as they might choose, and they cannot control when one or the other intrudes, demanding attention. In the midst of the crisis in relations with Great Britain, President Tyler and Secretary Webster also had a major domestic problem that seemed to be getting worse: "Dorr's rebellion" in Rhode Island. That state retained its highly restrictive property requirements for voting, in accordance with its seventeenth-century British colonial charter.[10] It was virtually the only state falling well short of universal adult white manhood suffrage. At about the same time as the *Creole* was heading to Nassau, Thomas Dorr, a Rhode Island lawyer, was engaged in a meeting in Providence of the "People's Convention." A month later, in December 1841, the People's Constitution was adopted; it provided for near universal white adult male suffrage, under which elections were scheduled for mid-April 1842. Rhode Island governor Samuel King turned to the federal government—to President Tyler—for help to suppress this "rebellion" against his charter government.

On April 4, 1842, the day that Lord Ashburton arrived in Washington, Governor King sent a delegation to Washington seeking Tyler's assurance that the federal military would be on the governor's side in the event that Dorr's followers got out of hand. A few days later, a delegation arrived representing the Dorr position. In terms of political instinct, Tyler probably was sympathetic to Dorr's goal of broader suffrage, and since northern Democrats rhetorically supported Dorr's efforts to change Rhode Island's ruling structure, but Tyler could not openly attack the People's Constitution.[11] The Whigs in Congress would probably incline toward Governor King's position. Tyler sent the governor a letter on April 11, explaining that he had no authority to anticipate insurrectionary activity; but at the same time, Tyler privately instructed General Winfield Scott to ensure that the US army fort at Newport was secure.

Events in Rhode Island continued to get worse. In another letter to President Tyler, Governor King—who "seemed at times to be on the verge of a nervous breakdown"—added that a large "deluded" portion of the citizenry had "declared their intention to put down the existing government."[12] Supreme Court Justice Joseph Story wrote on April 26 to his old friend Daniel Webster to urge him to have Tyler send troops to Fort Adams in Newport at once. Dorr's assembly moved into session, and on May 4, the governor again appealed to Tyler for federal help. Once again, Tyler brushed off the governor. On May 9, a warrant was issued for Dorr's arrest.

On May 10, Dorr met in the White House with President Tyler for four hours. Tyler told Dorr that his activity was "treasonable against the state and if [he] committed any overt acts and resisted the force of the U.S., [he] would then commit treason against the U.S. and as sure as [he] did so [he] should be hanged."[13] Daniel Webster confirmed this conclusion. On May 14, Secretary of State Webster broke from his negotiations with Lord Ashburton and was dispatched by Tyler to chair a secret meeting in New York City in an unsuccessful attempt to resolve the dispute. (This was not unlike Webster's successful role in easing the McLeod problem in New York a year earlier; see chapter 2.)

Southern newspapers, interestingly, connected the ideology of Dorr's Rebellion and the slave revolt on the *Creole*, in part because of the temporal coincidence of the two events. The *Madisonian*, published in Washington, DC, asserted on May 21 that those who "encouraged the commission of outrage against the existing government [in Rhode Island were] . . . of the same class that instigated the slaves on board the *Creole* to commit murder and mutiny."[14]

By mid-June, charter militias patrolled the streets of Providence night and day. Meanwhile, Dorr assembled a small force in the Gloucester village of Chepachet, close to the Connecticut border, on June 25. On the same day, the Rhode Island General Assembly placed the entire state under military rule. On June 29, Tyler ordered Secretary of War John Spencer to Rhode Island just in case federal military intervention became necessary.[15] In the end, Dorr was forced to leave Chepachet, and he fled the state. After several moves, Dorr ended up settling in New Hampshire on July 8, though he returned to Rhode Island in October 1843. The Dorr Rebellion, however, was over.

In the fall of 1842, the Rhode Island Assembly wrote a new state constitution granting greatly expanded voting rights. Thus, the Rhode Island crisis of opposing governments contending for legitimacy finally ended. However, the ultimate US constitutional issue of the federal role ended up in the US Supreme Court six years later, in a case won by none other than Daniel Webster (see the epilogue).

When Lord Ashburton wrote to Webster about his appointment, he asked for Webster's assistance in finding appropriate housing for him and his staff. Not surprisingly, Webster found a place for Ashburton right in Webster's own neighborhood—the best in the nation's capital.

On his nomination to be secretary of state, early in 1841, Webster felt he simply had to have a grand house in Washington. "Webster was venal even by the standards of his own day, since he encouraged the solicitation of funds from wealthy Bostonian constituents to maintain his lavish life-style in Washington."[16] He borrowed[17] funds to buy the elegant Swann House, on H Street, facing the Executive Mansion (not formally called the White House until 1901) across from President's Square, later known as Lafayette Square.[18] At the western corner of that square stood Decatur House, which had been the home of three previous secretaries of state: Henry Clay (under John Quincy Adams), Martin Van Buren (under Andrew Jackson) and Edward Livingston (also under Jackson); at various times, it had also been the home of the ministers of France, Russia, and Britain. One hundred yards to the east of Swann House on H Street was a great house that had been constructed only five years earlier. Webster selected that house for Ashburton, who leased it for ten months for $12,000.[19] One can imagine Webster walking over to Ashburton's residence, walking up the few steps to the front door, and being greeted by Lord Ashburton. Perhaps the two men looked across the park to where President Tyler lived and worked.

Just fifty feet to the east of Ashburton's new residence was Dolly Madison's house—an ironic situation, since that First Lady had fled the Executive Mansion in 1814, just before the British burned it. Mrs. Madison was not living in the house when Ashburton arrived, since she had rented it to former attorney general John J. Crittenden. Just a few dozen yards along Madison Place, along the square from Ashburton's new residence, was the most fashionable boarding house in Washington. John C. Spencer, whom President Tyler appointed secretary of war less than five months earlier, lived in that boarding house.

Finally, at the southeast corner of President's Square, about three hundred yards across the square from Webster's Swann House, was the location of the State Department, housed in the Northeast Executive Building. John Quincy Adams was secretary of state when the building was completed; the State Department moved into seventeen of the thirty-one rooms. By Webster's time, the full staff of the department consisted of about a dozen clerks.[20] It was in the secretary's office in the southeast corner that the Webster-Ashburton Treaty was signed some four months after Lord Ashburton arrived on the square.[21]

By the fall of 1841, when the renovation to Swann House was completed, and when Caroline Webster arrived, Webster hosted lavish dinner parties—as he felt necessary and appropriate for a secretary of state. However, Webster never conducted government business at these functions; rather, they were designed to cultivate "relationships" with members of Congress, diplomats, and other important members of society. Webster personally would select the food and wine, and often ended the evening by leading his guests in song.[22] More than once, the president, the diplomatic corps, the justices of the Supreme Court, and members of Congress would join in. Once Lord Ashburton arrived at his house in April 1842, one hundred yards to the east on H Street, the lavish entertaining moved into high gear. Ashburton offered rare wines and seductive French desserts prepared by his French chef. Ashburton used his elegant table to help smooth negotiations with his American interlocutors.

Even before Lord Ashburton arrived in the United States, Webster had privately consulted his friend from Massachusetts, Justice Joseph Story. Story was a giant on the Supreme Court, having served there for thirty-one years. (He had authored the court's Opinion in the *Amistad* case almost exactly one year earlier.) Story shared Webster's fundamental interest in the importance to society of the protection of property—even property in slaves. Story advised Webster that, in the absence of an extradition treaty with Britain, there was no legal basis to compel the return to the United States of the nineteen *Creole* slaves jailed in Nassau. Webster asked Story to draft articles that might go into a treaty, dealing with the problem of a ship being driven into a foreign port, and also dealing with extradition.[23]

Ashburton and Webster wasted no time in beginning their negotiation. They talked often, mostly at Ashburton's house, just yards from Webster's Swann House, and also in the State Department's offices. Neither man was young: Alexander Baring was sixty-eight, and Daniel Webster was sixty. They even looked somewhat the same: "Both had large heads, high foreheads [i.e., balding], piercing dark eyes with heavy brows. Ashburton's complexion, however, was 'clear red and white,' Webster's a dark dusky hue."[24]

The American lawyer and the British banker ran through all the issues: the boundary, the African slave ship inspection problem, the *Caroline*, and the *Creole*. They decide to concentrate on the pressing issue of the Northeast boundary issue. This was extremely complicated, since it involved—on the American side—the participation in some fashion of delegations from Maine and Massachusetts, and there was the almost comical periodic surfacing of old maps, each presenting a different boundary line. Even though the *Creole* issue was not in the instructions given by Lord Aberdeen, Ashburton—and Webster—simply had to discuss it, since there was a great deal of public excitement about it. Ashburton sought guidance from London, and explained that he thought security for the future was more important for the Southern slaveholders than compensation for past injuries.

On April 28, Ashburton wrote to the secretary of state for foreign affairs, Earl Aberdeen, and explained that Webster hoped to connect the *Creole* issue to a general extradition treaty. Webster's proposal would have "compelled British colonial officials not only to abstain from all interference with slave vessels driven by stress of weather into British ports, but went still further in cases of mutiny by slaves, requiring colonial officials to aid the officers and owners to recover possession of their ships."[25] Ashburton opined that "some" agreement had to be found. In the meantime, the British Foreign Office advised Minister Everett that the colonial officials in Nassau were to be commended for their conduct of the *Creole* situation.

By mid-May, there were reports of "warm debates" between Webster and Ashburton. Ashburton was of good demeanor and was "quite well received," whereas Webster looked "grave, and a little care-worn."[26] The two sides kept their negotiations strictly secret, and so the rumors had little to seize upon except appearances.[27] Nevertheless, by June, there were reports that Lord Ashburton was authorized to make "some *prospective* arrangement to guard against future cases, but not to allow any indemnification for the *Creole.*"[28] Lord Aberdeen approved in principle an extradition arrangement, except that he refused to accept, among the list of crimes, "mutiny and revolt on board ship," which the negotiators wanted to cover the *Creole* situation.[29]

On June 29, Ashburton sent a dispatch to Lord Aberdeen in London. With respect to the *Creole*, Ashburton "assured Aberdeen that failure to give satisfaction for the future would be a serious disappointment to the American President and Congress, and threatened the successful conclusion of other matters under discussion."[30]

Lord Ashburton found the Executive branch and the Congress locked in a bitter power struggle over policy, and he thought Tyler was "a bit testy" about the *Creole* issue. The negotiations continued into the hot summer of 1842. Ashburton enjoyed amiable dinners with the Websters and glittering official functions at the White House—one of which was a wedding reception for James Monroe's granddaughter, during which Tyler asked John Quincy Adams to escort Mrs. Tyler, while the president escorted the bride.

Tyler and Webster, and also Ashburton, used secret funds to "soften up" local authorities in Maine and Massachusetts, in order to get them to welcome a compromise borderline that gave more than half of the disputed territory to the American side, but gave the British a fifty-mile-wide buffer between the border and the St. Lawrence River—to permit a military road to defend Quebec and the maritime provinces. That helped to resolve the contentious Northeast border dispute, and a compromise was reached in early July. The matter of the British detaining and inspecting US vessels off the African coast, in connection with repressing the slave trade, was resolved by a decision to form joint cruising squadrons to reflect the common effort to end the international slave trade. That would be contained in the proposed treaty.

Webster proposed a provision in the treaty to deal with extradition. He tried to add "mutiny and revolt on board ship" to the standard list of crimes, and Ashburton at first seemed agreeable. But then Ashburton realized the implications for the *Creole* issue and refused. Later, when Tyler sent the treaty to the Senate, he explained that his purpose in including an extradition provision was to assist governors of states along the Canadian border in dealing with requests from Canada to surrender fugitives. He explained that the provision excluded "all political offenses or criminal charges arising from wars or intestine commotions."

By mid-July, Webster and Ashburton had agreed on a framework for an exchange of notes defusing the *Caroline* issue, along with the more recent but less important McLeod matter. Webster initiated the exchange of notes on July 27. He attached a copy of his note to Minister Fox of April 24, 1841, and a relevant extract from President Tyler's Message to Congress of December 7, 1841, both dealing with the *Caroline.* Webster pointed out that the attack was "an offense to the sovereignty and dignity" of the United States and "a wrong for which, to this day, no atonement, or even apology, has been made." It was almost as if being ignored by the British were a greater affront to American pride than the destruction of the vessel and the loss of life.

Ashburton replied the next day. He agreed with Webster's statement of the applicable general principles of international law and also with Webster's presentation of the exception of self-defense (i.e., whether there was "that necessity of self-defense, instant, overwhelming, leaving no choice of means"). More personally, Ashburton said that he had "admiration" for Webster's "very ingenious discussion of the general principles." On the other hand, Ashburton asserted that Webster had presented a "highly coloured picture" of the facts. That allowed Ashburton to present the facts as viewed from the British perspective. He also complained about the difficulty of dealing with the McLeod problem arising out of the federal/state system.[31]

Critically, Ashburton explained that "no slight of the authority of the United States was ever intended, yet it must be admitted that there was in the hurried execution of this necessary service a violation of territory." Finally, Ashburton explained that what was "perhaps most to be regretted is that some explanation and apology for this occurrence was not immediately made." Thus, Ashburton in effect claimed that the *Caroline* facts were on the side of the British, that the British actions were justified, and that the only fault was in not making this point clear years earlier.

Webster's reply note was dated August 6, 1842. He was masterful in cherry-picking Ashburton's note, and selecting for acknowledgment only those elements that would allow the US side to rid the parties of this problem. Webster noted that the president was pleased that the British: (1) admitted the American statement of the principles applicable, including the statement of the self-defense exception; (2) solemnly declared that no slight or disrespect was intended toward the United States; (3) acknowledged that, whether or not justified, there was a "violation of the territory of the United States"; and, finally, (4) "it is now admitted that an explanation or apology for this violation was due at the time." As a result of this reading of Ashburton's note, the president was "content" to receive those assurances in a conciliatory spirit, and therefore there will be no further discussion about this subject.

Thus, America's national honor over the *Caroline* affair could be said to have been restored. Lost in the euphoria, however, was the fact that the British never actually apologized or accepted responsibility or offered compensation. This outcome reflected brilliant diplomacy.

In June and July, the parties turned again and again to the problematic *Creole* case. Ashburton wrote to Lord Aberdeen on June 29 that this was his "real difficulty." He further reported that the "President, as a Virginian, has a strong opinion about *Creole* case, and is not a little disposed to be obstinate on the subject."[32] Ashburton was inclined to offer some reparations for the slaves, but he lacked authorization and was sure that London would not agree.[33]

In mid-July, Webster called the attorney general into the discussion with Lord Ashburton on the subject of the *Creole*. Hugh Swinton Legare had been a political figure in South Carolina and was a recognized expert in the law of nations (today's international law). Legare had studied in the United Kingdom and elsewhere in Europe, and was quite familiar with Continental views of maritime rights and obligations. At the end of the discussion, Ashburton asked Legare to reduce his remarks to writing, and the attorney general agreed.

Legare's position was clear and compelling. He acknowledged that in the eyes of English law, slaves are not things but persons, and they have a right to the protection of that law. Accordingly, England could prohibit the importation of slaves, but that does not give England the right to take possession of a ship in distress and to set the persons on board at liberty. American ships driven into English harbors by the dangers of the seas are not to be held accountable for what they contain when they are driven in. Legare flatly protested the interference of British authorities, who had no right to interfere on any matter of municipal law. America had every right to insist that other countries acknowledge personal capacity or status, such as marriage or slavery. Continental lawyers maintain that such laws follow the person, and so interference with persons on a foreign ship on the basis of status is "a gross violation of international comity."[34]

Legare explained that a ship at anchor in a foreign harbor preserves its jurisdiction and laws—and this proposition would command universal assent, but for the "peculiar feelings" that attach to all matters relating to domestic slavery. Hypothetically, if a man were to commit murder on the high seas, and was chained, and the ship entered a British port, and if that man sought a writ of habeas corpus, claiming that he was imprisoned within British territory for no offense against English law, no judge or lawyer in England would free him. Legare would concede, for the sake of argument, that a ship voluntarily entering British ports with an awareness of English law may be taken to have voluntarily submitted to that law. But in the case of compulsory entry, "no authority, or principle, or analogy of the law of nations, will justify" the enforcing of local English law on board that ship. All nations agree that a ship in distress is not bound to pay local duties, and English law specifically makes that clear.

The power of the attorney general's lengthy Opinion must have had an impact on Lord Ashburton, not only because of Legare's recognized stature in the law, but also because he was a politician from slaveholding South Carolina.[35] In addition, Ashburton came to understand the fears of the Southerners that the British action in Nassau exposed the entire American maritime domestic slave trade to great risks.

At the very end of July, after the Northeast boundary issue was resolved, but before the final resolution of the *Creole* matter, Webster hosted a grand dinner at his house to celebrate. The president and the entire cabinet attended, along with a few select senators and delegations from Maine and Massachusetts. Webster toasted Queen Victoria; Ashburton's reply toast was to the president and to the perpetuity of the institutions of the United States. Finally, President Tyler addressed the Maine and Massachusetts delegations, and toasted: "Blessed are the peacemakers."[36]

The heat and humidity in Washington must have been oppressive for the two negotiators, fraying their nerves and adding to their discomfort with the political problems.[37] One can imagine Ashburton and Webster sitting together in Webster's Swann House, or at Ashburton's nearby residence, or across the park at the State Department's offices. One scholar explained the procedure: "These friendly conferences, to which Webster willing assented, took the place of formal negotiations and were carried on without the exchange of written papers, until the time came to cast the final results into shape for presentation."[38] There are no minutes of these meetings, and no official record was kept.

The result of these exhausting and frustrating deliberations was an exchange of diplomatic notes in early August, the effect of which was to resolve the *Creole* problem and so to permit the logjam of other issues to be incorporated into treaty form. The notes are quite fascinating, and reflect important issues of international law; they are also interesting political documents. They are set out in full in appendix III.

It is not clear whether each side shared with the other a draft of each note and welcomed suggestions for improvement. It would not be surprising if that were how they conducted themselves, given their trusting working relationship. It is also possible that each note was prepared and exchanged at arm's length. In any event, both men must have been fully aware that the notes would become available to the public and eventually would have many different audiences. For Webster, he had to keep one eye on how the Senate would take them, for the Senate was a necessary actor in the entry into force of the treaty. He also had to walk the thin political line between not offending too much the liberal and abolitionist interests in his New England political base, while at the same time ensuring that he delivered the message to the South that he was protecting their interests.

For Ashburton, the political elements were somewhat less important, since he did not look for any personal political future. Of course, he had to ensure that his actions would not be rejected by Parliament, since that too would lead to the scuttling of the treaty. He had to be mindful of the very strong antislavery sentiment in the United Kingdom, and so he had to avoid any steps that might suggest that he was endorsing or cooperating with the evils of slavery. Ashburton also suffered the disadvantage of being alone, three thousand miles from his government, and confronting the problem of some six weeks' duration between the time he would ask a question of London and would receive London's answer. He must have envied Webster's ability to walk across the park to consult with President Tyler.

Secretary Webster's note was dated August 1. It is long, and mostly reads like a lawyer's brief. He set the groundwork by acknowledging that Ashburton was not empowered to put the *Creole* issues into the treaty, by not asking for compensation for the loss of the slaves, by acknowledging that the facts are "controverted" and so he would ignore them, and by explaining that his approach is future oriented only and desirous of "practical means of giving security to the coasting trade" of the United States. Webster's note makes no claim for the return of the slaves, because they had vanished, and could not have been returned even if the British were so inclined. In a smart political gesture, Webster also explained the importance of the coastal trade by pointing to the products of the Mississippi Valley, "a region of vast extent and boundless fertility," which were exported along that route—a nod to the Westerners that he was looking out for their interests too. In a bow to the South, Webster pointed out that slavery exists "under the guarantee of the Constitution of the United States." (He also must have had a twinkle in his eye as he reminded Ashburton that America's slaves were introduced and maintained by Britain during the colonial period.)

While pointing out that the facts are controverted, Webster introduced the term "officious[39] interference" to describe the actions of the Nassau authorities in setting the *Creole*'s slaves free. He used the term twice in the first few paragraphs, but only there. He did not define the term.

The core of the note is a brilliant lawyer's brief setting out the legal regime in which the *Creole* existed while it was at anchor in Nassau's harbor (i.e., it remained as if it were part of US territory, under US jurisdiction, although that was not exclusive jurisdiction in the sense that persons on board might not violate local law). Thus, if a murder took place on the vessel while in port, "the offense is cognizable and punishable by the proper court of the United States." (Webster wisely did not charge the British with a gross violation of law by not permitting the return of the seventeen slaves from British custody to the United States for trial.) On the other hand, Webster made clear that when American slaves escape into British territories, no one in the United States expects them to be returned; similarly, if persons who are charged with crimes seek asylum in British territory, their return is not expected, since the United States had no extradition treaty with the United Kingdom.

Near the end of his long note, Webster complimented Ashburton, and at the same time brought in the notion of the threat to trade and commerce: "Your Lordship's discernment and large experience in [commercial] affairs can not fail to suggest to you how important it is to merchants and navigators . . . that they should feel secure against all but the ordinary causes of maritime loss."

Then, at the very end of the note, Webster made a proposal: yes, we know that you are not empowered to treat this topic in the treaty, but you surely know your government's views well enough to "engage that instructions shall be given to the local authorities in the islands, which shall lead them to regulate their conduct in conformity with the rights of [US citizens] and the just expectations of their Government." This last offering was quite in contrast to the style and content of most of the document, and it introduced a completely new approach. It is not known whether this was solely Webster's idea, or whether both men fashioned it collaboratively, and structured it as an invitation by Webster. Webster closed his note with a reminder that it would be "with the most profound regret" that these negotiations should conclude with nothing being done on this topic, which would be a "dangerous source of future collisions" between the two countries.

Lord Ashburton responded with a note dated August 6. It is less than half the length of Webster's note, and is a very strange document.

Ashburton began by explaining why he was not empowered to deal with the *Creole* issues in the treaty: the case of the *Creole* was known in London only a few days before his departure for the United States, and so it was not a subject that immediately concerned his mission, and no complaint had yet been made by Minister Everett. This was probably a stretch of the time line facts, though technically accurate. Webster's long dispatch to Minister Everett was not sent until January 29, 1842, and Ashburton left the United Kingdom for Washington in mid-February, and so it is likely that Webster's complaint did in fact arrive only days before Ashburton's departure. On the other hand, Governor Cockburn reported the *Creole* incident immediately, and that information was at the disposal of Aberdeen no later than mid-December, and, unquestionably, it played a significant role in the decision to send Ashburton on his mission to Washington. Thus, there was ample time to provide instructions to Ashburton before he left. Nevertheless, Ashburton quickly acknowledged in his note that he understood the importance of the issue.

In the second paragraph of his note, Ashburton stated his "conclusion" that the issue would be better dealt with in London, not in Washington. Just in case this conclusion was missed, Ashburton repeated it twice in the very next paragraph: "I strongly recommend this question of the security of the Bahamas channel being referred for discussion in London." Ashburton explained the reasons for his insistence that the topic be addressed in London and not in Washington: the real issues are ones of national and international law, and in London the "highest authorities" are available to consult. In somewhat more personal terms, Ashburton explained that he—as an extremely successful investment banker—would be comfortable dealing with the usual commercial issues, but he was uncomfortable with these deep legal matters. In contrast, Ashburton complimented Webster on his "very elaborate" legal argument, to which Webster's professional "authority necessarily gives great weight." Finally, these broad and important legal principles—which were now being considered only in the very narrow case of the Bahamas—could have a global impact on British interests (for example, in Singapore, Cape Town, or Bombay).

Ashburton acknowledged Webster's admission that the United States did not seek the return of any escaped slave, and, reciprocally, Ashburton promised that the British would not act as "decoys" to attract slaves in violation of American law. On the other hand, when a slave reaches British territory, the law is clear (though Ashburton wisely does not state the law). To make the point, Ashburton stated that a slave reaching the shore of Nassau would be treated exactly the same as a "foreign" slave reaching Boston under any circumstances. The qualifying term "foreign" is ambiguous, perhaps intentionally so. Surely, Ashburton knew the obligations of authorities in Boston under the Fugitive Slave provision of the Constitution and the 1793 statute with respect to the return of fugitive slaves.

Once again, Ashburton complimented Webster on his "evident ability" in presenting the range of legal principles engulfing the *Creole*, and explained that he would not "pretend to judge them." For the fourth time in this note, Ashburton confirmed his opinion that the "subject be referred to where it will be perfectly weighed and examined"—London. Thus, for the first nine paragraphs of the note, Ashburton drove home the single message: I can't deal with this subject; it has to be moved to London for resolution.

The tenth paragraph seems to have absolutely nothing to do with the previous nine paragraphs, as if someone else had written it in a totally different context. It states:

> *In the meantime, I can engage that instructions shall be given to the Governors of her majesty's colonies on the southern borders of the United States to*

> *execute their own laws with careful attention* to the wish of their Government to maintain [a] good neighborhood, and *that there shall be no officious interference with American vessels driven by accident or by violence into those ports*. The laws and duties of hospitality shall be executed, and these seem neither to require nor to justify any further inquisition into the state of persons or things on board of vessels so situated, than may be indispensable to enforce the observance of the municipal law of the colony, and the proper regulation of its harbors and waters. (emphasis added)

Ashburton's "engagement" thus picked up on Webster's hint at the end of his long note of five days earlier that his Lordship might be able to "engage that instructions be given" to the colonial authorities so as to take away all reasonable American complaints. Ashburton concluded by expressing the hope that these new rules will avoid "any excitement or agitation on this very sensitive subject of slavery."

Two days later, Webster sent his brief reply ote. He explained that there "may be weight" to Ashburton's recommendation to refer the matter to London—if we really need to have this resolved by formal treaty.

Nevertheless, the president relied on the principles of law set out in Webster's first note, and also on Ashburton's "engagement"—which is then quoted in full. Thus ends this diplomatic exchange. And the logjam that had held up the treaty was broken.

What, exactly, did Ashburton promise? Little more than the following: local law would be executed in a manner that was not annoying, and any inquiry—about whether anyone on board was a slave—would be permitted only when it was absolutely necessary to comply with local law. One hundred and thirty years later, the value of diplomatic "constructive ambiguity" was reestablished in the Nixon-Mao "Shanghai Communiqué";[40] perhaps Webster and Ashburton had anticipated that idea.

On August 9, Lord Ashburton sent his correspondence with Webster to London for Lord Aberdeen and offered an explanation for its contents. Ashburton said that some official statement about the *Creole* had become "essential to the safety of the treaty [and it] had proved the most difficult of all the topics"[41] that he had to deal with. Interestingly, Ashburton claimed that Webster's note was designed to protect his popularity in the South, and Ashburton's own note was designed to "evade any engagement," while at the same time maintaining British principles with respect to slavery. In short, Ashburton asserted: "To say something conciliating was indispensable to the safety of our other objects."[42] Finally, Ashburton expressed the hope that his extremely vague "pledge" as to the future conduct of British colonial authorities would not be disavowed by London. Clearly, Ashburton was signaling that the entire treaty house of cards could come tumbling down if this cornerstone were withdrawn.

Webster and Ashburton signed two treaties on August 9. One dealt with the boundary issue, and the other dealt with all other issues. This arrangement was to satisfy Ashburton, who feared that opposition in the Senate to the African slave and extradition articles might sink the boundary settlement. However, the next day Ashburton yielded, and the two treaties were combined into one, retaining the August 9 date. The Treaty of Washington, as it was then called, contained ten articles: the first seven concerned boundary issues, VIII and IX concerned the establishment of joint antislavery squadrons off the African coast; Article X provided for extradition for a series of crimes including murder (but not mutiny). The last two articles dealt with the treaty's duration and site for the exchange of ratifications. Ashburton wrote to Aberdeen on that day and reported that it was not one of the happiest days of his life, because of the *Creole* "plague."[43] Ashburton was chagrined that no real conclusion could be reached on the *Creole* matter and that the topic could not be included in the treaty. Nevertheless, the fact that the treaty was not imperiled is a tribute to the skill of the negotiators.

President Tyler sent the treaty to the Senate on August 11. In his Special Message, Tyler also included the texts of notes exchanged in the context of the negotiation dealing with the *Caroline*, impressment, and the subject of the "interference of the colonial authorities of the British West Indies with American merchant vessels driven by stress of weather or carried by violence into the ports of those colonies." (Tyler neglected to mention that the "merchant vessels" that sparked the controversy were in fact slave ships.) Tyler explained that "a confident hope is entertained that the correspondence . . . showing the grounds taken by this Government and the engagements entered into by the British Minister, will be found such as to satisfy the just expectation" of the American people.

The late historian of the House of Representatives put his finger on the new dilemma: "The Whigs controlled the Senate and had cast out the President. In their eyes Webster was almost as bad. Would they now approve the handiwork of these two outcasts?"[44]

In the beginning, there seemed to be trouble in the Senate, where the debate was held in secret, in accordance with the procedures of the Foreign Relations Committee. Senator Thomas Hart Benton, a Democrat from Missouri, attacked the treaty as a dishonorable betrayal of the national interest. With respect to the *Creole* matter, Benton claimed that the freeing of the slaves in Nassau threatened the Mississippi Valley and the South, and the growing insecurity of the shipment of slaves from the Southeast to New Orleans would damage the West as well.[45] Webster coordinated closely with the chairman of the Foreign Relations Committee, Senator William C. Rives of Virginia.

But, in the end, it was an endorsement from Senator John C. Calhoun of South Carolina that proved decisive. He was prepared to support the treaty,

Figure 6.3. The Senate chamber, viewed from the gallery, several years after the Senate consented to the Treaty of Washington, the Webster-Ashburton Treaty.

because it would bring peace to US-British relations, and that peace was essential for the United States to return to prosperity. Left unstated was that Britain was the largest export market for the South's cotton, and war with Britain would further damage the already problematic economy of the South, which was still suffering from the Panic of 1837. With respect to the *Creole*, Calhoun said that he found Lord Ashburton's assurances to be satisfactory safeguards for American coastal shipping.

On Saturday night, August 20, the Senate voted 39–9 in favor of the treaty. Never before had the US Senate given a treaty such a large majority.[46] This substantial Senate vote somewhat surprised Webster. He gave appropriate credit to President Tyler in a note to Tyler of August 24:

> Your steady support and confidence, your anxious and intelligent attention to what was in progress, your exceedingly and pleasant intercourse both with the British minister and the commissioners of the States, have given every facility to my agency in this important transaction.[47]

This treaty is usually held up as the most important achievement of the Tyler presidency. However, for John Tyler personally, this must have been a bittersweet time, since twenty days later, his dear wife, Letitia, died of a second stroke, at age fifty-one.

For the next two decades, there were no further *Creole*-like incidents in the Caribbean. After that, the Civil War and the Thirteenth Amendment made the issue moot.

Daniel Webster left the Tyler cabinet in May 1843, and he returned to the Senate on March 4, 1845. A year later, after a variety of attacks on the Treaty of Washington and Webster's negotiation of it, Webster took to the floor of the Senate for two full days, April 6–7, 1846, to defend the treaty and his role in its negotiation. He noted that there had been "disparaging [and] disapproving" remarks in Congress, and he doubted that anyone expected that he "should sit [in the Senate] from day to day . . . hearing erroneous statements, entirely erroneous as to matters of fact, and deductions from those supposed facts quite as erroneous, all tending to produce unfavorable impressions respecting the treaty . . . and of everybody who had a hand in the treaty. . . . it could hardly have been expected that I should sit here and hear all this and keep my peace."[48] He noted sharply that the treaty had received a vote of five-sixths of the Senate, a greater majority than any previous disputed treaty.

Webster then proceeded to deal mostly with the Northeast boundary matter (whether the United States gave too much to the British), the *Caroline* controversy, the McLeod issue (whether he put undue pressure on the New York governor), and the African squadron (whether he gave the British the right to search American vessels). Near the end of the second day, he referred to the "coasting vessels" and the Bahamas, and specifically the *Encomium* case. He sought the agreement of Senator Calhoun that Webster had sought to solve the problem by preventing future occurrences. Calhoun quickly expressed his assent. Finally, Webster said:

> And in regard to the *Creole* case, I put it to the gentlemen and every citizen of the country whether everything intended to be accomplished by correspondence and negotiation on that subject has not been accomplished. And then I will put it to the country, finally, whether what was done on that occasion—whether the result of talent or fortune (I claim no merit for talent)—has not been favorable to the maritime rights of the United States and to the civilized world—whether it is not so regarded by all the civilized world.[49]

III

Afterward: Post-November 1841

Chapter Seven

Insurance for Slave "Property"

The United States and Great Britain went toe to toe over the *Creole* affair, but that conflict was dealt with in the context of other pressing bilateral issues and interests, and was handled diplomatically. Compensation for the freed slaves was pressed—but lightly—by the US side; and it was flatly rejected by the UK side. It would be another decade before the compensation question would be definitely settled (see the next chapter). In some ways, more important than compensation was the alleged injury to America's national honor. Ultimately, the American side settled for a vague promise that the British authorities would take steps to ensure that such an event would not happen again as a result of actions by British authorities. There was never an admission of liability or responsibility by the British, and there was never a mutually agreed and definitive statement of the facts.

The owners of the slaves who were freed in Nassau and their respective insurance carriers also went toe to toe, but in great contrast to the US and UK governmental conflict, this was a conflict over money and contract interpretation. The slave owners had taken out insurance policies on their slaves, as usual, and now they wanted the insurance companies to pay for their loss. Not surprisingly, the insurance companies argued that this particular type of loss was one not covered by the insurance policies, and so they refused to pay any claims.

The *Creole* came into New Orleans on December 2, 1841, and the word spread that all but five slaves were gone. It did not take long for the slave owners and their insurance companies to consult lawyers and start the process of adjudication. Some of the insurance companies formally received the initial claim on December 8. Seven separate lawsuits eventually were brought against four different insurance companies.[1] The cases were heard and initially decided by the Commercial Court of New Orleans. The slave owners generally were successful in that court. The insurance companies appealed to the Louisiana Supreme Court. The Supreme Court sat in New Orleans between November and August, in Government House on the New Orleans riverfront.[2]

Three of the four insurance companies hired the legal team of F. B. Conrad, Thomas Slidell, and Judah Benjamin to represent their interests. They were not a single partnership, but had separate offices.[3] Thomas Slidell and Judah Benjamin were young but very prominent in the Louisiana legal and political communities. Judah P. Benjamin was born in 1811 to a Portuguese Sephardic Jewish family in St. Croix, the Danish West Indies (now the Virgin Islands) and grew up in the American Carolinas. Benjamin entered Yale Law School at age fourteen but left after two years without obtaining a degree. In 1832, he moved to New Orleans, and was admitted to practice the same year. A year later, he married Natalie St. Martin of a prominent New Orleans Creole family. In 1834, he wrote, together with Tom Slidell, a digest of some 6,000 cases of the Supreme Court of Louisiana; this was the first comprehensive treatment of Louisiana's "uniquely cosmopolitan and complex legal system, derived from Roman, Spanish, French and English sources."[4] It became the standard text for lawyers in Louisiana. Benjamin also established a sugar plantation in Belle Chase, Louisiana, and became the owner of some 140 slaves. His professional rise was meteoric.

Benjamin was personally and professionally close to Tom Slidell with whom he coauthored the digest. Tom Slidell was appointed US attorney for the Eastern District of Louisiana in 1837, and, in 1844, he was elected to the state senate. More importantly—in a sense—Benjamin was also close to Tom's older brother, John Slidell. John was a commercial and maritime lawyer but was also the political "boss" of New Orleans. John "adopted Benjamin as his protégé."[5] In 1842, when the *Creole* lawsuits began, Benjamin was elected to the lower house of the Louisiana state legislature, as a Whig—with the help of John Slidell.

Benjamin's law practice concentrated on the Louisiana Supreme Court. In 1839, he appeared there in nine cases, in 1841, he had eleven cases, and in 1844, he had thirty-five cases; he won the overwhelming majority of these cases.[6] The insurance companies made good choices in selecting Judah Benjamin and Thomas Slidell as their lawyers to argue the cases in the Supreme Court. Benjamin was the lead and wrote the brief. Benjamin's brief was later printed and circulated as a pamphlet.[7]

The state Supreme Court rendered its decisions in March 1845. The main case was *McCargo v. the Merchants Insurance Company of New Orleans.*[8] The report of the cases covers more than 150 pages, beginning with the court's review of the lower court's decision (more than fifty pages) and roughly equal space for the arguments of the insurance companies, the slaveholders, and the Opinion by Judge Bullard. Crew members from the *Creole*

Figure 7.1. Judah P. Benjamin. This photo was taken about ten years after he won the *Creole* insurance case in the Louisiana Supreme Court.

testified, and so did the former US consul, John F. Bacon. Depositions were taken of other Americans in Nassau in April 1842 and were presented at trial, as well as those of the attorney general of the colony (George Campbell Anderson), the British inspector-general, a police sergeant, and four lieutenants of the British troops. Several pages of Benjamin's brief were in French and in Latin (quoting Roman legal sources). As he began his Opinion, Judge Bullard noted that the *Creole* affair had been "the subject of so much diplomatic, as well as forensic discussion [and] was elaborately argued."[9] That was quite an understatement. At the trial in the Commercial Court of New Orleans, the slave owner (McCargo) claimed that he had taken out an insurance policy for the shipment of his twenty-six slaves, valued at $800 each. The policy protected him against loss from the "perils of pirates" and arrests and other detainments and all other risks of "foreign influence." Thus, McCargo claimed that the insurance company owed him $20,800 (plus interest at 5 percent), because his slaves were lost due to the actions of the British authorities. The verdict in the Commercial Court was in McCargo's favor. He was awarded $18,400 (not the $20,800 he claimed): the jury had deducted $800 because one of his slaves reached New Orleans, and another $1,600 was deducted because it amounted to half the value of four slaves who had been part of the nineteen slaves involved in the insurrection, apparently because the jury felt that their loss should be shared equally between the insurers and McCargo. The insurance company appealed the decision to the state's Supreme Court.

It is sometimes a litigator's tactic to begin with an offensive move, and Benjamin made that move. He claimed that McCargo had an obligation under the contract to maintain a seaworthy vessel, and that the *Creole* was not seaworthy, considering the nature and purpose of her voyage, and therefore the insurance company's obligations were discharged. The elements of the claim were these: there was a failure of arms (the whites should have been armed), and failure to take proper precautions and discipline (the slaves were not searched for potential weapons upon boarding, and were free to move about). This was especially important, because of the great physical disparity between the ninety male slaves and the handful of whites in the context of the "nature of the slave, and his ever-wakeful and ever active longing after liberty." The third element of the unseaworthy claim rested on the assertion that too many slaves were crowded into a small space. Benjamin cited an 1819 federal law that limited the number of passengers to two for every five tons of the vessel, and noted that the *Creole* had a ratio of sixty-three "passengers" per five tons. That position permitted Benjamin to ask rhetorically:

> Will this court be disposed to recognize one standard of humanity for the white man, and another for the negro. Will any reasonable man say that 135 negroes would be as cheerful, contented and indisposed to insurrection, under such circumstances of discomfort, as they would have been in a larger and more commodious vessel?[10]

This statement of a principle of humanity—insisting on a single standard for black and white—was asserted by a man who held 140 slaves on his plantation.

The slave owners argued that their loss was as a result of piracy—which was a loss covered by the insurance policy—that the slaves were pirates. Rebutting, Benjamin pointed out "these slaves were instigated, not by thirst for plunder, but by the mere desire of liberty."[11] In any event, he argued, the intent was to cover an external attack and the carrying off of slaves by pirates. The court did not buy the piracy claim.

Ultimately, the question came down to whether the cause of the loss was the "interference" by the British authorities in Nassau (which was a covered loss), or it was due to an insurrection of the slaves (which was exempt from the coverage in the insurance policies). Although the testimony of the witnesses was largely contradictory (the American versus the British positions), the slaveholders argued that it was the British who "liberated" their slaves, and, but for that foreign interference, the *Creole* might well have been able to bring them to New Orleans. Benjamin explained that all the evidence clearly showed that the slaves' mutiny was successful on the high seas, and that, at the moment the *Creole* entered the port at Nassau, the slaves were in control. They were, in effect, fugitive slaves. In contrast, the earlier episodes involving the *Hermosa*, the *Comet*, the *Encomium*, and the *Enterprise* were fundamentally different because the slaves were all under the control of the whites. The freedom of the *Creole* slaves was acquired by their escape from slavery into a free country, claimed Benjamin.

Benjamin took the position that the British did not "intervene," but that, in effect, the slave status of those 130 people on the *Creole* vanished because there was no Slave Law in the Bahamas. He said:

> Slavery is against the law of nature; and although sanctioned as a local or municipal institution, of binding force within the limits of the nation that chooses to establish it, and on the vessels of such nations on the high seas, but as having no force or binding effect beyond the jurisdiction of such nation.[12]

This sounds much like the Resolutions offered in 1842 by Congressman Giddings—for which he was formally censured—and, of course, the formal position of the British government.

The evidence from the witnesses was sharply contradictory as to exactly what happened on the *Creole* after it came into the harbor but just before the slaves climbed overboard to freedom. The statements of the Americans—including Bacon, Merritt, the other members of the crew—were all essentially the same: they clearly put the blame on the British authorities for having, in effect, pushed the slaves into the arms of the locals. This rendition of the "facts" had been reflected in the formal protest and also in the statements made by the US authorities, including Secretary of State Webster. The "British" view of the facts was sharply contrary. George Campbell Anderson, the Bahamas attorney general who boarded the *Creole* on November 12 to check whether the investigation by the magistrate had terminated, claimed that Gifford made it clear to all the slaves that he, Gifford, had no intention of detaining any slaves who wanted to leave, and that Merritt had made the same offer. Anderson stated that the contrary claims made in the protest were "wholly untrue" and a "complete fabrication."[13]

Similar statements were made by Magistrate Hamilton, who was also a lieutenant in the British Navy; Pinder, the inspector-general of the police; Dalzell, a police sergeant; John Grant Anderson, the treasurer of the colony; four lieutenants in the Second West India Regiment of British troops; and Cobbe, their major. These witnesses explained why the Americans, in effect, invited the slaves to leave the *Creole*, rather than to resist the alleged invitation of the British authorities: the passengers and crew were convinced that "their lives were in danger" if they tried to resume the voyage with the slaves on board.[14] They claimed they simply would not resume the voyage with the slaves on board. Given the horror of the bloody mutiny that they had already experienced, their apprehension must have seemed far from unreasonable. On reexamination, Gifford and other Americans claimed that the statements of the British personnel were a "fabrication" and "utterly false." Thus, the "facts" of the events on the *Creole* were completely contradictory.

Judge Henry A. Bullard rendered his Opinion. He reviewed the Webster-Ashburton exchange of notes of August 1842 (see appendix III), and accepted the general principles that British law with respect to slavery did not operate on the *Creole* while it was lying in the port of Nassau. The judge noted that Lord Ashburton did "not pretend to combat the general principles thus expressed."[15]

However, Bullard took the position that the British "interfered" only at Consul Bacon's request, and solely for the purpose of singling out and confining the guilty, and that, after that had been accomplished, there would be no purpose for any restraint upon the others left on board.

What about the attempt, sponsored by Consul Bacon, to gain the assistance of some crew from the *Louisa* and the *Congress*, which culminated in the effort of Captain Woodside and his men to board the *Creole*—with their muskets and cutlasses wrapped in an American flag—only to be ordered by the British guard to withdraw? Judge Bullard answered that point with sarcasm: the British guard had been placed on the *Creole* at the US consul's request, and it would "hardly have comported with the good faith to have made an attempt at that time, by force of arms, to rescue the brig from the [British] guard."[16] But what about the "public prejudice" of the place (i.e., the large black population that swarmed near the vessel and "evidently intimidated and overawed the officers and crew of the brig")? Yes, reported the judge, the British authorities were generally sympathetic with the crowds, but the attorney general went to the boats that were assembled near the *Creole* and cautioned them against any violence.

The judge found that the statements of all the witnesses contained "irreconcilable contradictions," but he found some facts that were clear: there was no violence, not a single person from on shore or from the surrounding boats boarded the *Creole*, neither Gifford nor Merritt gave any orders to the slaves to go below and remain on board after the guard was withdrawn, and only the nineteen mutineers were taken on shore by the British with the consent of all concerned.[17]

The judge made it clear that his role had nothing to do with whether there was a violation of international comity, since that was a question of redress between the US and UK governments. His only inquiry was what was the proximate case of the loss under the insurance contract. He concluded that:

> the insurrection of the slaves was the cause of breaking up the voyage, and prevented that part of the cargo, which consisted of slaves, from reaching the port of New Orleans; and, consequently, the defendants [the insurance companies] are not liable on the policy.[18]

Thus, the insurance companies won, and the slave owners were not compensated.[19] But more than a decade later, the British government compensated the slave owners (see the next chapter).

Apart from settling the monetary liability question between the parties, this case served a valuable purpose. It was decided in a relatively calm and dispassionate context, years removed from the emotion and stresses of the actual events of November 1841. Most importantly, it produced a record that revealed a substantial amount of testimony from the British side, testimony that undercut the factual position taken by the crew and others in the formal Protest. The usual inquiry into the *Creole* affair ends with the diplomatic resolution in August 1842—or, perhaps with a brief note of the 1855 Anglo-American Claims settlement—and thus tends to project the American rendition of the facts as accurate. This insurance case from 1845 helps to explain that there was an alternative narrative of the events of November 1841 in Nassau's harbor.

Chapter Eight

Should the British Have Freed the Slaves?

It is customary for nations periodically to gather up private claims the citizens of one country have had against the government of another and to create a general claims settlement tribunal or commission, under which these claims are adjudicated. On February 8, 1853, the United States and the United Kingdom signed a convention in London establishing such a claims commission. The secretary of state was Edward Everett, Webster's old friend and former American minister in London. The agreement entered into force on July 26, 1853,[1] and was formally proclaimed by President Franklin Pierce on August 20, 1853. The convention covered all claims "on the part of corporations, companies, or private individuals, citizens of the United States, upon the Government of her Britannic Majesty" that had been presented since the Treaty of Ghent that ended the War of 1812, on December 24, 1814—almost forty years of accrued claims. Reciprocally, British claims against the United States were also to be covered.

Claims were to be presented to two commissioners, one American and one British. The two commissioners were required to subscribe to a "solemn declaration" of their impartiality and to decide cases based solely on "justice and equity" without "fear, favor, or affection to their own country." If they could not agree on a decision, they would appoint "some third person to act as an arbitrator or umpire," in accordance with Article I of the Convention. The United States appointed Nathaniel G. Upham as its commissioner; he was a Democrat from New Hampshire, a Dartmouth graduate who had become a judge of the state's Superior Court when he was only twenty-seven years old. The British appointed a diplomat, Sir Edmond Grimani Hornby, as its commissioner.[2]

The two commissioners met in London on September 15, 1853, and signed their joint Declaration of Impartiality. They met again on October 13, and agreed to propose to former US president Martin Van Buren that he act as the umpire in cases where they could not agree. Even though Van Buren was at that time living in Florence, this must have been seen by the American side as quite a positive gesture on the part of the British—or, perhaps to the contrary, if one assumes that Van Buren would have bent over backward not to be seen as unfairly favoring a US claim. On Friday, October 28, the commissioners received a letter dated October 22 from the seventy-one-year-old Van Buren in which he declined the appointment. Van Buren noted that no one could "appreciate more highly than [he does] the importance, not to themselves only, but to the world, of the maintenance of friendly relations between" the United States and United Kingdom. But, he explained, he had for several years withdrawn himself from public affairs and even from business "of every description," and that had given him "a degree of repose" suitable to his age and condition. Yes, if the matter were only a single question, he might agree to be umpire, but his experience taught him that these claims matters carry on beyond the expected time, and he could not agree to such delay, which in turn would force him to postpone his return to the United States.

The following Monday, October 31, the British commissioner proposed sixty-five-year-old Joshua Bates as the umpire. Bates was an American, born in Massachusetts, but he spent most of his time in London—"his adopted home"—where he joined the great financial house of Baring Brothers; he later became Barings' senior partner, just as Lord Ashburton had been. (Alexander Baring, the Lord Ashburton, died in 1846.) In 1828, Bates toured the United States with Francis Baring, Lord Ashburton's second son (the 3rd Baron Ashburton), and focused on the bank's great interests in New Orleans.[3] In 1830, Bates negotiated a loan to provide funds to compensate slave owners in the British West Indies when their slaves were emancipated. Early in the second half of the 1830s Bates began to lose confidence in the American and English financial system, anticipating the financial collapse that began in 1837. The year before the claims agreement was signed, Bates founded the Boston Public Library and gave it $50,000 (about $1.4 million today).

The US commissioner quickly agreed to Bates. Here was a man who really understood the United States, slavery, and the needs that underlay national and international commerce. Bates formally accepted the appointment on November 2, and two weeks later, Bates signed his formal Declaration of Impartiality. The final administrative actions were the arrival of the two agents: John A. Thomas for the United States and James Hannen for the British. The task of the agents was to present their respective national claims to the commission.

The commission was presented with more than one hundred claims that had arisen over decades, and the two governments had to agree to extend the life of the commission to hear them all. The claims ranged from those arising out of US military actions in Mexico to Texas bonds. But three claims are especially relevant, all of which were discussed earlier, in chapter 2.

McLEOD

Alexander McLeod of Upper Canada was arrested 1840 in New York State following his engagement in the destruction in 1837 of the US steamer *Caroline*. He was ultimately released in October 1841, and the matter was also dealt with between Webster and Ashburton. Nevertheless, McLeod himself—without counsel—appeared at the Claims Commission's hearing on September 27, 1854, and was supported by the UK agent, Hannen. The UK commissioner agreed with McLeod that the United States owed him compensation for the undue period he was detained, after the United Kingdom had acknowledged that his actions were on behalf of the UK government; McLeod also claimed compensation because his detention was longer than necessary, because of "public excitement," and the United States had failed to meet its obligation to repress that public excitement. The US commissioner, not surprisingly, decided that McLeod's claim was outside the scope of the commission, and so the matter was put to Umpire Bates for decision.

Another hearing was held on December 11, 1854, before the umpire, and, once again, McLeod personally testified in his own behalf. Bates disposed of the McLeod claim rather quickly on January 15, 1855. He noted that the entire episode related to the *Caroline*—including McLeod's arrest—was "all amicably and finally settled by the diplomatic agents [Webster and Ashburton] of the two governments in 1841 and 1842." In rejecting the claim, Bates closed summarily: "The question, in my judgment, having been so settled, ought not now to be brought before this Commission as a private claim. I therefore reject it." Later that year, the British government awarded McLeod an annual pension equal to about $20,000 in today's currency to compensate him for his suffering while imprisoned in New York.[4]

THE SLAVE SHIPS

The three slave ship claims were dealt with as a package, since most of the issues were related. On March 14, 1854, the US agent, John A. Thomas, presented some thirty claims on behalf of the United States, and included were those for the *Enterprise*, *Hermosa*, and *Creole*. Hearings were held on October 19 and 21 dealing with all three claims.

Enterprise

The US agent, John Thomas, argued that the British should compensate the owners of the thirty-eight slaves on board the ship, just as they did with the *Comet* and the *Encomium* in 1830 and 1834, respectively. But the British government refused payment on the grounds that, at the time the *Enterprise* arrived in Bermuda, slavery had been abolished throughout the British Empire. Thomas noted that the UK abolition act in 1833 contained a large proviso that exempted large portions of the Empire, such as Ceylon, St. Helena, and the territories of the East India Company. In any event, Thomas argued, when a vessel in distress comes into another nation's waters, that nation's authority does not attach to that vessel; indeed, the vessel is guarded by international law. Thus, the enforcement of the British Emancipation Act upon the *Enterprise* was a violation of the law of nations. Thomas offered a hypothetical illustration: if Turkish law permitted a husband to have multiple wives, and a distressed Turkish ship is forced into a British port, could a British sheriff go on board and remove one of the captain's wives?

The US commissioner, Nathaniel Upham, presented a lengthy and learned opinion, relying on extensive citations to international law authorities, and, of course, concluded that the British must compensate the Americans for the loss of their slaves. The British commissioner, Edmund Hornby, cited the 1842 US Supreme Court case of *Prigg v. Pennsylvania* (see chapter 5) for the proposition that no nation is bound to recognize the state of slavery or of foreign slaves found within its territory. At the time the *Comet* and *Encomium* came into British waters, it was not unlawful to have slaves, while it was unlawful in the Bahamas at the time the *Enterprise* arrived, and so no compensation is required for the act of freeing the slaves.

The umpire began his discussion of the claim with the general statement that no one can deny that "slavery is contrary to the principles of justice and humanity," but he also noted that slavery in fact existed in several countries by local law. As a result, slavery "could not then be contrary to the law of nations, and the *Enterprise* was as much entitled to protection as though her cargo consisted of any other description of property." Therefore, Bates concluded, the conduct of the British in Bermuda "was a violation of the laws of nations, and of those laws of hospitality which should prompt every nation to afford protection and succor to the vessels of a friendly nation that may enter their ports in distress." On December 23, 1854, the umpire decided the claim for the *Enterprise*. He awarded $16,000 to the Augusta Insurance Banking Company and $33,000 to the Charlestown Marine Insurance Company, effective January 15, 1855. Since there were thirty-eight slaves "lost" [freed] to the owners who had been indemnified by the insurance companies, that sum amounted to $1,290 per slave or about $35,000 per slave in current dollars.

Hermosa

Having dealt with similar issues in the *Enterprise* claim, Bates supported the claim, explaining that the captain of the *Hermosa* required simply "that aid and assistance which was due from one friendly nation, to the citizens or subjects of another friendly nation, engaged in a business lawful in their own country, and not contrary to the law of nations." The authorities in the Bahamas in 1840 failed to render that minimal assistance. On January 11, 1855, the umpire rendered his decision in the *Hermosa* claim, and awarded $8,000 to the Louisiana State Marine and Fire Insurance Company and $8,000 to the New Orleans Insurance Company, effective January 15, 1855. Since seventy-two slaves were "lost" [freed], that sum amounted to only $222 per slave. However, the umpire explained his rationale for the substantial difference in slave valuation: he made allowance for a reasonable salvage amount for the wreckers.

Creole

The case was presented March 14, 1854, and heard June 3, 10, and 14, 1854, after which the commissioners disagreed, and the claim was heard by the umpire on October 19 and 20. On January 9, 1855, the umpire rendered his decision.

Umpire Bates explained the facts of the *Creole* claim, sometimes in racially explicit terms. For example: on November 9, 1841, "twenty African soldiers, with an African sergeant and corporal, commanded by a white officer" came on board; on November 12 "a large number of boats assembled near the *Creole*, filled with colored persons armed with bludgeons. They were under the immediate command of the pilot who took the vessel into the port, who was an officer of the government, and a colored man." Bates's opinion laid out the dramatic scene in the harbor, where men with clubs were passing clubs around to others, and a "vast concourse of people were collected on shore opposite the brig." Bates explained that the British government officers, during the whole time they were on board, "encouraged the insubordination of the slaves."

The umpire noted that the British identified those slaves who were implicated in the mutiny and murder, brought them to shore, and detained them in jail. To make unmistakably clear the role of the British authorities—as opposed to the "vast concourse of people on shore"—Bates quoted the statement of the Bahamas attorney general to the remaining slaves assembled on deck: "My [men], you have been detained a short time on board the *Creole* for the purpose of ascertaining what individuals were concerned in the murder. They have been identified, and will be detained. The rest of you are free, and at liberty to go on shore, and wherever you please." Bates completed that portion of the story by pointing out that the liberated slaves, once on shore, were conducted "by a vast assemblage" to the police station for registration. Thus were the slaves lost to the claimants, concluded Bates.

As he did in the *Enterprise* case, the umpire once again pointed out that slavery is not a violation of the law of nations. The voyage of the *Creole* was sanctioned and protected by the laws of the United States and by the law of nations. It had a right to seek shelter in case of distress or any unavoidable necessity. In such a case, Bates asked rhetorically, what were the duties of the authorities in Nassau? Since the crimes of the mutineers were committed on the high seas, those men could not be tried in Nassau. Therefore, their responsibility was to comply with the request of the US consul and to keep them in custody until a vessel could be obtained to send them to the United States. With respect to the other slaves, the responsibility of the authorities was to afford the protection required by the law of nations. Once again, Bates was crystal clear:

> The municipal law of England cannot authorize a magistrate to violate the law of nations by invading with an armed force the vessel of a friendly nation that has committed no offence, and forcibly dissolving the relations which by the laws of his country the captain is bound to preserve and enforce on board.

The umpire did not explain the basis for his assertion that the British invaded with an armed force when there was agreement on the fact that the US consul requested that a British force board the ship.

Umpire Bates then announced his conclusion: "the conduct of the authorities at Nassau was in violation of the established law of nations, and that the claimants are justly entitled to compensation for their losses." Bates then awarded a total of $110,330, divided among eight claimants.[5] If there were 135 slaves on the vessel when it left Richmond, and five elected to remain on the *Creole* and continue to New Orleans, the award amounted to about $883 per lost slave.

One distinguished scholar has noted that Bates's decision, aside from legal technicalities, "cast serious doubt on the later widespread assumption that by the 1850s justification for slavery had been wholly repudiated in the nonslaveholding world."[6] Another writer asserted that Bates's decision "erased the agency of the rebels—and Nassau's black population—by figuring the conflict as a struggle between armed national entities."[7]

Thus, the US-UK Claims Commission resolved the *Creole* claim in 1855. But there was one more *Creole* claim controversy—this time, three years later. The US Supreme Court resolved it.

The Merchants' Insurance Company of New Orleans,[8] which had insured some of the slaves on board the *Creole*, was dissolved, and a liquidator was appointed, John Pemberton of New Orleans. In that capacity, Pemberton had two claims—identified by the commission, creatively, as first and second claims. In January 1855, the umpire awarded Pemberton $12,460 and $16,000, respectively, for a total of $28,460. That sum was then duly transmitted to the State Department in Washington, where it was to be paid to Pemberton, as liquidator, with a deduction of 5 percent for expenses. So far, the system was working as expected. But when Pemberton sought the $28,460 (less 5 percent) from the State Department, Secretary of State William Marcy explained that he was permitted to provide only half of that sum, because he was constrained by an injunction issued in June 20, 1855, by the US Circuit Court for the District of Columbia, and had to refuse to pay the other half of that sum.

Three people had successfully obtained that injunction: Edward Lockett, James G. Berret, and Henry D. Johnson. They lived in the District of Columbia, and on December 23, 1851, they had signed a contract in New Orleans with Pemberton in which they undertook to prosecute Pemberton's claims for the value of the slaves freed in Nassau, for which they would be paid one-half of any money that might be recovered for those losses. Since Pemberton's two claims were awarded a total of $28,460, the three Washingtonians wanted their half. They secured the injunction to achieve that goal. It is not clear whether these three were lawyers, lobbyists, or simply claims consultants.

The case ended up in the Supreme Court in the December term, 1858.[9] Justice Samuel Nelson, an admiralty expert[10] appointed at the end of the Tyler term, wrote the Opinion. Pemberton argued that, in 1851, he needed counsel in Washington to press his claim but that the subsequent action, in 1853, of the two governments to establish an International Claims Commission to settle this claim, among others, effectively put an end to the 1851 contract. When the commission got under way, one of the three wrote to Pemberton asking for a power of attorney to represent him before the commission, but Pemberton never responded. Senator Judah Benjamin—the lawyer in the New Orleans *Creole* insurance case—advised Pemberton to hire English solicitors (Trinder & Eyre of London) to represent his claim before the commission. Pemberton did so, and the London lawyers were present at the argument before the commission and aided the US agent. Pemberton compensated them.

Justice Nelson found that one of the three Washingtonians, Henry D. Johnson, had in fact drawn up a memorial to the commissioners—without authority from Pemberton—but, in any event, Nelson thought it was "a very trifling matter." Moreover, Nelson pointed out, the arguments in that memorial had already been presented by the United States. In any event, Nelson noted, the central issues of international law, which formed the basis for the award by the commission, had already been "the subject of repeated discussion between this Government and Great Britain, and also in Congress, by some of the most distinguished statesmen and jurists of the country." Therefore, the court decided that there was "no legal or just ground" for half of Pemberton's award to go to the three Washingtonians. The injunction was then lifted, and the State Department paid the full $28,460 to Pemberton. The *Creole* case was finally over.

Chapter Nine

A Former Slave's Heroic Slave

As the *Creole* affair began in late 1841, the former slave from Maryland's Eastern Shore, Frederick Douglass (nee Fred Bailey), was living in New Bedford, Massachusetts. It was there that he gave his first major antislavery speech, encouraged by the abolitionist William Lloyd Garrison. Douglass then moved throughout the North, lecturing on the abolitionist cause. Four years later, when the Louisiana Supreme Court decided the *Creole* insurance claims, Douglass published the first of his autobiographies, the eloquent *Narrative of the Life of Frederick Douglass, an American Slave*, which became a best seller. Unfortunately, this notoriety brought with it increased threats of harm. Some thought that slave catchers might capture him and return him to his "owner," Thomas Auld. Therefore, Garrison and others urged Douglass to make his first trip abroad, to embark on a lecture tour of Ireland, England, and Scotland.

In August 1845, Douglass left the United States for Ireland, the first stop on what would become a two-year lecture tour of the British Isles. In some ways, his period in Ireland was awkward for him, since he was an Anglophile—in part because of the enormous leadership the English provided in the drive for abolition—in a place where most people had only bitter feelings toward their English and Anglo-Irish ruling class. Moreover, Irish Americans and the Irish Catholic Church in the United States were far from warm toward the cause of black freedom and equality.[1] Douglass's arrival in Ireland coincided with the arrival of the Great Famine provoked by a potato disease known as the potato blight. In part because of the blight, Douglass witnessed poverty in Ireland greater than he had seen anywhere in the United States.

On the positive side, his white hosts treated Douglass as an equal, an extraordinary experience for the young former slave. Perhaps as important,

Figure 9.1. Frederick Douglass, the great American abolitionist and orator (1818–1895). This photo was taken about seventeen years after he published *The Heroic Slave*.

Douglass met Daniel O'Connell, the great Irish Liberator. O'Connell was from an Irish Catholic aristocratic family and was the most famous barrister in Ireland. He was the leader of the fight that, in 1829, led the British Parliament to grant Catholic emancipation, which in turn enabled O'Connell to be elected to the Parliament from Kerry. A decade later, O'Connell became the first Catholic lord mayor of Dublin. Douglass and O'Connell met at a huge rally in Dublin. A prominent novelist described the meeting:

> [O'Connell's] words shot up out of him, huge, fearsome, brimming. It astounded Douglass, the logic, the rhetoric, the humor. . . . O'Connell held the crowd in the well of his outstretched arms. . . . Douglass stood, transfixed. . . . Douglass forced his way through, excused himself past dozens of pairs of shoulders. O'Connell looked up, knew immediately who he was. They shook hands.—An honor, said O'Connell. Douglass was taken aback.—Mine alone, he said. There was so much Douglass wanted to speak of: repeal, pacifism, the position of the Irish clergy in America, the philosophy of agitation. . . . Two days later . . . O'Connell brought him on stage and he thrust Douglass's hand in the air: *Here*, he said, *the black O'Connell.* Douglass watched the hats go up into the rafters.[2]

It is not difficult to imagine the energy that united the twenty-seven-year-old former slave and the seventy-year-old lawyer and political agitator. Both sought liberation by peaceful means.

In the spring of 1847, Douglass left Britain and returned to the United States. British abolitionists collected funds to purchase his freedom from Thomas Auld, and so the risk of attempts by slave catchers to return him to bondage was eliminated. Douglass settled in Rochester, New York—hundreds of miles from Garrison in Boston, where he published an abolitionist newspaper, the *North Star*; in 1851, he changed the name of the paper to the *Frederick Douglass Paper*.

The United States had changed significantly in the decade since the *Creole* affair began. Texas had been admitted as a state, and vast lands were acquired as a result of the war with Mexico—and so, the size of the United States increased by one-third. The California "gold rush" of 1849, and the question of the admission of California as a state, resulted in the "Compromise of 1850," fathered by Henry Clay and shepherded by Daniel Webster and Stephen Douglas.[3] It was designed to achieve a political settlement by ensuring that the free state-slave state balance of interests was maintained. The compromise entailed a series of five laws that included the admission of California as a free state, the abolition of the slave trade in the District of Columbia, and a very strict Fugitive Slave law.[4]

One effect of the adoption of the new Fugitive Slave law was the conversion of "thousands of previously conservative and law-abiding northerners to the cause of abolition."[5] This conversion was motivated by the public's increasing awareness of a series of violent captures and rescues of fugitive slaves.[6] Even greater passion for abolition was created by the publication of Harriet Beecher Stowe's *Uncle Tom's Cabin*. It first appeared serially in an antislavery weekly beginning in June 1851, and then was quickly published as a book in March 1852, even before serialization was complete. The book went on to become the highest-selling book first in the United States and then throughout the English-speaking world.[7] Mrs. Stowe did not attack the South, or most slave owners; the most vicious person in the book, Simon Legree, is a transplanted Northerner. But her book attacked slavery and the impact of laws, such as the new Fugitive Slave Act. The idea of slaves running away to freedom, and then being caught and returned, was saluted and condemned, respectively.

Seven months before the *Creole* left Richmond bound for New Orleans, a free black man from New York was captured and sold into slavery. He too sailed on a brig from Richmond, but unfortunately for Solomon Northup, the ship deposited him in New Orleans into brutal slavery. In January 1853, Solomon Northup was brought home to New York to rejoin his wife and children—once again a free man. A white man who brought him to freedom was from New York: Henry B. Northup, whose relatives held Solomon's forefathers as slaves. Henry B. Northup was a lawyer who was formally authorized by the governor of New York to prove that Solomon had been captured and wrongfully sold into slavery. In 1853, Solomon wrote an autobiography detailing his brutal capture, his horrible life on Louisiana plantations, and then his release and return to freedom. Solomon's book was titled *Twelve Years a Slave: Narrative of Solomon Northup, a Citizen of New-York, Kidnapped in Washington City in 1841, and Rescued in 1853, From a Cotton Plantation Near the Red River, in Louisiana.*

This was the context in which Frederick Douglass wrote his only work of fiction, a novella titled *The Heroic Slave, a Thrilling Narrative of the Adventures of Madison Washington, in Pursuit of Liberty*. In late 1852, Julia Griffiths, a founder of the Rochester Ladies' Anti-Slavery Society, an organization that raised funds to support antislavery actions (including Douglass's newspaper), asked Douglass to submit an essay to be included in the Society's compilation of antislavery essays, *Autographs for Freedom.*[8] During the second half of the 1840s, Douglass had mentioned Madison Washington in at least six speeches, but this essay/novella was his first and only portrayal of the "heroic" Madison Washington as the leader of the revolt on the *Creole.*[9]

The Heroic Slave, published in 1853, is very loosely patterned on the actual events of the *Creole* affair, though with a vastly greater backstory.[10] While it is a story of black heroism in resistance to slavery, it ironically minimizes the role of blacks in the United States and in the Bahamas in securing their own freedom.[11] The story of Madison Washington is presented by Douglass in four parts.[12]

In the introduction, the author explains what a great state Virginia was, as the birthplace of heroes such as Thomas Jefferson and Patrick Henry, but, for some reason ("strange neglect") the story of the one of the "truest, manliest and bravest" of Virginia's children has been reflected "only in the chattel records of his native State." This, then, is his story.

In part I, the narrator is a man from Ohio (a white man, presumably, but unstated), named Listwell—aptly named, because his role in this part is simply to listen to Madison Washington, a slave who has come to the edge of a pine forest in Virginia on a Sunday morning in 1835 and engages in a soliloquy. Living as a slave—"under the constant dread and apprehension of being sold"—is too much for him, and so he decides to free himself. But he is tormented by the fact that he would be abandoning his wife, Susan; he quickly resolves the dilemma by explaining to himself that, when he gets free, he then will be able to figure out how to rescue her. Madison is described as "black, but comely" having "arms like polished iron" with "Herculean strength; yet nothing savage or forbidding in his aspect." Thus, Madison seems to have stepped out of the Bible or from Greek mythology.

The impact on Mr. Listwell is immediate. Madison's soliloquy "rung through the chambers of his soul, and vibrated through his entire frame." It was as if he were Paul of Tarsus having a vision on the road to Damascus. And from that moment, the Ohioan becomes an abolitionist, resolved to atone for his past indifference to this "ill-starred race" to achieve the "speedy emancipation of every slave in the land."

Part II is the longest section. It is set in the winter of 1840, in the Ohio home of the Listwells, a "happy pair." The Virginia slave shows up at their door, and Mr. Listwell has a flash of recognition: here is the man he had observed at the edge of the Virginia forest five years earlier. The visitor introduces himself: "My name is Madison, Madison Washington, my mother used to call me." The two Listwells and Madison talk around the fire, after a fine meal, and Madison is offered the best bed for the night. Before retiring, Madison reveals that he had tried to escape five years ago but decided to simply to hide in the nearby woods and meet his wife in secret once a week. But a fire of apocalyptic proportions forced him on the run again, guided by his "beloved" North Star—which was the first name of Frederick Douglass's newspaper and the stellar compass for slaves fleeing north to freedom. En route, Madison observed the horrible beating of a deeply religious old slave whose crime was that he might have assisted a fugitive slave.

Madison plans to proceed from the Listwells' to Canada. After fully considering that aiding a fugitive slave is a serious offense in Ohio, the Listwells decide to help Madison. They provide him with clothes and money, and bring him to Cleveland, where they make arrangements with a steamer's captain to deliver Madison to Canada safely and at no charge. Madison feels himself, finally, as a passenger, not a piece of merchandise. In less than a week, the Listwells receive a letter, dated Windsor, Canada, December 16, 1840, from their grateful friend. It reported: "I nestle in the mane of the British lion, protected by his mighty paw from the talons and the beak of the American eagle."

Part III begins in 1841, about fifteen miles south of Richmond. Mr. Listwell, paying his second visit to Virginia, plans to spend the night at a tavern—a metaphor for Virginia—that has seen better days. Virginia too has "lost much of its ancient consequence and splendor; yet it keeps up some appearance." The wooden pillars "are all rotten." The deadbeats who loaf around the tavern rattle off stories like "the guides at Dryburgh Abbey."[13] Listwell learns from one of the loafers in the tavern that there will be a large slave auction the next day in Richmond and is told that the slave trade is "a money making business." On cue, that night, hundreds of persons arrive at the tavern, amid the "cracking of whips, and the noise of chains," along with weeping and mourning. Listwell's conscience demands that he cry out against this slavery, but he thinks it wiser to hold his tongue: "Bodily fear, not conscientious scruples, prevailed."

Finally, Listwell encounters Madison, "the noble fugitive." He has become the leader of the slaves "by that mesmeric power, which is the invariable accompaniment of genius." Madison explains his terribly sad story. Hoping to rescue his wife, he returned from Canada to his old master's house and climbed a ladder to reach his wife's room. But she became frightened, screamed, and fainted; Madison carried her down the ladder and into the woods, but the master and his sons shot her and captured him. He was then sold to a slaver and put with the others headed for New Orleans. After an unsuccessful attempt to buy Madison, Listwell follows the slave coffle to the wharf in Richmond and manages to slip three strong files into Madison's pocket just moments before the slaves are loaded on the vessel. Listwell watches the ship sail down the river, wishing farewell to the "brave and true man."

Part IV is set in a Richmond coffeehouse two months after the *Creole* sailed from Richmond. The chief narrator is named Grant—the fictional version of the first mate, Gifford. One of the local salts chides Grant for having allowed the slaves to get away with the insurrection on the vessel, especially since Negroes are inherently cowards who would withdraw in the presence of a whip. Grant quickly denies the cowardice charge, noting that it is wise of a slave to pretend cowardice on a plantation, but on the high seas, he's no coward. Grant explains that he is resolved never to serve again on a slave ship; his conscience simply does not approve: "this whole slave-trading business is a disgrace and scandal to Old Virginia." Douglass changes some of the facts: the slaves are in chains, Madison Washington cuts nineteen of them free, and they kill the captain and the master of the slaves; their bodies are washed overboard in a storm.

Not surprisingly, Madison Washington is portrayed as a classic hero-leader: the shrewdest man Grant had ever met, his manner was dignified and his speech eloquent, all the officers had confidence in him, and the other slaves "fairly worshipped" him. Grant felt himself "in the presence of a superior man." The hero claims that, as "God is my witness . . . LIBERTY, not malice, is the motive for this night's work." It is Madison who takes the helm and sails to Nassau, while the terrorized sailors were clinging in the rigging like "frightened monkeys." In a key sentence, Douglass has Grant point out that Madison's principles "are the principles of 1776." Thus, Frederick Douglass wraps Madison Washington's efforts toward freedom for the enslaved in the same cloth as those who revolted sixty-five years earlier against British oppression.

Madison sails the *Creole* right up to the wharf in Nassau, and Grant sends two men to see the US consul, after which a company of black soldiers comes on board to protect the ship's property; Grant asserts that the slaves are as much property as the barrels of flour (not tobacco) on board. The soldiers roll their eyes at the absurd idea that slaves are the same as flour and stand aside while the slaves pour through the gangway into the streets of Nassau "under the triumphant leadership of their heroic chief and deliverer, MADISION WASHINGTON." Thus, with the words of the first mate describing the deliverance, the novella ends.

The Heroic Slave is well written, at times poetic. It presents a story that in some respects draws upon Douglass's own personal story of enslavement and freedom. It is a heart-wrenching narrative. If it were to be set to music, it would be an opera by Puccini, perhaps analogous to *La Boheme* or *Madame Butterfly*, at least the story of Susan's death. The story is powerful but not subtle. Douglass's message is clear:

- The slave's struggle for freedom is exactly the same as the Founders' struggle for independence from Great Britain in 1776. In this context, the slave freed by his own effort stands in the shoes of Jefferson and Patrick Henry.
- A black man can be comely, powerful but not savage, brave not cowardly, a genius, a superior man.
- By permitting slavery and the slave trade, Virginia today (a symbol for the South) is a scandal to the Old Virginia, which respected human dignity and the struggle for freedom. While the people controlling today's Virginia seem to be culturally alive, they are in fact decaying.
- In contrast to the Virginia of the South, the Ohio of the North sets the right example. Note that Harriet Beecher Stowe was from Ohio—dear Eliza

crossed the Ohio River from Kentucky—as were Joshua Giddings and Salmon Chase, among other leading abolitionists.

- Once a white man genuinely encounters the savagery of slavery, conversion to abolition comes with some ease and power, despite the risks (Listwell violates the law by aiding Madison's escape, and Grant abandons his slave ship position).
- Finally, and ironically, it is the British Lion—whether in the Bahamas, or in Windsor, Canada—that offers safety, unlike the situation in 1776.

Ultimately, the message to slaves was: right is on your side, your own leaders are worthy, and you will succeed. And the message to whites was: have the courage to follow the nation's basic principles, and you will gain the rewarding experience of helping the slaves lead themselves to freedom.

Epilogue

The *Creole* affair is important because, from the slaves' standpoint, the *Creole* affair was the most successful slave revolt in American history. In contrast, the most unsuccessful slave revolt was the 1811 German Coast uprising near New Orleans, where almost one hundred slaves were killed by militia. From a diplomatic standpoint, the successful Webster-Ashburton diplomacy that resolved the affair eliminated the threat of war with Great Britain, at least until near the end of the first year of the Civil War.

However, the tensions and issues that were exposed during that period grew in the years ahead and led to the Civil War. The slavery issue began to dominate public discourse. Northern abolitionists became more aggressive and insistent. Southerners feared not only more slave rebellions closer to home, but also that their ebbing political strength in Washington would lead to restrictions on their coastal slave trade (sought by Giddings) and then to even banning their slave trade in interstate commerce on land. Such restrictions on their "legitimate" activity would lead to the suffocation of slavery, exactly at a time when an expansion of slavery to the west and south was required. More compromises were fashioned to avoid fracture: the Compromise of 1850 and the Kansas-Nebraska Act of 1854, but by 1859, the raid by John Brown designed to arm and free Virginia's slaves cast the die.

After Tyler's administration, all of the presidents until Lincoln (except for Polk) were weak, and none had a second term: Polk, Taylor, Fillmore, Pierce, and Buchanan. Sectionalism grew. Political parties realigned: the Whigs collapsed, giving way to the Republicans—a Northern party only—and the Democrats split on sectional lines. This led to Lincoln's election. And to civil war.

What happened to some of the key figures prominent in the *Creole* affair? Here is a summary in alphabetical order:

John Quincy Adams: On June 17, 1843, there was a great celebration at the Bunker Hill Monument in Massachusetts. The chief orator at the ceremony was Daniel Webster, who had made a famous speech at that site in 1825, at the fiftieth anniversary of the Battle of Bunker Hill. There was a crowd of one hundred thousand to hear Webster, and also President Tyler. But John Quincy Adams and other abolitionist congressmen boycotted the event. Adams wrote in his diary that the arrival of Webster and Tyler "and his cabinet of slave drivers, [would] desecrate the solemnity" of the celebration. How could he have "witnessed all this at once, without an unbecoming burst of indignation, or of laughter?"[1] Adams wrote: "My life must be militant to its close."[2] Attorney General Legare, who had just arrived in Boston for the Bunker Hill ceremony, died suddenly, possibly from appendicitis; the presidential party carried Legare's body back to South Carolina for burial.

In December 1844, at the beginning of the 2nd Session of the 28th Congress, the seventy-seven-year-old Adams finally succeeded in securing a vote (108–80) to abolish the House Gag Rule. In September 1845, Adams suffered a mild stroke, but within a few months he was back in the House, where he had been assigned the most accessible desk. By July 1846, at seventy-nine, he was back swimming in the Potomac River each morning for thiry minutes. In late November 1846, while in Boston, Adams suffered another stroke, but on February 13, 1847, he returned to the House, where the members rose as one to greet their patriarch. Congressman Andrew Johnson—later, Lincoln's vice president and successor—immediately vacated Adams's former seat.

On March 2, 1847, the day before the adjournment of the 29th Congress, Adams delivered his only speech of the second session—on a subject he knew well—the only subject that stirred him to anything like his old-time passion.[3] Spain was demanding $50,000 in reparations for the loss of the *Amistad* and its Africans. Secretary of State Buchanan recommended payment, but Adams was strongly opposed: "God forbid that any claim should ever be allowed by Congress which rested on such a false foundation." After Adams spoke, the House defeated the reparations motion, 94–28. That summer of 1847, Adams turned eighty, and he and his wife Louisa celebrated their fiftieth wedding anniversary. In November, when he left Massachusetts for Washington to attend the 30th Congress, Adams had an uneasy premonition that he was leaving home on his last journey.

On February 21, 1848, at his desk in the House, Adams suddenly flushed and became unconscious. He was moved to the Speaker's office in a coma. All congressional activities and Washington's Birthday celebrations were canceled. Two days later, Adams died in the Speaker's office. (Lincoln was appointed to the large House committee on funeral arrangements.) Some said the eighteenth century died with him. The outpouring of public grief was the greatest since the death of Washington and until the death of Lincoln.[4] For two days, 15,000 people filed past his bier in the Capitol rotunda. Daniel Webster wrote the words for the plaque on his casket, including the statement that Adams had served his country for fifty years and "enjoyed its highest honors."

Adams's legal arguments against the gag rule and his defense of the right of self-emancipation of the African slaves on board the *Amistad* formed the basis for the arguments by abolitionists before and during the Civil War. "Indeed, after the abolitionist senator from Massachusetts Charles Sumner learned of the Confederate attack on Fort Sumter, he waved copies of Adams's speeches in President Lincoln's face, defying him to live up to Adams's arguments."[5]

Lord Ashburton died six years after his negotiation with Webster, leaving nine children; his eldest son, Bingham Baring, became the 2nd Baron Ashburton. The great financial House of Baring fell apart in 1995 as a result of a massive fraud arising out of its Singapore branch. The Dutch bank ING bought the bankrupt Barings in 1995.

John F. Bacon was replaced as US consul in Nassau by Timothy Darling in April 1842. It is unclear whether this move was a normal rotation of personnel, or whether the Bacon-Cockburn relationship had so frayed during the *Creole* incident that Bacon could no longer work effectively in Nassau. But

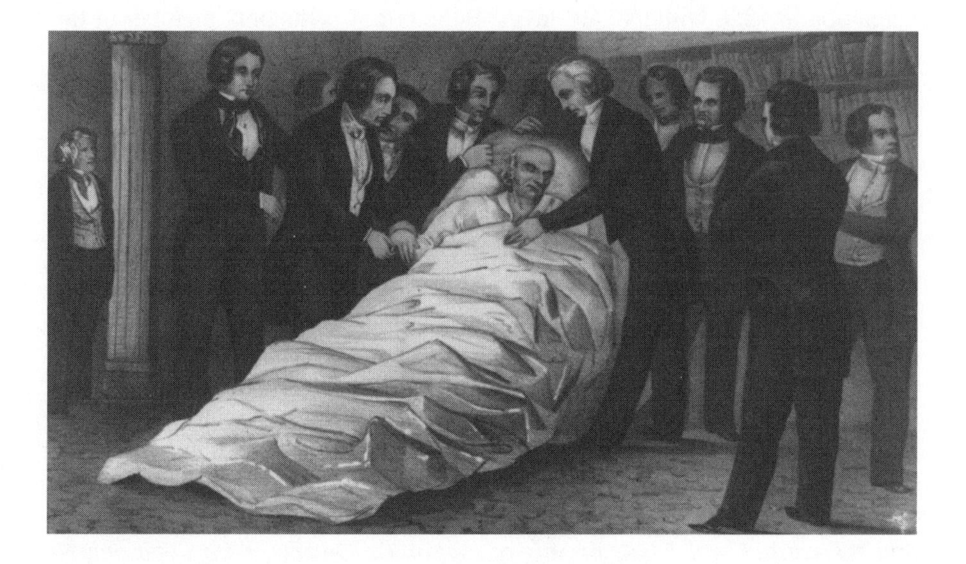

Figure 9.2. The death of John Quincy Adams, February 23, 1848, in the office of the speaker of the House of Representatives.

Bacon returned to serve again as US consul in Nassau 1845–1850 and 1852–1853—when he, once again, was succeeded by Timothy Darling. Bacon died in Nassau on February 25, 1860, at age seventy-one.

Judah P. Benjamin was elected in 1852 by the Louisiana state legislature to serve as a US senator; he took office, as a Whig, in March 1853. Just before his term began, outgoing President Millard Fillmore proposed to nominate him as associate justice of the US Supreme Court, but Benjamin declined, preferring to serve in the Senate. Benjamin was the first acknowledged Jew to hold a US Senate seat.[6] He served again, as a Democrat, in 1859. During the debate on the issue of extending slavery to Kansas, the abolitionist senator from Ohio (and former law partner of Joshua Reed Giddings), Benjamin F. Wade,[7] goaded Benjamin, pointing out that Moses had "enticed a whole nation of slaves" to run away, and that he was probably denounced as an abolitionist, and that Benjamin was "an Israelite in Egyptian clothing" to which Benjamin replied: "It is true that I am a Jew, and when my ancestors were receiving their Ten Commandments from the immediate Deity, amidst the thundering and lightning of Mt. Sinai, the ancestors of my opponent were herding swine in the forests of Great Britain."[8]

Benjamin withdrew from the US Senate in February 1861 and became the attorney general in the Provisional Confederate States of America (CSA). From August 1861 to February 1862, Benjamin was CSA secretary of war, and then became CSA secretary of state until the end of the Civil War. Benjamin's face was pictured on the Confederate $2 bill. Having sold his plantation in 1850 with its 140 slaves, Benjamin was the only member of the CSA cabinet who did not own slaves. Near the end of the war, John Surratt Jr.—the son of Mary Surratt—was a dispatch runner for Benjamin's agents in Canada. One scholar suggests that it might have been Benjamin, who "had the mindset, motive, means, and opportunity to execute this plan during the last week of March in 1865," who ordered the execution of President Lincoln.[9]

After Lee's surrender at Appomattox Courthouse in April 1865, Benjamin advised CSA President Jefferson Davis that surrender was the only option, but Davis disagreed. At that point, Benjamin fled to Florida, took an open boat to the Bahamas Islands (Bimini), and landed at Nassau.[10] From Nassau, he made his way to Havana, St. Thomas, and then to Liverpool, England. Liverpool was home to the largest number of Confederate sympathizers, and they would welcome Benjamin's legal services. He was called to the bar at Lincoln's Inn on January 13, 1866, and quickly published the first comprehensive treatise on English commercial law two years later, *Benjamin's Treatise On the Law of Sale of Personal Property, With Reference to the American Decisions, And to the French Code and Civil Law.* Today, his treatise is commonly known as *Benjamin's Sale of Goods.* The eighth edition of that book was published by Sweet & Maxwell Ltd. in London in 2010.[11] Most English law students and lawyers have no idea that the original author had a prior political and legal career in the United States.

Benjamin became Queen's Counsel in 1872—an elevated status conferred by the Crown, recognized by the courts, and permitting the "QC" to wear a silk gown and full-bottomed wigs. Benjamin is reputed to have earned more than any member of the bar of his time, some GBP 480,000 during his sixteen years of practice in the UK—the equivalent to almost $17 million today. He retired in 1883 and moved to Paris, where his wife and daughter lived. He died there the following year.

US Supreme Court Justice Ruth Bader Ginsburg noted that Benjamin "rose to the top of the legal profession twice in one lifetime, on two continents, beginning his first ascent as a raw youth and his second as a fugitive minister of a vanquished power."[12]

Sir Francis Cockburn was promoted to major general in 1846, lieutenant general in 1854, and general in 1860. He died in 1868 in Dover, England, at age eighty-eight. His brother, Sir James Cockburn, the 9th Baronet, was governor of Bermuda; another brother, Sir George, the 10th Baronet, served as Admiral of the Fleet and First Sea Lord; his nephew, Sir Alexander, the 12th Baronet, was the Lord Chief Justice of England. Cockburn Town, on San Salvador Island in the Bahamas, is named in honor of Sir Francis.

Charles Dickens published *American Notes* in October 1842. It was, in the words of one scholar, "an unforgiving portrait of a troubled republic: ambitious, cruel, ungenerous, brutal, and divided. . . . Dickens's humor about America was black."[13] He retained his status as the super-celebrity of the English-speaking popular literary world, although he did suffer a public scandal in 1858 when he decided to separate from his wife, Catherine—in sort of a midlife crisis. They had been married for more than two decades, and she had borne him seven sons and three daughters over sixteen years. Ellen Ternan, a nineteen-year-old actress (Dickens was forty-six), became his protégé and probably his lover.[14]

Dickens returned to America in November 1867, the most successful author in the English-speaking world: he virtually invented the Victorian Christmas, and was also a journalist, philanthropist, actor, orator, and public conscience.[15] Unlike his 1842 "tour from hell," this time his American tour was managed like a modern, professional, speaking tour, and it was a lucrative venture. Tickets for his readings sold for three times the price of a play. He gave seventy-six readings and earned a total of $228,000—the rough equivalent today of $50,000 per night. More than 40,000 people heard Dickens read in New York City alone; 5,000 people waited for tickets in the cold in a line a half mile long.

During his Washington visit in February 1868, where he celebrated his fifty-sixth birthday, he again met with an unelected American president, who also was unpopular with Congress, Andrew Johnson. Johnson was preoccupied with the congressional situation: on February 24, the House voted (126–47) to impeach him. (Dickens's readings had to be canceled in March due to the president's trial in the Senate.) Dickens, this time, left all politics aside and did not speak about international copyright or the plight of the Negro freedman. Unlike 1842, this second, and final, visit to America was a commercial and artistic success. Dickens, this time, was sick, hobbled on a stick, and dosed himself with laudanum in order to sleep.

Back in England, on June 9, 1870, while trying to finish *Edwin Drood*, Charles Dickens died. In England, his death was as momentous as those of Prince Albert and the Duke of Wellington.

Frederick Douglass: In 1855, he published a second autobiography, *My Bondage and My Freedom.* The fiery abolitionist John Brown stayed at Douglass's home in Rochester in 1858, while Brown was developing his plan to cause a slave revolt in the South. Just prior to Brown's raid at Harpers Ferry in 1859, Douglass met with Brown in nearby Maryland, but Douglass declined to participate in Brown's raid. After the bloodshed at Harpers Ferry, Douglass's name was found among Brown's papers, and an arrest warrant was issued for Douglass. Douglass fled to Canada, and then to Europe, to avoid capture. He returned to the United States the following year, after his daughter Annie died. During the Civil War, Douglass was active in improving the position of Negro soldiers, and in pushing Lincoln to end slavery.

After the war, in 1871, Douglass moved to Washington, DC, and was appointed US marshall of the District (1877), and then recorder of deeds (1881). Also in 1881, he published his third autobiography, *Life and Times of Frederick Douglass*. Three years later, Douglass married his secretary, Helen Pitts, a cousin to John Quincy Adams. In 1888, President Benjamin Harrison—the grandson of President William Henry Harrison, whose untimely death in 1841 caused Vice President Tyler to become president—appointed Douglass US consul general in Haiti, and the following year US minister to Haiti.

At seventy-seven, Douglass died of a massive heart attack at his home (Cedar Hill) in Anacostia, in the District of Columbia, February 20, 1895.

On June 19, 2013, a statue of Frederick Douglass was installed at the Capitol building in the National Statutory Hall. It joined fifty statues, each representing a state; Douglass's bronze statue—seven feet tall and weighing 1,700 pounds—was the first to represent the District of Columbia.[16] (A statue of Daniel Webster represents New Hampshire.) The hall, famous for its ability to carry echoes of conversations, was the meeting place of the House of Representatives from 1807 until 1857.

Edward Everett, after serving as Tyler's envoy to Great Britain, 1841–1845, returned home to Massachusetts and became president of Harvard University. In 1852, he succeeded Daniel Webster as secretary of state, and then was a US senator, 1853–1854. In the election of 1860, he was the vice presidential candidate for the Constitutional Union Party. Everett is most renowned as the featured speaker at the November 19, 1863, dedication ceremony in Gettysburg, Pennsylvania, where his formal two-hour oration (13,508 words) preceded the two-minute (280 words) address of President Lincoln. The next day, Everett wrote to Lincoln, "I should be glad if I could flatter myself that I came as near to the central idea of the occasion, in two hours, as you did in two minutes."[17]

Everett died in January 1865. The town of Everett, Massachusetts, is named in his honor.

Henry S. Fox, the unpopular British minister in Washington from 1837—over whose head Lord Ashburton negotiated with Secretary of State Webster—was finally asked to retire in 1843 by Lord Aberdeen, in part to ease negotiations with the United States over the divided Oregon territory. Fox stayed in Washington and died three years later from a morphine overdose. Fox is buried in the Congressional Cemetery, located less than two miles from the Congress. The bodies of President Harrison and John Quincy Adams lay temporarily at the Public Vault at the same cemetery.

Joshua Reed Giddings spent seventeen more years in the House of Representatives, where he led congressional opposition to the expansion of slavery. In April 1848, following the unsuccessful escape of seventy-seven slaves on a schooner, the *Pearl*, down the Potomac River, and the consequent three-day riot in downtown Washington, Giddings introduced a resolution asking why, in light of the popular struggles for freedom in Europe,[18] the *Pearl* fugitives were being jailed for attempting to enjoy the freedom for which America's forefathers had died.

Giddings condemned the annexation of Texas (1846), the Mexican War (1845–1848), the Compromise of 1850, and the Kansas-Nebraska Act (1854). He left the Whig Party and became one of the founders of the Republican Party. From his law office in Ashtabula, Ohio, Giddings wrote the Republican Party's first national platform, adopted at Philadelphia on June 17, 1856. He retired from the House on March 3, 1859. At the outset of the Lincoln administration in March 1861, Giddings was appointed by Lincoln to be the US consul general in Canada [the British North American Provinces]. He died in Montreal in May 1864.

In 1889, the first all-black public school was built on Capitol Hill (315 G Street SE), and was named the J. R. Giddings School. In the late 1990s, the DC government sold it as surplus; the historic building is now a gym.

Nassau, the Bahamas: Emancipation Day, celebrated on the first Monday of August, is a public holiday in the Bahamas.[19] On Emancipation Day in 1850, marching Bahamian celebrants offered three cheers for the Queen of England, the governor of the Bahamas, and freedom. But when they came to the US consulate, they instead gave out three groans against American slavery.[20]

During the American Civil War, the Bahamas was a primary transshipment point for blockade runners. Large, slow ships brought goods to the Bahamas, and smaller, swifter vessels carried the cargo from the Bahamas to the Confederate ports, and vice versa.[21] During the American Prohibition era, "rum-running" also found that Nassau was a convenient location for smuggling activity.

In 1936, King Edward VIII abdicated the British throne and became HRH, Prince Edward, Duke of Windsor. The following year, he married Wallis Simpson, who became the Duchess of Windsor. Great Britain was soon in the midst of World War II, and so the British government arranged for the duke and duchess to be transported to Nassau, where they would be safe. The duke served as governor of the Bahamas from August 1940 to March 1945.

In 1973, the Bahamas became an independent nation, and Nassau is its capital. The United States formally recognized the Bahamas on July 11, 1973, when the US embassy in Nassau was established. Today, the Bahamas is a fairly successful middle-income country with a GDP per head close to that of Spain or Italy.[22]

Winfield Scott, the general who helped to defuse the tense Canadian border areas with New York and with Maine, led the US invasion of Mexico in 1847, and five years later became the last Whig candidate for president. In 1856, Scott was promoted to lieutenant general, the first officer to hold that rank since George Washington. In 1861, after Fort Sumter, Scott established the largest army in US history (to that point), and devised the famous Anaconda Plan to strangle the Confederacy by blockade.[23] After the first battle of Bull Run, President Lincoln decided that the seventy-four-year-old general was not up to the task and replaced him with thirty-five-year-old General George McClellan, as head of the Army of the Potomac. On October 13, 1861, Scott submitted his resignation as general-in-chief of the Union Army. There is some speculation that later that year, while visiting Europe, Scott played a role in defusing the tense situation with Great Britain over the *Trent* affair.[24] Scott died in May 1866 and is buried at West Point.

Slavery: On December 13, 1865, Secretary of State William H. Seward announced that the Thirteenth Amendment had been ratified, and thus slavery ended in the United States. The last major nation to abolish slavery was Brazil, on May 13, 1888. On December 10, 1948, the General Assembly of the United Nations adopted the Universal Declaration of Human Rights. Of the thirty articles in the declaration, the first and the fourth provide: "Article 1. All human beings are born free and equal in dignity and rights. . . . Article 4. No one shall be held in slavery or servitude; slavery and the slave trade shall be prohibited in all their forms." The 1958 Convention on the High Seas provides in Article 13: "Every State shall adopt effective measures to prevent and punish the transport of slaves in ships authorized to fly its flag, and to prevent the unlawful use of its flag for that purpose. Any slave taking refuge on board any ship, whatever its flag, shall *ipso facto* be free."[25] The United States ratified the convention on April 12, 1961.

Slidells: Judah Benjamin's coauthor and law partner, Thomas Slidell, was appointed an associate justice of the Louisiana Supreme Court in 1846, and in 1852 was elected to a ten-year term as chief justice. He resigned in 1855 for health reasons. Thomas died in 1864. His older brother, John Slidell, who was Judah Benjamin's political mentor, was elected to the US House of Representatives for the 1843–1845 term and then served as US minister to Mexico. John Slidell was elected to the US Senate in 1853 but resigned in February 1861 to join the Confederacy. He was appointed CSA minister to France in 1861 and was part of the "Trent Affair," which involved the United States capturing him and James Mason (CSA envoy to London) on the high seas. John Slidell died in the United Kingdom in 1871 and was buried there. The city of Slidell, Louisiana, is named in honor of both John and Thomas.

Lord Stanley, the British secretary of state for war and the colonies during the *Creole* affair, later became the 14th Earl of Derby and prime minister three times during the period 1852–1868. His second son, Frederick, became Canada's governor general (1888–1893), after whom the famous hockey trophy, the Stanley Cup, is named.

John Tyler continued to have difficulties with Congress, especially with the Whig-controlled Senate. The Senate turned down four of Tyler's cabinet nominees and four of his Supreme Court nominees. In early March 1843, Tyler sent Congressman Caleb Cushing's name to the Senate for secretary of the treasury, but the Senate rejected Cushing three times on the same day, each time by larger margins. This three-time rejection remains the worst one-day loss of cabinet nominations by any president, before or since. Later that year, Tyler was successful in securing the confirmation of Cushing as US ambassador to China; Cushing then negotiated the first China-US treaty, one of the few successes of the Tyler term. The secretary of the US legation in China, under Cushing, was Daniel Webster's elder son, Fletcher.

His new Democratic-Republican Party renominated Tyler for the presidency on May 27, 1844. The Democrats nominated (on the ninth ballot) James K. Polk, a slave owner from Tennessee, and a former Speaker of the House of Representatives. Fearing that, if he stayed in the race, he would split votes with Polk, and, therefore, his archenemy, Henry Clay, might win, Tyler withdrew his nomination. A month later, Tyler became the first president to marry while in office (Julia Gardner, younger than his daughter, in June 1844.) Among his last acts as president was to push Congress to annex Texas through Joint Resolution, which he signed just before leaving office in 1845. After leaving the White House on March 3, 1845, he practiced law in Virginia and served on the board of visitors for the College of William and Mary.

In early 1861, as the Civil War loomed, Tyler met with President Buchanan, and urged that he abandon Fort Sumter. Tyler was unanimously elected president of the Washington Peace Convention, composed of twenty-seven states (seven of which were from the South) on February 5, 1861, in a last effort to resolve the crisis.

The conference did not proceed well, and by February 9, six more Deep South states seceded. Concerned that the draft constitutional amendment being proposed by the conference would not permit slavery to grow in Latin America and the West Indies, Tyler joined the seceding radicals, and tried to persuade the border states to join the Confederacy in the hope that the Confederacy would be strong enough to deter the incoming Lincoln administration from choosing war. During a heated meeting on February 26 with Lincoln, Tyler was persuaded that Lincoln did in fact want war. Two days later, Tyler was back in Richmond, urging Virginia to secede. On April 27, Tyler joined eighty-seven other delegates to the Virginia State Convention in approving the Ordinance of Secession. Thus, he became the only president to take action to dismember the United States and thus to betray his country.

Later that same year, after the formation of the Confederacy, Tyler was elected to the Confederate House. But he died on January 18, 1862, before he could take his seat. President Lincoln did not issue a proclamation marking the death of the former president; the passing of the disgraced ex-president was greeted with official US government silence. However, Tyler's coffin, draped in a Confederate flag, lay in state in Richmond's Hall of Congress while thousands passed by in mourning. Confederate President Jefferson Davis and his cabinet attended the church memorial service.[26]

Daniel Webster remained secretary of state for almost a year following the Webster-Ashburton Treaty. He resigned from the Tyler cabinet on May 8,

1843. In 1844, he was elected senator from Massachusetts for the second time.

After the initial conclusion of the 1842 "Dorr's Rebellion" in Rhode Island, one of Dorr's supporters, Martin Luther, sued a Rhode Island militiaman, Luther Borden, who had entered Luther's house wrongfully under the state's martial law. The case ended up in the US Supreme Court, where arguments were held over several days in late January 1848. Daniel Webster argued the case on behalf of Borden and the charter government. The ultimate legal issue was the constitutional provision (in Art. IV, Sec. 4) in which the federal government guarantees to each state a "Republican Form of Government." In political terms, the case was seen as a contest between the Whigs (Borden and the established charter government) and the Democrats (Luther and the Dorr faction). Webster argued "brilliantly."[27] Since 1848 was an election year, the court delayed its decision until January 1849, where in *Luther v. Borden*[28] the court held 8 to 1 that this was a "political question" and declined to intervene. This doctrine, pronounced by Chief Justice Taney, remains a cornerstone of constitutional law.[29] Daniel Webster won.

Later in 1848, Webster sought the Whig nomination for president but lost to Zachary Taylor. Webster, once again, was offered the vice presidential nomination but declined. (President Zachary Taylor died after sixteen months in office, and so, had Webster accepted the vice presidential nomination, Webster would have become president.) He played a pivotal role in achieving the great Compromise of 1850, an effort led by Henry Clay and Stephen Douglas to avoid civil war. In March 1850, Webster gave a famous speech in support of the Compromise, which included the Fugitive Slave law. In that act of support, he destroyed his political base in New England, and he resigned from the Senate in July 1850.

He became secretary of state once again, under President Millard Fillmore (1850–1852). Webster had been somewhat reluctant to serve again, largely because he felt he could not afford to take a great reduction in his income. To accept Fillmore's offer would also mean giving up twenty important cases he had pending at the Supreme Court.[30] In 1851, there were political charges that he had accepted "voluntary contributions" from major American bankers—specifically including Baring Brothers' agent—as an inducement to take the secretary of state position, for which they were rewarded by Webster with contracts relating to the installment payments to Mexico due by the United States under the 1848 Treaty of Guadalupe Hidalgo, which ended the US-Mexican War. A House Resolution to formally investigate the charges was rejected 119 to 35, over the passionate objections of Congressman Joshua Giddings.

Senator John F. Kennedy, in his *Profiles in Courage* (1955), called Webster's defense of the Compromise of 1850, despite the certainty that it would create denunciations from the North, one of the greatest acts of courageous principle in the Senate's history. Webster died on October 24, 1852.

Daniel Webster's grandson, the son of Fletcher, was born in Boston in 1847, five years after the signing of the Webster-Ashburton Treaty. His name: Ashburton Webster.

Henry A. Wise continued to duel verbally with John Quincy Adams over the Gag Rule. Wise was reelected to the House as a Tyler Democrat in 1843, and then he served as US minister in Brazil, 1844–1847. In 1855, he was elected governor of Virginia (1856–1860). He rushed to Harpers Ferry in the fall of 1859 to interview John Brown, and later signed Brown's death warrant as one of his final acts in office. Wise was a member of the Virginia secession convention in 1861, where he opposed immediate secession. After Virginia's secession, he became a general in the Confederate army and was with Lee at Appomattox Courthouse, where he advised Lee to surrender to Grant. After the war, Wise was a successful lawyer. He died in 1876.

Madison Washington stepped out of jail in Nassau in April 1842 and vanished from history.

Appendix I

Chronology

1772

June 22: Lord Mansfield delivered his famous opinion in *Somerset v. Stewart*, which concluded that a slave brought into England could be set free, since there was no law in England establishing slavery.

1775

The Royal Governor of Virginia promised freedom to slaves owned by rebels if those slaves would join His Majesty's troops.

1779

Royal Governor Clinton in New York declared that slaves serving the rebels would be sold, but those who deserted the rebels would be offered full security.

1807

February 23: The British Parliament voted, 283 to 16, to end British participation in the international slave trade; the act passed on March 25, effective May 1.

March 7: President Jefferson signed into law the elimination of US participation in the international slave trade, effective in 1808.

1814

August 24: Rear Admiral Sir George Cockburn reportedly stood on the chair of the Speaker of the House and asked: "Shall this harbor of Yankee democracy be burned?" Then he ordered British troops to "destroy and lay waste" to the public buildings in Washington, DC. Slaves obtained freedom by serving the British forces.

December 24: The Treaty of Ghent was signed, ending the War of 1812. Among the US signers was John Quincy Adams.

1816

The American Colonization Society was formed.

1817

The Anglo-Spanish Treaty banned the importation of African slaves into Cuba.

1819

Congress authorized the president to create the Africa Squadron of US armed vessels to interdict slavers off the African coast.

1820

March 6: The Missouri Compromise was signed by President Monroe, under which Missouri was admitted as a slave state and Maine as a free state, preserving the North-South equality in the Senate.

Congress enacted a law to make those involved in the international slave trade punishable as pirates.

1822

May: Charleston, South Carolina, was rocked by an ambitious, but thwarted, slave rebellion organized by the freed slave Denmark Vesey, designed to seize Charleston and to drive out the whites.

1824

The United Kingdom and United States signed a treaty in London mutually agreeing that participants in the slave trade would be treated as pirates. The treaty failed Senate ratification.

1827

In England, Lord Stowell delivered his Opinion in the case of *The Slave, Grace*, in which he concluded that a slave who had been returned to the British colony of Antigua had not been emancipated by her stay in England.

1830

The *Comet* was wrecked near Bermuda, and its slaves were freed.

1831

August: A slave, Nat Turner, led a slave rebellion in Southampton, Virginia, that led to the killing of some sixty people. Later fifty-six slaves were executed, and at least another 100 slaves, or free blacks, were killed by mobs. The rebellion sent shock waves through the South.

1833

August: The British Parliament enacted the Slavery Abolition Act, effective August 1, 1834, which abolished slavery in most of its colonies and possessions. The abolition took place gradually, over five years, and slaveholders were to be compensated for their loss.

December: The American Anti-Slavery Society was founded in Philadelphia by William Lloyd Garrison. It called for immediate abolition.

1834

The *Encomium* was wrecked near Bermuda, and its slaves were freed.

1835

January: The *Enterprise*, sailing from the District of Columbia to Charleston, South Carolina, was driven by seas to Bermuda, where her seventy-three slaves were freed.

1836

May 26: The Pinckney petitions, including the Gag Resolution, were enacted in the House of Representatives, 117 to 68. (The 24th Congress had 141 Democrats and 95 Whigs.)

November: Vice President Martin Van Buren was elected president.

1837

February 6: Congressman Waddy Thompson of South Carolina moved to censure Adams, but the attempt failed on February 10.

March 4: President Van Buren was inaugurated.

May: The Van Buren administration reached agreement with the United Kingdom for compensation for the slaves freed on the *Comet* and the *Encomium*.

May 10: The beginning of the financial crisis known as the Panic of 1837, which continued for some five years. It was caused by speculative lending in the western states, a decline in cotton prices, a property price bubble, and restrictive lending prices in the United Kingdom. On this day, the banks in New York City suspended specie payments.

November: Beginning of the rebellion in Lower Canada, followed by the rebellion in Upper Canada.

December 21: The 25th Congress (129 Democrats and 119 Whigs) enacted the Gag Resolution.

December 29: British/Canadian forces burned the US ship the *Caroline*.

1838

January 4: President Van Buren received the news of the burning of the *Caroline*.

January 9: Senator Henry Clay of Kentucky, a former secretary of state, charged in a Senate speech that the burning of the *Caroline* was an outrage.

May 22: Andrew Stevenson, the US minister to the United Kingdom, and former congressman from Virginia and Speaker of the House, demanded reparations for the burning of the *Caroline*.

August 1: All slaves in the British Caribbean colonies were freed.

September 3: Frederick Bailey escaped from Baltimore and moved to New Bedford, Massachusetts, where he took the name Frederick Douglass.

November: Joshua Giddings was elected to the House of Representatives from Ohio, the first avowed abolitionist congressman.

December 12: The Atherton Gag Resolution was passed in the House, 126 to 78.

1839

January–August: The Aroostook "War" took place in Maine and New Brunswick.

March: General Winfield Scott arrived in New England to defuse the Maine border confrontation.

August 27: The *Amistad* was taken to New London, Connecticut, and a criminal trial for murder and piracy was begun two days later against the Africans.

November 19: The civil trial against the *Amistad* began.

December 2: The 26th Congress opened, with 126 Democrats and 116 Whigs.

December 30: Rep. Henry Wise of Virginia moved to enact a permanent gag rule.

1840

January 13: The *Amistad* federal district court ruled that the Africans were "born free" and were kidnapped in violation of international law.

January 28: The permanent Gag Rule 21 passed the House, 114 to 108.

July: The Act of Union, formally the British North America Act, was enacted by the United Kingdom, with effect from February 10, 1841, creating a new political entity. The Province of Canada replaced Upper Canada and Lower Canada.

October: The schooner *Hermosa*, while en route from Richmond to New Orleans, was wrecked in the Bahamas, and its thirty-eight slaves were freed.

November: Whigs won the election and would control both Houses; William Henry Harrison was elected president.

November 12: Alexander McLeod, a deputy sheriff from Upper Canada, was arrested in Lewiston, New York, in connection with the *Caroline* affair.

1841

February: Arguments heard in the Supreme Court on the 12th in *Groves v. Slaughter*, and on the 22nd in the *Amistad* case.

March 4: William Henry Harrison was inaugurated.

March 9: The Supreme Court decided the *Amistad* case.

March 10: The Supreme Court decided *Groves v. Slaughter*.

April 4: President Harrison died.

April 6: President Tyler sworn in, the third president in 1841.

April 24: Secretary of State Webster wrote to the British minister in Washington, Henry Fox, setting out the famous international law formulation concerning limits on the use of force relating to the *Caroline* incident.

September 11: All Whigs, except Secretary of State Webster, resigned from Tyler's cabinet.

October 4: The trial of McLeod began in Utica, New York.

October 12: McLeod was acquitted. US-UK tensions began to relax.

October 25: The *Creole* left Richmond bound for New Orleans.

November 7: The *Creole* mutiny took place 130 miles northeast of Abaco Island in the northern Bahamas.

November 9: The *Creole* entered Nassau harbor. First Mate Gifford met with US Consul Bacon. Bacon wrote to Cockburn; Cockburn responded twice. Gifford gave his sworn deposition before Bacon. Merritt gave his sworn deposition before Bacon.

November 10: Stevens (second mate) gave his sworn deposition before Bacon. Curtis (seaman) gave his sworn deposition before Bacon, as did McCargo.

November 12: Bacon wrote to Cockburn about threatened invasion of the vessel by locals.

November 14: Bacon wrote to Sir Francis Cockburn, governor of the Bahamas, protesting the freeing of the slaves.

November 15: Cockburn wrote to Bacon that the British authorities had no role in the freeing of the slaves. Cockburn attached the official report, dated November 13, of the attorney general. A passenger (Leitner) gave his sworn deposition before Bacon.

November 17: Governor Cockburn wrote a dispatch to London about the *Creole*. Consul Bacon wrote to Secretary Webster; Consul Bacon certified the formal protest of Ensor, Gifford, Stevens, and Curtis.

November 18: Captain Ensor gave his sworn deposition in front of Bacon.

November 20: Secretary Webster, unaware of the *Creole* incident, wrote to the new American envoy in London, Everett, that the two most important bilateral issues were the *Caroline* matter and the search of American vessels off the African coast.

November 24: Governor Cockburn wrote to London about the inadequacy of Fort Charlotte in the event of an American attack on Nassau.

November 26: Bacon certified the copies of the depositions he had taken of Woodside, Merritt, Gifford, and Stevens on November 13. Cockburn's secretary provided Bacon with a list of the nineteen slave leaders, along with the affidavits taken November 9 and 10 by the police magistrate.

November 27: The thirty-five surviving Africans from the *Amistad* left New York and sailed to Sierra Leone in west Africa.

November 30: Bacon wrote to Webster a fuller letter about the *Creole* events.

December 2: The *Creole* arrived in New Orleans.

December 6: The second session of the 27th Congress opened.

December 7: The president's message addressed the *Caroline* and a host of US-UK problems. Gifford and seven others swore the formal protest in New Orleans.

December 16: The *New Orleans Bulletin* reported that the city was in flames over the incident.

December 18: The collector of customs in New Orleans transmitted the protest to Treasury Secretary Walter Forward.

December 24: Queen Victoria approved the proposal to send Lord Ashburton to Washington to resolve all disputes with the United States.

1842

January 3: Minister Everett wrote to Webster about Ashburton's appointment.

January 7: Lord Stanley replied to Cockburn's November 17 dispatch.

January 18: Senator John C. Calhoun introduced a Resolution urging Tyler to defend US interests arising from the *Creole* affair.

January 19: President Tyler sent to the Senate a report by Webster with attachments, dealing with the *Creole* affair, as requested by a Senate Resolution.

January 21: The beginning of the "trial" of John Quincy Adams in the House of Representatives over the Gag Rule.

January 22: Charles Dickens arrived in Boston.

January 29: Webster directed US Minister Edward Everett to support the Calhoun resolution and to demand indemnification for the freed slaves. In London, the law officers reported to Lord Stanley.

January 31: Lord Stanley wrote to Cockburn, enclosing the legal Opinion.

February 7: Adams won the censure "trial" by winning a vote (106 to 93) to table the censure motion.

February 8: Counsel for Maryland and Pennsylvania began their arguments in the first fugitive slave case at the US Supreme Court, *Prigg v. Pennsylvania.* In London, Lord Aberdeen gave negotiating instructions to Ashburton for his diplomacy in Washington.

Mid-February: Lord Ashburton left the United Kingdom for the United States.

March 1: Supreme Court decided *Prigg*, in an Opinion by Justice Story.

March 9: Dickens arrived in Washington.

March 16: Dickens left Washington for Richmond.

March 17: Dickens arrived in Richmond.

March 20: Dickens left Richmond for Baltimore without stopping in the District of Columbia.

March 21: Representative Giddings introduced nine Resolutions regarding the *Creole.*

March 22: Giddings was censured by a vote of 125 to 69. Giddings submitted his resignation.

March 29: Cockburn wrote to Lord Stanley, acknowledging Stanley's letter of January 31, but sought more instructions.

April 2: Lord Ashburton arrived in Annapolis, Maryland, on board the British frigate *Warspite*, after his ship from New York has been blown off course.

April 4: Rhode Island governor King wrote to President Tyler seeking assurance of federal assistance for the "Dorr Rebellion."

April 5: Cockburn wrote to Lord Stanley that the grand jury would not indict the Americans being held in jail.

April 11: President Tyler wrote to Governor King declining federal assistance not authorized for "anticipatory insurrection."

April 16: Cockburn released the seventeen mutineers from jail (two had died), on orders from London, at the special session of the Bahamian Court of Admiralty.

April 17: Cockburn reported to Stanley that the seventeen Americans from the *Creole* were out of custody.

April 26: Justice Story wrote to Secretary Webster urging him to press President Tyler to send troops to Fort Adams.

April 30: Lord Stanley gave guidance to Cockburn for future cases.

May 10: Dorr met with President Tyler for four hours at White House.

May 14: Secretary Webster held secret meeting in New York City in an effort to resolve the Door Rebellion.

June 7: Dickens left New York for England.

June 25: Martial law was declared for the entire state of Rhode Island.

July 20: US Attorney General Hugh Swinton Legare rendered his Opinion on the international law elements of the *Creole* case.

July 27: Webster's note to Ashburton concerning the *Caroline*.

July 28: Ashburton's reply note to Webster on the *Caroline*.

August 1: Webster note to Ashburton on the *Creole*.

August 6: Ashburton's note to Webster on the *Creole*, and Webster's note to Ashburton on the *Caroline*.

August 8: Webster's note to Ashburton settling the *Creole*.

August 9: Webster and Ashburton signed the Treaty of Washington.

August 11: President Tyler in a Special Message submitted the treaty and diplomatic correspondence to the Senate.

August 20: The Senate ratified the treaty, 39 to 9.

October 15: Ratifications of the treaty were exchanged in London.

October 19: Dickens's *American Notes for General Circulation* was published in London.

November 10: President Tyler formally proclaimed the Treaty of Washington.

1843

March 3: Calhoun resigned from the Senate.

May 8: Webster resigned as secretary of state and returned to law practice.

December 21: Wise announced he would no longer fight the gag rule.

1844

April 1: Calhoun became Tyler's secretary of state, upon Upshur's death.

December 3: Second session of the 28th Congress opened; Rule 25 rescinded, 108 to 80.

1845

March: The Louisiana Supreme Court decided *McCargo v. New Orleans Insurance Co.*

Frederick Douglass published *Narrative of the Life of Frederick Douglass, An American Slave.*

August: Frederick Douglass left the United States for his stay in Britain.

1846

April 6–7: Having returned to the Senate, Webster launched a two-day defense of the Treaty of Washington, particularly with respect to charges relating to the Maine border settlement.

1852

March 20: Harriet Beecher Stowe published *Uncle Tom's Cabin.*

1853

Frederick Douglass published his novella, *Heroic Slave: A Thrilling Narrative of the Adventures of Madison Washington, in Pursuit of Liberty.*

Solomon Northup wrote and had published *Twelve Years a Slave: Narrative of Solomon Northup, a Citizen of New York, Kidnapped in Washington City in 1841, and Rescued in 1853, From a Cotton Plantation Near the Red River, in Louisiana.* Published by Derby and Miller in Auburn, New York, in 1853.

February 8: The United States and the United Kingdom signed in London the Convention for the Establishment of a Commission to settle claims between the two governments.

August 20: President Franklin Pierce formally proclaimed the Claims Convention.

1855

January 15: The Anglo-American Claims Commission granted $110,330 in compensation to the United States for the owners of the slaves freed on the *Creole*.

Herman Melville published in serialized form his novella *Benito Cereno*, resembling the *Amistad* event.

1858

The US Supreme Court decides the final step in the legal battle relating to the *Creole*.

Appendix II

Message from the President of the United States to the Two Houses of Congress at the Commencement of the Second Session of the Twenty-seventh Congress, December 7, 1841

[The first paragraph is a statement of the good fortune of the country, and a prayer: "[W]e are all called upon . . . to renew our thanks and devotion to our Heavenly Parent. . . . [L]et us ever remember our dependence for all these, on the protection and merciful dispensations of Divine Providence."]

Since your last adjournment Alexander McLeod, a British subject, who was indicted for the murder of an American citizen, and whose case has been the subject of a correspondence heretofore communicated to you, has been acquitted by the verdict of an impartial and intelligent jury, and has under the judgment of the court been regularly discharged.

Great Britain having made known to this Government that the expedition which was fitted out from Canada for the destruction of the steamboat Caroline, in the winter of 1837, and which resulted in the destruction of said boat and in the death of an American citizen, was undertaken by orders emanating from the authorities of the British Government in Canada, and demanding the discharge of McLeod upon the ground that, if engaged in that expedition, he did but fulfil the orders of his Government, has thus been answered in the only way in which she could be answered by a Government, the powers of which are distributed among its several departments by the fundamental law. Happily for the people of Great Britain as well as those of the United States, the only mode by which an individual, arraigned for in a criminal offence, before the courts of either, can obtain his discharge, is by the independent action of the judiciary, and by proceedings equally familiar to the courts of both countries.

If in Great Britain a power exists in the Crown to cause to be entered a *nolle prosequi*, which is not the case with the Executive power of the United States upon a prosecution pending in a State court, yet *there* no more than *here*, can the chief Executive power rescue a prisoner from custody without an order of the proper tribunal, directing his discharge. The precise stage of the proceedings at which such order may be made is a matter of municipal regulation exclusively, and not to be complained of by any other Government. In cases of this kind, a Government becomes politically responsible only when its tribunals of last resort are shown to have rendered unjust and injurious judgments in matters not doubtful. To the establishment and elucidation of this principle, no nation has lent its authority more efficiently than Great Britain. Alexander McLeod having his option either to prosecute a writ of error from the decision of the supreme court of New York, which has rendered upon his application for a discharge, to the Supreme Court of the United States, or to submit his case to the decision of a jury, preferred the latter, deeming it the readiest mode of obtaining his liberation; and the result has fully sustained the wisdom of his choice. The manner in which the issue submitted was tried will satisfy the English Government that the principles of justice will never fail to govern the enlightened decision of an American tribunal. I cannot fail, however, to suggest to Congress the propriety, and in some degree the necessity, of making such provisions by law, so far as they may constitutionally do so, for the removal at their commencement, and at the option of the party, of all such cases as may hereafter arise, and which may involve the faithful observance and execution of our international obligations, from the State to the Federal Judiciary. This Government, by our institutions, is charged with the maintenance of peace and the preservation of amicable relations with the nations of the earth, and ought to possess, without question, all the reasonable and proper means of maintaining the one and preserving the other. Whilst just confidence is felt in the Judiciary of the States, yet this Government ought to be competent in itself for the fulfilment of the high duties which have been devolved upon it, under the organic law, by the States themselves.

In the month of September, a party of armed men from Upper Canada invaded the territory of the United States, and forcibly seized upon the person of one Grogan, and, under circumstances of great harshness, hurriedly carried him beyond the limits of the United States, and delivered him up to the authorities of Upper Canada. His immediate discharge was ordered by those authorities, upon the facts of the case being brought to their knowledge—a course of procedure which was to have been expected from a nation with whom we are at peace, and which was not more due to the rights of the United States than to its own regard for justice. The correspondence which passed between the Department of State and the British Envoy, Mr. Fox, and with the Governor of Vermont, as soon as the facts had been made known to this Department, are herewith communicated.

I regret that it is not in my power to make known to you an equally satisfactory conclusion in the case of the Caroline steamer, with the circumstances connected with the destruction of which, in December, 1837, by an armed force fitted out in the province of Upper Canada, you are already made acquainted. No such atonement as was due for the public wrong to the United States by this invasion of her territory, so wholly irreconcilable with her rights as an independent Power, has yet been made. In the view taken by this Government, the inquiry whether the vessel was in the employment of those who were prosecuting an unauthorized war against that province, or was engaged by the owner in the business of transporting passengers to and from Navy island in hopes of private gain, which was most probably the case, in no degree alters the real question at issue between the two Governments. This Government can never concede to any foreign Government the power, except in a case of the most urgent and extreme necessity, of invading its territory, either to arrest the persons or destroy the property of those who may have violated the municipal laws of such foreign Government, or have disregarded their obligation arising under the law of nations. The territory of the United States must be regarded as sacredly secure against all such invasions, until they shall voluntarily acknowledge their inability to acquit themselves of their duties to others. And, in announcing this sentiment, I do but affirm a principle which no nation on earth would be more ready to vindicate, at all hazards, than the people and Government of Great Britain.

If, upon a full investigation of all the facts, it shall appear that the owner of the Caroline was governed by a hostile intent, or had made common cause with those who were in the occupancy of Navy island, then, so far as he is concerned, there can be no claim to indemnity for the destruction of his boat which this Government would feel itself bound to prosecute—since he would have acted not only in derogation of the rights of Great Britain, but in clear violation of the laws of the United States: but that is a question which, however settled, in no manner involves the higher consideration of the violation of territorial sovereignty and jurisdiction. To recognise it as an admissible practice, that each Government, in its turn, upon any sudden and unauthorized outbreak, which, on a frontier the extent of which renders it impossible for either to have an efficient force on every mile of it, and which outbreak, therefore, neither may be able to suppress in a day, may take vengeance into its own hands, and without even a remonstrance, and in the absence of any pressing or overruling necessity, may invade the territory of the other, would inevitably lead to results equally to be deplored by both. When border collisions come to receive the sanction or to be made on the authority of either Government, general war must be the inevitable result.

While it is the ardent desire of the United States to cultivate the relations of peace with all nations, and to fulfil all the duties of good neighborhood towards those who possess territories adjoining their own, that very desire would lead them to deny the right of any foreign power to invade their boundary with an armed force. The correspondence between the two Governments on this subject, will, at a future day of your session, be submitted to your consideration; and, in the mean time, I cannot but indulge the hope that the British Government will see the propriety of renouncing, as a rule of future action, the precedent which has been set in the affair at Schlosser.

I herewith submit the correspondence which has recently taken place between the American minister at the Court of St. James, Mr. Stevenson, and the Minister of Foreign Affairs of that Government, on the right claimed by that Government to visit and detain vessels sailing under the American flag, and engaged in prosecuting lawful commerce in the African seas. Our commercial interests in that region have experienced considerable increase, and have become an object of much importance, and it is the duty of this Government to protect them against all improper and vexatious interruption. However desirous the United States may be for the suppression of the slave trade, they cannot consent to the interpolations into the maritime code at the mere will and pleasure of other Governments. We deny the right of any such interpolation to any one, or all the nations of the earth without our consent. We claim to have a voice in all amendments or alternations of that code; and when we are given to understand, as in this instance, by a foreign Government, that its treaties with other nations cannot be executed without the establishment and enforcement of new principles of maritime police, to be applied without our consent, we must employ a language neither of equivocal import, nor susceptible of misconstruction. American citizens prosecuting a lawful commerce in the African seas, under the flag of their country, are not responsible for the abuse or unlawful use of that flag by others; nor can they rightfully, on account of any such alleged abuses, be interrupted, molested, or detained while on the ocean; and if thus molested and detained, while pursuing honest voyages in the usual way, and violating no law themselves, they are unquestionably entitled to indemnity. This Government has manifested its repugnance to the slave trade, in a manner which can not be misunderstood. By its fundamental law, it prescribed limits in point of time to its continuance; and against its own citizens, who might so far forget the rights of humanity as to engage in that wicked traffic, it has long since, by its municipal laws denounced the most condign punishment. Many of the States composing this Union had made appeals to the civilized world for its suppression, long before the moral sense of other nations had become shocked by the iniquities of the traffic. Whether this Government should now enter into treaties containing mutual stipulations upon this subject, is a question for its mature deliberation. Certain it is, that if the right to detain American ships on the high seas can be justified on the plea of a necessity for such detention, arising out of the existence of treaties between other nations, the same plea may be extended and enlarged by the new stipulations of new treaties, to which the United States may not be a party. This Government will not cease to urge upon that of Great Britain full and ample remuneration for all losses, whether arising from detention or otherwise, to which American citizens have heretofore been or may hereafter be subjected, by the exercise of rights which this Government cannot recognize as legitimate and proper. Nor will I indulge a doubt but that the sense of justice of Great Britain will constrain her to make retribution for any wrong or loss which any American citizen, engaged in the prosecution of lawful commerce, may have experienced at the hands of her cruisers or other public authorities, This Government, at the same time, will relax no effort to prevent its citizens, if there may be any so disposed, from prosecuting a traffic so revolting to the feelings of humanity. It seeks to do no more than to protect the fair and honest trader from molestation and injury; but while the enterprising mariner, engaged in the pursuit of an honorable trade, is entitled to its protection, it will visit with condign punishment others of an opposite character.

I invite your attention to existing laws for the suppression of the African slave trade, and recommend all such alternations, as may give to them greater force and efficacy. That the American flag is grossly abused by the abandoned and profligate of other nations is but too probable. Congress has, not long since, had this subject under its consideration, and its importance well justifies renewed and anxious attention.

[One sentence relating to US-UK correspondence on rice duties.]

At the opening of the last annual session, the President informed Congress of the progress which had then been made in negotiating a convention between this Government and that of England, with a view to the final settlement of the question of the boundary between the territorial limits of the two countries. I regret to say that little further advancement of the object has been accomplished since last year; but this is owing to circumstances no way indicative of any abatement of the desire of both parties to hasten the negotiation to its conclusion, and to settle the question in dispute as early as possible. In the course of the session, it is my hope to be able to announce some further degree of progress towards the accomplishment of this highly desirable end.

The commission appointed by this Government for the exploration and survey of the line of boundary separating the States of Maine and New Hampshire from the conterminous British provinces is, it is believed, about to close its field labors, and is expected soon to report the results of its examinations to the Department of State. The report, when received, will be laid before Congress.

[Discussion of other relations with other nations, a report on tax, revenue and debt matters. Beginning of a report on the Navy.]

We look to no foreign conquests, nor do we propose to enter into competition with any other nation for supremacy on the ocean; but it is due, not only to the honor, but to the security of the people of the United States, that no nation should be permitted to invade our waters at pleasure, and subject our towns and villages to conflagration or pillage. . . . [I recommend] the increase and prompt equipment of that gallant navy, which has lighted up every sea with its victories, and spread an imperishable glory over the country.

Appendix III

Exchange of Diplomatic Notes between Secretary Webster and Lord Ashburton, August 1842

Department of State
Washington, August 1, 1842

My Lord: The President has learned with much regret that you are not empowered by your Government to enter into a formal stipulation for the better security of vessels of the United States, when meeting with disaster in passing between the United States and the Bahama [*sic*] islands, and driven, by such disasters into British ports. This is a subject which is deemed to be of great importance, and which can not, on the present occasion, be overlooked.

Your Lordship is aware that several cases have occurred within the last few years which have caused much complaint. In some of these cases compensation has been made by the English Government for the interference of the local authorities with American vessels having slaves on board, by which interference these slaves were set free. In other cases, such compensation has been refused. It appears to the President to be for the interest of both countries that the recurrence of similar cases in the future should be prevented as far as possible.

Your Lordship has been acquainted with the case of the "Creole," a vessel carried into the port of Nassau last winter by persons who had risen upon the lawful authority of the vessel, and, in the accomplishment of their purpose, had committed murder on a person on board.

The opinions which that occurrence gave occasion for this Government to express, in regard to the rights and duties of friendly and civilized maritime states, placed by Providence near to each other, were well considered, and are entertained with entire confidence. The facts in the particular case of the

"Creole" are controverted: positive and officious interference by the colonial authorities to set the slaves free being alleged on one side and denied on the other.

It is not my present purpose to discuss this difference of opinion as to the evidence in the case, as it at present exists, because the rights of individuals having rendered necessary a more thorough and a judicial investigation of facts and circumstance attending the transaction, such investigation is understood to be now in progress, and its result, when known, will render me more able than at the moment to present to the British Government a full and accurate view of the whole case. But it is my purpose, and my duty, to invite your Lordship's attention to the general subject, and your serious consideration of some practical means of giving security to the coasting trade of the United States against unlawful annoyance and interruption along this part of their shore. The Bahama [*sic*] islands approach the coast of Florida within a few leagues, and, with the coast, form a long and narrow channel, filled with innumerable small islands and banks of sand, and the navigation difficult and dangerous, not only on these accounts, but from the violence of the winds and the variable nature of the currents. Accidents are of course frequent, and necessity often compels vessels of the United States, in attempting to double Cape Florida, to seek shelter in the ports of these islands. Among this passage the Atlantic States hold intercourse with the States on the Gulf and the Mississippi, and through it the products of the valley of that river (a region of vast extent and boundless fertility) find a main outlet to the sea, in their destination to the markets of the world.

No particular ground of complaint exists as to the treatment of which American vessels receive in the these ports, unless they happen to have slaves on board; but, in cases of that kind, complaints have been made, as already stated, of officious interference of the colonial authorities with the vessel, for the purpose of changing the condition in which these persons are, by the laws of their own country, and of setting them free.

In the southern States of this Union slavery exists by the laws of the States and under the guarantee of the Constitution of the United States; and it has existed in them from a period long antecedent to the time when they ceased to be British colonies. In this state of things, it will happen that slaves will be often on board coasting vessels, as hands, as servants attending the families of their owners, or for the purpose of being carried from port to port. For the security of the rights of their citizens, when vessels, having persons of this description on board, are driven by stress of weather, or carried by unlawful force, into British ports, the United States propose the introduction of no new principle into the law of nations. They require only a faithful and exact observance of the injunctions of that code, as understood and practiced in modern times.

Your Lordship observes that I have spoken only of American vessels driven into British ports by the disasters of the seas, or carried in by unlawful force. I confine my remarks to these cases, because they are the common cases, and because they are the cases which the law of nations most emphatically exempts from interference. The maritime law is full of instances of the application of that great and practical rule, which declares that that which is the clear result of necessity ought to draw after it no penalty and no hazard. If a ship be driven, by stress of weather, into a prohibited port, or into an open port, with prohibited articles on board, in neither case is any forfeiture incurred. And what may be considered a still stronger case, it has been decided by eminent English authority, and that decision has received general approbation, that if a vessel be driven, by necessity, into a port strictly blockaded, this necessity is good defense, and exempts her from penalty.

A vessel on the high seas, beyond the distance of a marine league from the shore, is regarded as part of the territory of the nation to which she belongs, and subjected, exclusively, to the jurisdiction of that nation. If against the will of her master, or owner, she be driven or carried nearer to the land, or even into port, those who have, or who ought to have, control over her, struggling all the while to keep her upon the high seas, and so within the exclusive jurisdiction of her own Government, what reason or justice is there in creating a distinction between her rights and immunities, in a position, thus the result of absolute necessity, and the same rights and immunities before superior power had forced her out of her voluntary course?

But, my Lord, the rule of law, and the comity and practice of nations, go much further than these cases of necessity, and allow even to a merchant vessel, coming into any open port of another country voluntarily, for the purpose of lawful trade, to bring with her, and keep over her, to a very considerable extent, the jurisdiction and authority of the laws of her own country, excluding to this extent, by consequence, the jurisdiction of the local law. A ship, say the publicists, though at anchor in a foreign harbor, preserves its jurisdiction and its laws. It is natural to consider the vessels of a nation as parts of its territory, though at sea, as the state retains its jurisdiction over them; and, according to the commonly-received custom, this jurisdiction is preserved over the vessels, even in parts of the sea subject to a foreign dominion.

This is the doctrine of the law of nations, clearly laid down by writers of received authority, and entirely comfortable, as it is supposed, with practices of modern nations.

If a murder be committed on board of an American vessel, by one of the crew upon another or upon a passenger, or by a passenger on one of the crew or another passenger, while such vessel is lying in a port within the jurisdiction of a foreign state or sovereignty, the offence is cognizable and punishable by the proper court of the United States, in the same manner as if such offense had been committed on board the vessel on the high seas. The law of England is supposed to be the same.

It is true that the jurisdiction of a nation over a vessel belonging to it, while lying in the port of another, is not necessarily wholly exclusive. We do not so consider or so assert it. For any unlawful acts done by her while thus lying in port, and for all contracts entered into while there, by her master or owners, she and they must doubtless be answerable to the laws of the place. Nor, if her master or crew, while on board in such a port, break [*sic*] the peace of the community by the commission of crimes, can exemption be claimed for them. But, nevertheless, the law of nations, as I have stated it, and the statutes of Governments founded on that law, as I have referred to them, show that enlightened nations, in modern times, so clearly hold that the jurisdiction and laws of a nation accompany her ships, not only over the high seas, but into ports and harbors, or wheresoever else they may be water-borne, for the general purpose of governing and regulating the rights, duties, and obligations of those on board thereof, and that, to the extent of the exercise of this jurisdiction, they are considered as parts of the territory of the nation herself.

If a vessel be driven by weather into the ports of another nation, it would hardly be alleged by any one that, by the mere force of such arrival within the waters of the state, the law of that state would so attach to the vessel as to affect existing rights of property between persons on board, whether arising from contract or otherwise. The local law would not operate to make the goods of one man to become the goods of another man. Nor ought it to affect their personal obligations, or existing relations between themselves; nor was it ever supposed to have such effect, until the delicate and exciting question which has caused these interferences in the British islands arose. The local law in these cases dissolves no obligations or relations lawfully entered into or lawfully existing according to the laws of the ship's country. If it did, intercourse of civilized men between nation and nation must cease. Marriages are frequently celebrated in one country in a manner not lawful or valid in another; but did anybody ever doubt that marriages are valid all over the civilized world, if valid in the country in which they took place? Did any one ever imagine that local law acted upon such marriages to annihilate their obligation, if the party should visit a country in which marriages must be celebrated in another form?

It may be said that, in such instances, personal relations are founded in contract, and therefore to be respected; but that the relation of master and slave is not founded in contract, and therefore is to be respected only by the law of the places which recognizes [*sic*] it. Whoever so reasons encounters the authority of the whole body of public law from Grotius down; because there are numerous instances in which the law itself presumes or implies contracts; and prominent among these instances is the very relation which we are now considering and which relation is holden by law to draw after it mutuality of obligation.

Is not the relation between a father and his minor children acknowledged, when they go abroad? And on what contract is this founded, but a contract raised by general principles of law, from the relation of the parties?

Your Lordship will please to bear in mind that the proposition which I am endeavoring to support is, that by the comity of the law of nations, and the practice of modern times, merchant vessels entering open ports of other nations, for the purpose of trade, are presumed to be allowed to bring with them, and to retain, for their protection and government, the jurisdiction and laws of their own country. All this, I repeat, is presumed to be allowed; because the ports are open, because trade is invited, and because, under these circumstances, such permission or allowance is according to general usage. It is not denied that all this may be refused; and this suggests a distinction, the disregard of which may perhaps account for most of the difficulties arising in cases of this sort; that is to say, the distinction between what a state may do, if it pleases, and what it is presumed to do, or not to do, in the absence of any positive declaration of its will.

A state might declare that all foreign marriages should be regarded as null and void within its territory; that a foreign father, arriving with an infant son, should no longer have authority or control over him; that, on the arrival of a foreign vessel in its ports, all shipping articles and all indentures of apprenticeship between her crew and her owners or masters should cease to be binding. These, and many other things equally irrational and absurd, a sovereign state has doubtless the power to do; but they are not to be presumed. It is not to be taken for granted, *ab ante*, that if it is the will of the sovereign state thus to believe this to be its intention, when it formally announces that intention by appropriate enactments, edicts, or other declarations.

In regard to slavery within the British territories, there is a well-known and clear promulgation of the will of the sovereign authority; that is to say, there is a well-known rule of her law. As to England herself, that law has long existed; and recent acts of Parliament establish the same law for the colonies. The usual mode of stating the rule of English law is, that no sooner does a slave reach the shore of England than he is free. This is true; but it means no more than that when a slave comes within the exclusive jurisdiction of England he ceases to be a slave, because the law of England positively and notoriously prohibits and forbids the existence of such a relation between man and man. But it does not mean that English authorities, with this rule of English law in their hands, may enter where the jurisdiction of another nation is acknowledged to exist, and there destroy rights, obligations, and interests lawfully existing under the authority of such other nation. No such construction, and no such effect, can be rightfully given to the British law. It is also true that it is competent to the British Parliament, by express statute provision, to declare that no foreign jurisdiction of any kind should exist in or over a vessel after its arrival voluntarily in her ports. And so she might close all her ports to the ships of all nations. A state may also declare, in the absence of treaty stipulations, that foreigners shall not sue in her courts, nor travel in her territories, nor carry away funds or goods received for debts. We need not inquire what would be the condition of a country that should establish such laws, nor in what relation they would leave her toward the states of the civilized world. Her power to make such laws is unquestionable; but, in the absence of direct and positive enactments to that effect, the presumption is that the opposites of these things exist. While her ports are open to foreign trade, it is to be presumed that she expects foreign ships to enter them, bring with them the jurisdiction of their own Government, and the protection of its laws, to the same extent that her ships and the ships of other commercial states carry with them the jurisdiction of their respective Governments into the open ports of the world; just as it is presumed, while the contrary is not avowed, that strangers may travel in a civilized country in a time of peace, sue in its courts, and bring away their property.

A merchant vessel enters the port of a friendly state, and enjoys while there the protection of her own laws, and is under the jurisdiction of her own Government, not in derogation of the sovereignty of the place, but by the presumed allowance or permission of that sovereignty. This permission or allowance is founded on the comity of nations, like the other cases which have been mentioned; and this comity is part, and a most important and valuable part, of the law of nations, to which all nations are presumed to assent until they make their dissent known. In the silence of any positive rule, affirming or denying or restraining the operation of foreign laws, their tacit adoption is presumed, to the usual extent. It is upon this ground that the courts of law expound contacts according to the law of the place in which they are made; and instances almost innumerable exist, in which, by the general practice of civilized countries, the laws of one will be recognized and often executed in another. This is the comity of nations; and it is upon this, as its solid basis, that the intercourse of civilized states is maintained.

But while that which has now been said is understood to be the voluntary and adopted law of nations, in cases of the voluntary entry of merchant vessels into the ports of other countries, it is nevertheless true, that vessels in such ports, only through an overruling necessity, may place their claim for exemption from interference on still higher principles; that is to say, principles held in more sacred regard by the comity, the courtesy, or indeed the common sense of justice of all civilized states.

Even in regard to cases of necessity, however, there are things of an unfriendly and offensive character, which yet it may not be easy to say that a nation might not do. For example, a nation might declare her will to be, and make it by the law of her dominions, that foreign vessels, cast away on her shores, should be lost to their owners, and subject to the ancient law of wreck. Or a neutral state, while shutting her ports to the armed vessels of belligerents, as she has a right to do, might resolve on seizing and confiscating vessels of that description, which should be driven to take shelter in her harbors by the violence of the storms of the ocean. But laws of this character, however within the absolute competence of Governments, could only be passed, if passed at all, under willingness to meet the last responsibility to which nations are subjected.

The presumption is stronger, therefore, in regard to vessels driven into foreign ports by necessity, and seeking only temporary refuge, than in regard to those which enter them voluntarily, and for purposes of trade, that they will not be interfered with, and that, unless they commit, while in port, some act against the laws of the place, they will be permitted to receive supplies to repair damage, and to depart unmolested.

If, therefore, vessels of the United States, pursuing lawful voyages, from port to port, along their own shore, are driven by stress of weather, or carried by unlawful force, into English ports, the Government of the United States can not consent that the local authorities in those ports shall take advantage of such misfortunes, and enter them, for the purpose of interfering with the condition of persons or things on board, as established by their own laws. If slaves, the property of citizens of the United States, escape into the British territories, it is not expected that they will be restored. In that case, the territorial jurisdiction of England will have become exclusive over them, and must decide their condition. But slaves on board of American vessels, lying in British waters, are not within the exclusive jurisdiction of England; or under the exclusive operation of English law; and this founds the broad distinction between the cases. If persons, guilty of crimes in the United States, seek an asylum in the British dominions, they will not be demanded, until provision for such cases be made by treaty: because the giving-up of criminals, fugitive from justice, is agreed and understood to be a matter in which every nation regulates its conduct according to its own discretion. It is no breach of comity to refuse such surrender.

On the other hand, vessels of the United States, driven by necessity into British ports, and staying there no longer than such necessity exists, violating no law, nor having intent to violate any law, will claim, and there will be claimed for them protection and security, freedom from molestation, and from all interference with the character or condition of persons or things on board. In the opinion of the Government of the United States, such vessels, so driven and so detained by necessity in a friendly port, ought to be regarded as still pursuing their original voyage, and turned out of their direct course only by disaster, or by wrongful violence; that they ought to receive all assistance necessary to enable them to resume that direct course; and that interference and molestation by the local authorities, where the whole voyage is lawful, both in act and intent, is ground for just and grave complaint.

Your Lordship's discernment and large experience in affairs can not fail to suggest to you how important it is to merchants and navigators engaged in the coasting trade of a country so large in extent as the United States, that they should feel secure against all but the ordinary causes of maritime loss. The possessions of the two Governments closely approach each other. This proximity which ought to make us friends and good neighbors, may, without proper care and regulation, itself prove a ceaseless cause of vexation, irritation and disquiet.

If your Lordship has no authority to enter into a stipulation by treaty for the prevention of such occurrences hereafter as have already happened, occurrences so likely to disturb that peace between the two countries which it is the object of your Lordship's mission to establish and confirm, you may still be so acquainted with the sentiments of your Government as to be able to engage that instructions shall be given to the local authorities in the islands, which shall lend them to regulate their conduct in conformity with the rights of citizens of the United States, and the just expectations of their Government, and in such manner as shall, in future, take away all reasonable ground of complaint. It would be with the most profound regret that the President should see that, while it is now hoped so many other subjects of difference may be harmoniously adjusted, nothing should be done in regard to this dangerous source of future collisions.

I avail myself of this occasion to renew to your Lordship the assurances of my distinguished consideration.

DANIEL WEBSTER
Lord Ashburton
Etc., etc., etc.

Lord Ashburton to Mr. Webster
Washington, August 6, 1842

Sir: You may be well assured that I am duly sensible of the great importance of the subject to which you call my attention in the note which you did me the honor of addressing me the 1st instant, in which you inform me that the President had been pleased to express his regret that I was not empowered by my Government to enter into a formal stipulation for the better security of vessels of the United States, when meeting with disasters in passing between the United States and the Bahama [*sic*] islands, and driven by such disasters into British ports.

It is, I believe, unnecessary that I should tell you that the case of the Creole was known in London a few days only before my departure. No complaint had at that time been made by Mr. Everett. The subject was not, therefore, among those that it was the immediate object of my mission to discuss. But at the same time I must admit that, from the moment I was acquainted with the facts of this case, I was sensible of all its importance, and I should not think myself without power to consider of some adjustment of, and remedy for, a great acknowledged difficulty, if I could see my way clearly to any satisfactory course, and if I had not arrived at the conclusion, after very anxious consideration, that, for the reasons which I will state, this question had better be treated in London, where it will have a much increased chance of settlement, on terms likely to satisfy the interests of the United States.

The immediate case of the Creole would be easily disposed of; but [it] involves a class and description of cases which, for the purpose of affording that security you seek for the trade of American through the Bahama [*sic*] channel, brings into consideration questions of law, both national and international, of the highest importance; and, to increase the delicacy and difficulty of the subject, public feeling is sensitively alive to everything connected with it. These circumstances bring me to the conviction that, although I really believe that much may be done to meet the wishes of your Government, the means of doing so would be best considered in London, where immediate reference may be had to the highest authorities, on every point of delicacy and difficulty that may arise. Whatever I might attempt would be more or less under the disadvantage of being fettered by apprehensions of responsibility, and I might thereby be kept within limits which my Government at home might disregard. In other words, I believe you would have a better chance in this settlement with them than with me. I state this after some imperfect endeavors, by correspondence, to come at satisfactory explanations. If I were in this instance treating of ordinary material interests, I should proceed with more confidence; but anxious as I unfeignedly am that all questions likely to disturb the future good understandings between us should be averted, I strongly recommend this question of the security of the Bahama [*sic*] channel being referred for discussion in London.

This opinion is more decidedly confirmed by your very elaborate and important argument on the application of the general principle of the law of nations to these subjects—an argument to which your authority necessarily gives great weight, but in which I would not presume to follow you with my own imperfect means. Great Britain and the United States, covering all the seas of the world with their commerce, have the greatest possible interest in maintaining sound and pure principles of international law, as well as the practice of reciprocal aid and good offices in all their harbors and possessions. With respect to the latter, it is satisfactory to know that the disposition of the respective Governments and people leaves little to be desired, with the single exception of those very delicate and perplexing questions which have recently arisen from the state of slavery, and even these seem confined, and likely to continue to be confined, to the narrow passage of the Bahama [*sic*] channel. At no other part of the British possessions are American vessels with slaves ever likely to touch, nor are they likely to touch there otherwise than from the pressure of very urgent necessity. The difficulty, therefore, as well as the desired remedy, is apparently confined within narrow limits.

Upon the great general principles affecting this case we do not differ. You admit that if slaves, the property of American citizens, escape into British territories, it is not expected that they will be restored; and you may be well assured that there is no wish on our part that they should reach our shores, or that British possessions should be used as decoys for the violators of the laws of a friendly neighbor.

When these slaves do reach us, by whatever means, there is no alternative. The present state of British law is in this respect too well known to require repetition, nor need I remind you that it is exactly the same with the laws of every part of the United States where a state of slavery is not recognized; and that the slave put on shore at Nassau would be dealt with exactly as would a foreign slave landed, under any circumstances whatever, at Boston.

But what constitutes the being within British dominion, from which these consequences are to follow? Is a vessel passing through the Bahama [*sic*] channel, and forced involuntarily, either from storm or mutiny, into British waters, to be so considered? What power have the authorities of those islands to take cognizance of persons or property in such vessels? These are questions which you, sir, have discussed at great length, and with evident ability. Although you have advanced some propositions which rather surprise and startle me, I do not pretend to judge them; but what is very clear is, that great principles are involved in a discussion which it would ill become me lightly to enter upon; and I am confirmed by this consideration in wishing that the subject be referred to where it will be perfectly weighed and examined.

It behooves the authorities of our two Governments well to guard themselves against establishing by their diplomatic intercourse false precedents and principles, and that they do not, for the purpose of meeting a passing difficulty, set examples which may hereafter mislead the world.

It is not intended on this occasion to consider in detail the particular instances which have given rise to these discussions. They have already been stated and explained. Our object is rather to look to the means of future prevention of such occurrences. That this may be obtained, I have little doubt, although we may not be able immediately to agree on the precise stipulations of a treaty. On the part of Great Britain, there are certain great principles too deeply rooted in the consciences and sympathies of the people for any minister to be able to overlook; and any engagement I might make in opposition to them would be instantly disavowed; but, at the same time that we maintain our own laws within our own territories, we are bound to respect those of our neighbor, and to listen to every possible suggestion of means of averting from them every annoyance and injury. I have great confidence that this may be effectually done in the present instance; but the case to be met and remedied is new, and must not be too hastily dealt with. You may, however, be assured that measures so important for the preservation of friendly intercourse between the two countries shall not be neglected.

In the meantime, I can engage that instructions shall be given to the Governors of her majesty's colonies to the southern borders of the United States to execute their own laws with careful attention to the wish of their Government to maintain good neighborhood, and that there shall be no officious interference with American vessels driven by accident or by violence into those ports. The laws and duties of hospitality shall be executed, and these seem neither to require nor to justify any inquisition into the state of persons or things on board of vessels so situated, than may be indispensable to enforce the observance of the municipal law of the colony, and the proper regulation of its harbors and waters.

A strict and careful attention to these rules, applied in good faith to all transactions as they arise, will, I hope and believe, without any abandonment of great and general principles, lead to the avoidance of any excitement or agitation on this very sensitive subject of slavery, and, consequently, of those irritating feelings which may have a tendency to bring into peril all the great interests connected with the maintenance of peace.

I further trust that friendly sentiments, and a conviction of the importance of cherishing them, will, on all occasions, lead the two countries to consider favorably any further arrangements which may be judged necessary for the reciprocal protections of their interests.

I hope, Sir, that this explanation on this very important subject will be satisfactory to the President, and that he will see in it no diminution of that earnest desire, which you have been pleased to recognize in me, to perform my work of reconciliation and friendship; but that he will rather perceive in my suggestion, in this particular instance, that it is made with a well-founded hope of thereby better obtaining the object we have in view.
ASHBURTON
Hon. Daniel Webster, etc., etc. etc.

Mr. Webster to Lord Ashburton
Department of State
Washington, August 8, 1842

My Lord: I have the honor to acknowledge the receipt of your Lordship's note of the 6th instant, in answer to mine of the 1st, upon the subject of a stipulation for the better security of American vessels driven by accident or carried by force into the British West India ports.

The President would have been gratified if you had felt yourself at liberty to proceed at once to consider of some proper arrangement, by formal treaty, for this object; but there may be weight in the reasons which you urge for referring such mode of stipulation for consideration in London.

The President places his reliance on those principles of public law which were stated in my note to your Lordship, and which are regarded as equally well founded and important; and on your Lordship's engagement that instructions shall be given to the Governors of her majesty's colonies to execute their own laws with careful attention to the wish of their Government to maintain good neighborhood, and that there shall be no officious interference with American vessels driven by accident or by violence into those ports; that the laws and duties of hospitality shall be executed, and that these seem neither to require nor to justify any further inquisition into the state of persons or things on board of vessels so situated than may be indispensable to enforce observance of the municipal law of the colony, and the proper regulation of its harbors and waters. He indulges the hope, nevertheless, that, actuated by a just sense of what is due to the mutual interests of the two countries, and the maintenance of a permanent peace between them, her majesty's Government will not fail to see the importance of removing, by such further stipulations, by treaty or otherwise, as may be found to be necessary, all cause of complaint connected with this subject.

I have the honor to be, with high consideration, you Lord's obedient servant,

DANIEL WEBSTER

Lord Ashburton, etc., etc., etc.

Notes

INTRODUCTION

1. See Arthur T. Downey, *Civil War Lawyers: Constitutional Questions, Courtroom Dramas, and the Men Behind Them* (Chicago: ABA Books, 2010), 212–16.

2. See David Brion Davis, *In Human Bondage: The Rise and Fall of Slavery in the New World* (New York: Oxford University Press, 2006). See also George M. Fredrickson, "Redcoat Liberation," *New York Review of Books* 53, no. 13 (August 10, 2006): 51–53.

3. Mark S. Weiner, *Black Trials: Citizenship from the Beginnings of Slavery to the End of Caste* (New York: Knopf, 2004), 73. See also Joseph Ellis, *American Creation: Triumphs and Tragedies at the Founding of the Republic* (New York: Knopf, 2007), 268n53.

4. Jenny S. Martinez, *The Slave Trade and the Origins of International Human Rights Law* (New York: Oxford University Press, 2012), 22.

5. Alan Taylor, *The Internal Enemy: Slavery and War in Virginia, 1772–1832* (New York: Norton, 2013), 2.

6. Ibid., 5.

7. Ibid., 9.

8. Ibid., 10.

9. Ibid., 429–35.

10. Act of 1819, and Act of March 3, 1819, Relative to the Slave Trade.

11. Act of 1820, Statute I, May 15, 1820, chap. CXIII—An Act to continue in force "an Act to protect the commerce of the United States, and punish the crime of piracy," and also to make further provisions punishing the crime of piracy.

12. Martinez, *Slave Trade*, 50–51.

13. Ibid., 3–35.

14. Ibid., 52.

15. Message from the President of the United States, to Both Houses of Congress, at the Commencement of the Second Session of the Eighteenth Congress, 7 December 1824, 18th Cong. 2nd Secession.

16. The Treaty Between the Republic of Texas and Great Britain for the Suppression of the African Slave Trade was proclaimed by the president of the republic on September 16, 1842.

17. Taylor, *The Internal Enemy*, 349.

18. For a review of the most *un*successful slave revolt in American history, see Daniel Rasmussen, *American Uprising: The Untold Story of America's Largest Slave Revolt* (New York: HarperCollins, 2011). This deals with the 1811 uprising by 500 slaves around New Orleans. It resulted in disaster for all.

19. The only book that is devoted exclusively to the mutiny itself seems to be: George and Willene Hendrick, *The Creole Mutiny: A Tale of Revolt Aboard a Slave Ship* (Chicago: Ivan R. Dee, 2003). See also an article by Edward D. Jervey and C. Harold Huber in the *Journal of Negro History* 65, no. 3 (Summer 1980), "The *Creole* Affair." For a similar treatment, see Maggie Montesinos Sale, *The Slumbering Volcano: American Slave Ship Revolts and the Production of Rebellious Masculinity* (Durham: Duke University Press, 1997). For more of a diplomatic and political history, see Howard Jones, *To the Webster-Ashburton Treaty: A Study in Anglo-American Relations, 1783–1843* (Chapel Hill: University of North Carolina Press, 1977).

20. During America's first century (1789 to 1889), there were twenty-three presidents, of whom seventeen were lawyers; in the last century (1913 to 2013), the trend is reversed: there have been twenty presidents, but only nine of those were lawyers. Similarly, lawyers dominated the early Congress; for example, in the 30th Congress (1847–1849) in which Lincoln served, 74 percent of the members were lawyers. In contrast, in the 112th Congress law was the third-leading occupation.

THE REBELLION

1. A brig is a vessel with two square-rigged masts with the main mast aft. It was fast and maneuverable but required a relatively large crew for its size. In the early part of the nineteenth century, a brig was a standard cargo ship, and was larger than a schooner. (A brigantine is a vessel also with two masts, but only the foremast is square rigged.) A barque is a vessel with at least three masts, all of which are square rigged, except for the sternmost. A barque was the most common vessel in the mid-nineteenth century for deep water cargo carrying, because it required relatively smaller crews and therefore was less expensive to operate.

2. Solomon Northup, *Twelve Years a Slave* (New York: Miller, Orton & Mulligan, 1855; Eastford, Connecticut: Martino Publishing, 2010), 33.

3. David Nicholson, "First Slaves First Hope," *American History* 48, no. 2 (June 2013): 68. See also Lisa Rein, "Mystery of Va.'s First Slaves Is Unlocked 400 Years Later," *Washington Post*, September 3, 2006. The direct slave trade from Africa to North America did not start until the 1700s. For an interesting view of the Jamestown settlement, see Kieran Doherty, *Sea Adventure: Shipwreck, Survival, and the Salvation of the First English Colony in the New World* (New York: St. Martin's, 2007).

4. The fort was decommissioned in 2011, and portions of it were declared a national monument.

5. John V. Quarstein and Dennis P. Mroczkowski, *Fort Monroe: The Key to the South* (Mount Pleasant, OK: Arcadia, 2000), 26.

6. The official logbook of the ship noted that there were 186 slaves. Yet, all parties seem to have agreed that this was simply inaccurate, and that 135 was the correct number.

7. Interestingly, the famous free northern black, Solomon Northup, who was sold into slavery and carried on a brig from Richmond to New Orleans, also served as the slave cook. He also conspired to take control of his slave ship, perhaps trying to make his way back to New York.

8. The narratives of Madison Washington typically present as fact a personal history involving his flight to Canada, return to Virginia to rescue his wife, and so forth. One source for this biographical information is a brief unsigned article in the newspaper *Friend of Man* published in central New York, which was republished on April 4, 1842, in the *National Anti-Slavery Standard*, and in the *Liberator* of June 10, 1842. There was also an account offered by the black abolitionist, Robert Purvis, half a century later, to a journalist in Philadelphia. Purvis's version links Madison Washington to the *Amistad* affair by claiming that Washington was inspired by a painting of Cinque when Washington visited Purvis's home in the fall of 1841. (Purvis had been involved in Cinque's legal defense, and so this linkage may have been somewhat self-serving.) See Marcus Rediker, *The Amistad Rebellion: An Atlantic Odyssey of Slavery and Freedom* (New York: Viking/Penguin, 2012), 224–26 and 273n1. However, since

there is no verifiable support for the accuracy of this information, that biographical story is not repeated here. Chapter 9 reveals much of the fictional history.

9. This is a nautical procedure, which, by balancing the sails and rudder, leaves the vessel with little or no forward movement. It is generally used to permit the crew to have a break for the night or for a meal.

10. The description of the events and all the quotations are taken from the formal Protest sworn in New Orleans on December 2, 1842, by Gifford and all the crew members, as transmitted to the US Senate on January 19, 1842, by President Tyler in response to a Senate Resolution requesting copies of all documents relating to the *Creole* matter.

11. Quoted in the deposition of Jacob Leitner, sworn before the US consul on November 15, 1841, included in the collection of documents sent to the Senate by President Tyler.

12. Hog Island today is known as Paradise Island, a tourism area anchored by the Atlantis Resort, which has 4,000 hotel rooms and the largest gambling casino in the Caribbean with 50,000 square feet of gaming.

13. From the formal protest, sworn on December 7, 1841, in New Orleans, by Gifford and his crew.

14. The formal protest made in New Orleans on December 2 by Gifford identified the local officer as a quarantine officer, not the harbormaster.

1. THE UNITED STATES

1. The top five largest cities were New York City (312,710), Baltimore (102,313), New Orleans (102,193), Philadelphia (93,665), and Boston (93,383). At that time, Brooklyn, ranked seventh, was not a part of New York City. US Bureau of the Census, 1840.

2. In 1836, the Wisconsin Territory included the present states of Wisconsin, Minnesota, and Iowa, along with parts of the Dakotas east of the Missouri River. In 1838, the Iowa Territory was created.

3. Julia M. Klein, "An Edgar Allan Poe-pourri," *Wall Street Journal*, October 3, 2013, D4.

4. Stephen E. Ambrose, *Nothing Like it in the World: The Men Who Built the Transcontinental Railroad 1863–1869* (New York: Simon & Schuster, 2005), 28.

5. Ari Kelman, "Perimeters of Pain," review of *River of Dark Dreams* in *Times Literary Supplement*, July 26, 2013, 12.

6. Daniel Walker Howe, *What Hath God Wrought: The Transformation of America, 1815–1848* (New York: Oxford University Press, 2007), xv. The late, great historian of the US House of Representatives, and biographer of Andrew Jackson, Robert V. Remini, said that Jackson embodied the "new American": "This new man was no longer British. . . . He no longer wore the queue and silk pants. He wore trousers, and he stopped talking with a British accent." Quoted in the obituary for Remini in the *Washington Post*, April 5, 2013, B-7.

7. "Whereas merchants most commonly called the period between March and May 1837 a 'crisis,' American politicians preferred the word 'panic.' Labeling the crisis a panic worked for both Democrats and Whigs because it implied that it was manufactured, the product of politically assailable policies." Jessica M. Lepler, *The Many Panics of 1837: People, Politics, and the Creation of a Transatlantic Financial Crisis* (New York: Cambridge University Press, 2013), 154.

8. David S. Reynolds, *Waking Giant: American in the Age of Jackson* (New York: HarperCollins, 2008), 331. At that point, almost 40 percent of America's banks failed.

9. Lepler, *The Many Panics of 1837*, 232.

10. 5 Stat. 440. The first such statute was the Bankruptcy Act of 1800, but it dealt only with involuntary bankruptcy for merchants and was repealed three years later.

11. Dennis K. Berman, "When States Default: 2011, Meet 1841," *Wall Street Journal*, January 4, 2011, C-1.

12. Sean Wilentz, *The Rise of American Democracy: Jefferson to Lincoln* (New York: Norton, 2005), 456.

13. In 1834, the Maryland State Colonization Society established Maryland in Liberia, at Cape Palmas, near Liberia's current border with Côte d'Ivoire. For a scholarly review of that event, see Richard L. Hall, *On Africa's Shore: A History of Maryland in Liberia, 1834–1857* (Baltimore: Maryland Historical Society, 2003).

14. Edward B. Rugemer, "Slave Rebels and Abolitionists: The Black Atlantic and the Coming of the Civil War," *Journal of the Civil War Era* 2, no. 2 (June 2012): 184.

15. Alan Taylor, *The Internal Enemy: Slavery and War in Virginia, 1772–1832* (New York: Norton, 2013), 415.

16. Stanley Harrold, *Border War: Fighting over Slavery before the Civil War* (Chapel Hill: University of North Carolina Press, 2010), 70.

17. Rugemer, "Slave Rebels and Abolitionists," 187.

18. Daniel Howe, "Goodbye to the Age of Jackson," *New York Review of Books* 35 (May 28, 2009). Professor Howe is Rhodes Professor of American History Emeritus at Oxford and UCLA.

19. In President Lincoln's inaugural address in 1861, he dealt head-on with the "mail delivery" issue, promising that it would be "furnished in all parts of the Union."

20. Maggie Montesinos Sale, *The Slumbering Volcano: American Slave Ship Revolts and the Production of Rebellious Masculinity* (Durham: Duke University Press, 1997), 1.

21. Ironically, the British diplomat responsible for the papal negotiations and the British minister in Washington at the same time were both named Henry Fox. The one in Italy was Henry Edward Fox, while the one in Washington was Henry Stephen Fox.

22. The description of the Palmerston effort and the papal response is brilliantly treated in John T. Noonan Jr., *A Church That Can and Cannot Change* (Notre Dame, IN: University of Notre Dame Press, 2005), 104–8. Noonan's perspective on slavery in particular has been criticized. See Avery Cardinal Dulles, SJ, "Development or Reversal?" *First Things* (October 2005).

23. Noonan, *A Church*, 108.

24. For a magnificent study of this general issue, particularly as it ultimately impacted the Civil War, see Steven Deyle, *Carry Me Back: The Domestic Slave Trade in American Life* (New York: Oxford University Press, 2005).

25. Lepler, *The Many Panics of 1837*, 14.

26. Kelman, "Perimeters of Pain," 12.

27. Lepler, *The Many Panics of 1837*, 13.

28. Jason Berry, "Urban Gumbo: New Orleans became a Creole Society of Mingled Bloodlines," review of Ned Sublette, *The World that Made New Orleans: From Spanish Silver to Congo Square* in *New York Times Book Review*, February 17, 2008, 23.

29. For a full discussion of the New Orleans/Mississippi system of slavery, see Walter Johnson, *River of Dark Dreams: Slavery and Empire in the Cotton Kingdom* (Cambridge, MA: Belknap, 2013). See also the review of it: Kelman, "Perimeters of Pain," 12–13.

30. For a superb presentation of this issue and the Supreme Court, see David L. Lightner, "The Supreme Court and the Interstate Slave Trade: A Study in Evasion, Anarchy, and Extremism" *Journal of Supreme Court History* 29, no. 3 (2004): 229.

31. John Jay was one of the Founding Fathers: president of the Continental Congress (1778–1779), drafter of five of the *Federalist Papers*, negotiator of the 1795 Jay Treaty with Great Britain, chief justice (1789–1795) appointed by George Washington, and governor of New York (1795–1801). Importantly, Jay was the leading opponent of slavery in his state and, finally, in 1799, he was successful in passing legislation providing for gradual emancipation. His son, Judge William Jay, followed his father's passion for law and for abolition.

32. William Jay, *A View of the Action of the Federal Government, in Behalf of Slavery* (New York: J. S. Taylor, 1839).

33. The admiral was the older brother of Sir Francis Cockburn, the governor of the Bahamas. See chapter 4.

34. Jay, *A View of the Action*, 60–61.

35. A relatively minor foreign relations issue, but very sensitive in domestic political terms, was the matter of diplomatic relations with Haiti. Abolitionists in the North and in Congress demanded acceptance of the successful black republic, while the slaveholding states insisted

that the fruits of a successful slave insurrection should not be exhibited in the United States, and, in any event, Haitian diplomats could not be accepted as social equals in Washington. The Tyler administration, fearful of the contagion of slave uprisings spreading from the Caribbean to the American South, was opposed to diplomatic relations with Haiti. The United States did not diplomatically recognize Haiti until 1862.

36. Gail Collins, *William Henry Harrison* (New York: Time Books/Henry Holt, 2012), 83.

37. Ibid., 85–86.

38. Richard Brookhiser, "William Henry Harrison Showed Rich Presidential Candidates How to Win," *American History*, June 2012, 22.

39. Ibid., 88.

40. Mark O. Hatfield, with the Senate Historical Office, *Vice Presidents of the United States, 1789–1993* (Washington, DC: US Government Printing Office, 1997), 142.

41. Thomas Fleming, "How Presidential Politics Fastened Onto Buttons," *Wall Street Journal*, September 25, 2012, A-17.

42. Kathryn Allamong Jacob, *Capital Elites: High Society in Washington D.C., After the Civil War* (Washington, DC: Smithsonian Institution Press, 1995), 23.

43. Hatfield, *Vice Presidents*, 143.

44. Lynn Hudson Parsons, *John Quincy Adams* (Lanham, MD: Rowman & Littlefield, 2001), 246.

45. George Washington had only four cabinet members: state, treasury, war, and the attorney general. Today, the cabinet is composed of fifteen executive department heads: state, treasury, defense, justice, interior, agriculture, commerce, labor, health and human services, housing and urban development, transportation, energy, education, veterans affairs, and homeland security. In addition, the following positions have the status of cabinet rank: chief of staff, environmental protection agency, management and budget, US trade representative, ambassador to the UN, chair of the council of economic advisers, and the small business administration.

46. Collins, *William Henry Harrison*, 118.

47. William H. Rehnquist, "Daniel Webster and the Oratorical Tradition," *1989 Yearbook of the Supreme Court Historical Society*, 7.

48. Ibid.

49. *Dartmouth College v. Woodward*, 17 US 518 (1819).

50. 22 US 1 (1824).

51. S. W. Finley, "Constitutional Orator: Daniel Webster Packed 'Em In," *1979 Yearbook of the Supreme Court Historical Society*, 59.

52. Herman Belz, ed., *The Webster-Hayne Debate on the Nature of the Union: Selected Documents* (Indianapolis: Liberty Fund, 2000).

53. The Daniel Webster Memorial is a bronze statue of Webster, located in Washington, DC, dedicated in 1900 with funds appropriated by Congress. The main inscription on the granite pedestal is: "Daniel Webster, Liberty and Union Now and Forever One and Inseparable."

54. Gary May, *John Tyler* (New York: Times Books/Henry Holt, 2008), 59.

55. Ibid., 123.

56. Edward P. Crapol, *John Tyler: The Accidental President* (Chapel Hill: University of North Carolina Press, 2006), 8.

57. Daniel Webster's elder son, Daniel Fletcher Webster, was colonel of the 12th Regiment, Massachusetts Infantry, the "Webster regiment." Fletcher was killed at the Second Battle of Bull Run on August 30, 1862, at the age of forty-nine. Fletcher was named after his mother's maiden name, Grace Fletcher Webster.

58. William G. Clotworthy, *Homes and Libraries of the Presidents* (Granville, OH: McDonald & Woodward: 2008), 84.

59. Hatfield, *Vice Presidents*, 144.

60. Ibid., 145, citing Charles Francis Adams, ed., *Memoirs of John Quincy Adams*, 12 vols. (Philadelphia, 1876), 10:456–57.

61. This site is currently the location of the Newseum, a museum dedicated to the news media. The hotel had been the location of President Madison's second inaugural ball in 1813, and also the site for both of President James Monroe's inaugural balls in 1817 and 1821.

62. Collins, *William Henry Harrison*, 124.
63. Parsons, *John Quincy Adams*, 247.
64. Solomon Northup, *Twelve Years a Slave* (New York: Miller, Orton & Mulligan, 1855; Eastford, CT: Martino Publishing, 2010), 22.
65. Clotworthy, *Homes and Libraries of the Presidents*, 84.
66. See Forest McDonald, *States' Rights and the Union: Imperium in Imperio, 1776–1876* (Lawrence: University Press of Kansas, 2000), 124–26.
67. Robert V. Remini, *Daniel Webster: The Man and His Time* (New York: Norton, 1997), 529.
68. May, *John Tyler*, 74.
69. Hatfield, *Vice Presidents*, 148.
70. Remini, *Daniel Webster*, 530.
71. Ibid., 531.
72. Alexis de Tocqueville, *Democracy in America*, trans. and ed. Harvey C. Mansfield and Delba Winthrop (Chicago: University of Chicago Press, 2002), 191.
73. Wise had been a Jacksonian Democrat in the 23rd and 24th Congresses (1833–1837), but became a Whig in the 25th Congress (1837); in 1843, he became a Tyler Democrat.
74. The full title was "An Act Supplementary to the Act Entitled 'An Act to Amend the Judicial System of the United States.'"
75. Mary Ann Harrell and Burnett Anderson, *Equal Justice Under Law: The Supreme Court in American Life* (Washington, DC: Supreme Court Historical Society, 1994), 42.
76. See Don E. Fehrenbacher, *The Slaveholding Republic: An Account of the United States Government's Relations to Slavery* (New York: Oxford University Press, 2001), 192–93.
77. 23 US (10 Wheat.) 66 (1825).
78. Jenny S. Martinez, *The Slave Trade and the Origins of International Human Rights Law* (New York: Oxford University Press, 2012), 59.
79. Wirt still holds the record for the longest serving attorney general, 1817–1829, under Monroe and John Quincy Adams.
80. Galen N. Thorp, "William Wirt," *Journal of the Supreme Court Historical Society* 33, no. 3 (2008): 242.
81. *The Antelope*, 23 US (10 Wheat.) 66 (1825), 121.
82. Martinez, *Slave Trade*, 64.
83. *United States v. Skiddy*, 36 US 73 (1837).
84. *US v. Amistad*, 40 US 518 (1841). The full caption is: *The United States, Appellants v. Libellants and Claimants of the Schooner Amistad, Her Tackle, Apparel, and Furniture, Together with Her Cargo, and the Africans Mentioned and Describer in the Several Libels and Claims, Appellees.* Much of the description of the complex judicial proceedings is taken from the excellent essay by Bruce A. Ragsdale, the director of the federal judicial history office in 2002, prepared for inclusion in the project Federal Trials and Great Debates in United States History.
85. For an extraordinary account of the courageous Africans who rebelled, see Marcus Rediker, *The Amistad Rebellion: An Atlantic Odyssey of Slavery and Rebellion* (New York: Viking, 2012). Professor Rediker correctly notes that the "heroes" of the *Amistad* affair have been popularized as the legal system, lawyers, and political figures, rather than the courageous Africans. His book tells their story.
86. One might question why the commander brought the schooner to Connecticut rather than New York. The answer may lie in the fact that slavery ended in New York in 1827, while it remained legal in Connecticut until 1848. The commander may have thought that his claim for compensation for slave property might be easier to make in a state where slavery was still legal. See Arthur T. Downey, *Civil War Lawyers: Constitutional Questions, Courtroom Dramas, and the Men Behind Them* (Chicago: ABA Books, 2010), 213.
87. Baldwin later became governor of Connecticut (1844–1846) and US senator from Connecticut (1847–1851).
88. *US v. Amistad*, 40 US 518 (1841), at 522.
89. Daniel Walker Howe, *What Hath God Wrought: The Transformation of America, 1815–1848* (New York: Oxford University Press, 2007), 521.

90. Harlow Giles Unger, *John Quincy Adams* (Boston: Da Capo, 2012), 288–89.

91. Parsons, *John Quincy Adams*, 237.

92. Allen Sharp, "Presidents as Supreme Court Advocates: Before and After the White House," 28 *Journal of Supreme Court History* (no. 2, 2003), 121.

93. *Fletcher v. Peck* (1810) was a landmark case involving the Contract Clause. Adams had argued for the winning side. Adams argued in 1809, but the arguments continued into 1810, by which time Adams had left for Russia; Joseph Story took Adams's place for the final argument.

94. Parsons, *John Quincy Adams*, 239.

95. Sharp, "Presidents as Supreme Court Advocates, 120.

96. Parsons, *John Quincy Adams*, 240.

97. In the 1997 movie directed by Steven Spielberg, *Amistad*, retired supreme court justice Harry Blackmun played Justice Story.

98. In 1855, Herman Melville published in serialized form his novella titled *Benito Cereno*, loosely modeled after the *Amistad* event. See also Mark S. Weiner, *Black Trials: Citizenship from the Beginnings of Slavery to the End of Caste* (New York: Knopf, 2004), 133.

99. In 1844, Tyler asked Congress to consider the matter. A house committee proposed $70,000 for Spain, but Adams led the fight that defeated the measure. In 1847, at the request of Secretary of State Buchanan (under Polk), the Senate proposed a $50,000 payment to Spain, but the House killed the proposal (113–40) after Adams argued against it in his last House speech. Adams's colleague Joshua Giddings forcefully argued against the bill in a House speech on April 18, 1844. No reparations were ever paid, although Spain persisted in demanding them until the Civil War.

100. For a superb discussion of the interstate slave trade, including this Mississippi case, see David L. Lightner, "The Supreme Court and the Interstate Slave Trade: A Study in Evasion, Anarchy, and Extremism," *Journal of Supreme Court History* 29, no. 3 (2004): 229.

101. 40 US 449 at 502.

102. Ibid., 506.

103. Ibid., 508.

104. *Black's Law Dictionary*, 5th ed. (St. Paul: West Publishing, 1979), 408.

105. Ibid.

106. Ibid., 510.

107. For a discussion of both the *Prigg* and the *Groves* cases, see Tony A. Freyer and Daniel Thomas, "The *Passenger* Cases Reconsidered in Transatlantic Commerce Clause History," *Journal of Supreme Court History* 36, no. 3 (2011): 221.

108. The clause read: "No Person held to Service or Labor in one State, under the Law thereof, escaping into another, shall, in Consequence of any Law or Regulation therein, be discharged from such Service or Labor, but shall be delivered up on Claim of other Party to whom such Service or Labor may be due." For a full and interesting discussion, see Akhil Reed Amar, *America's Constitution: A Biography* (New York: Random House, 2005), 256–63.

109. "An Act more effectively to protect the free citizens of this State from being kidnapped, or reduced to slavery," chap. 375; May 14, 1840. The full text is found at Appendix A of Northup, *Twelve Years a Slave*. It was under this New York law that Solomon Northup was recused in Louisiana and returned to his home in New York State in 1853.

110. For an interesting discussion of slave life in western Maryland, see Constance M. McGovern, "'Liberty to Them Is as Sweet as It Is to Me': Slave Life in Allegany County, Maryland, 1789–1864," *Maryland Historical Magazine* 107, no. 4 (Winter 2012): 405. Professor McGovern noted, "the southwestern Pennsylvania countryside . . . had numbers of slave catchers, a 'despicable set' who 'drank whiskey, chewed tobacco, played cards, and loafed around village taverns, posted handbills and lay in wait for the runaways.'" Ibid., 421.

111. A clear and brief explanation of the case is available at Kermit L. Hall, ed., *The Oxford Companion to the Supreme Court of the United States* (New York: Oxford University Press, 1992), 669.

112. The most comprehensive treatment of this case can be found at H. Robert Baker, *Prigg v. Pennsylvania: Slavery, the Supreme Court, and the Ambivalent Constitution* (Lawrence: University Press of Kansas, 2012).

113. For a brilliant and riveting study of the problem of fugitive slaves in the decade before the Civil War, see Steven Lubet, *Fugitive Justice: Runaways, Rescuers, and Slavery on Trial* (Cambridge: Belknap, 2010).

114. This curious story is detailed in Stanley Harrold, *Border War: Fighting over Slavery before the Civil War* (Chapel Hill: University of North Carolina Press, 2010), 78–79.

2. US-BRITISH RELATIONS—AT THE BRINK

1. In 1790, the US population was 4 million, and in 1860, it was 31 million. The population had increased by one-third every decade.

2. The "Monroe Doctrine" was set out in President Monroe's seventh annual message to Congress on December 2, 1823. A key contributor was Secretary of State John Quincy Adams. Monroe stated: "[T]he American continents, by the free and independent condition which they have assumed and maintain, are henceforth not to be considered as subjects for future colonization by any European powers."

3. Michael Fathers, "Catastrophe at Kabul," review of William Dalrymple, *Return of a King: The Battle for Afghanistan, 1839–42* in the *Wall Street Journal*, April 13–14, C-6.

4. For an excellent and exhaustive treatment see Peter Hopkirk, *The Great Game: The Struggle for Empire in Central Asia* (New York: Kodansha America, 1994).

5. John Darwin, "The Men Who Would Be King," review of Dalrymple, *Return of a King* in the *New York Times Book Review*, May 26, 2013, 14.

6. Seth G. Jones, "Costly Mistakes in an Afghan Adventure," review of Dalrymple, *Return of a King* in the *Washington Post*, June 23, 2013, B-7.

7. William W. Freehling, *The Road to Disunion: Secessionists at Bay, 1776–1854*, vol. 1 (New York: Oxford University Press, 1990), 368.

8. Mark M. Smith, "More True Sons of Liberty," review of Alan Taylor, *The Internal Enemy* in the *Wall Street Journal*, September 14–15, 2013, C5.

9. David Brion Davis, *Inhuman Bondage: The Rise and Fall of Slavery in the New World* (New York: Oxford University Press, 2006) 269.

10. Ibid., 272.

11. The would-be killer was an eighteen-year-old barman from London; the attempt was theatrical, and his trial was a sensation. His plea of insanity carried the day, and he was sent to Bedlam. See John Sutherland, "How Not to Kill A Queen," review of Paul Thomas Murphy, *Shooting Victoria: Madness, Mayhem, and the Rebirth of the British Monarchy* in the *New York Times Book Review*, July 29, 2012, 10.

12. David Waller, "Worth Being Shot," review of Murphy, *Shooting Victoria* in the *Times Literary Supplement*, August 2, 2013, 25.

13. Confirmed on June 22, 1772, in the famous case of *Somerset v. Stewart,* written by Lord Mansfield, the chief justice of the King's Bench. See Norman S. Poser, *Lord Mansfield: Justice in the Age of Reason* (Montreal: McGill-Queen's University Press, 2013).

14. The 1827 case of *The Slave Grace.*

15. A regiment from Barbados and a battalion from Bermuda were sent to assist. In 1832, Parliament appointed a Select Committee on the Extinction of Slavery throughout the British Dominions, which was to consider the best way to effect abolition "whilst ensuring the safety of all classes in the colonies." The committee issued its report in 1833.

16. August 28, 1833, "An Act for Abolition of Slavery throughout British Colonies," with effect one year later.

17. The former slaves, of course, received no compensation. However, the Caribbean Community (Caricom), which includes former British colonies, together with Suriname and Haiti, currently are claiming reparations for the former slaves. Among the unsettled questions are who should pay, how much should be paid, and who should be paid. These issues are considered in *The Economist*, October 5, 2013, 42.

18. Howard Jones, *To The Webster-Ashburton Treaty: A Study in Anglo-American Relations, 1783–1843* (Chapel Hill: University of North Carolina Press, 1977), xii.

19. The formal caption is *The British North America Act, 1840* (3&4 Victoria, c. 35).

20. For an excellent and compressive study of the issues, see John E. Noyes, "*The Caroline*: International Law Limits on Resort to Force," in *International Law Stories* (New York: Foundation Press, 2007).

21. R. Y. Jennings, "The *Caroline* and McLeod Cases," *American Journal of International Law* 32, no. 1 (January 1938): 82.

22. Jones, *To The Webster-Ashburton Treaty*, 27.

23. Fillmore was not an unimportant political figure: in 1841, he came in second place in the race for speaker of the House, and was elected vice president under Zachary Taylor in 1848. Fillmore became president in 1850, when Taylor died.

24. Robert V. Remini, *Daniel Webster: The Man and His Time* (New York: Norton, 1997), 519.

25. Minister Fox's letter to Webster, and Webster's reply of April 24, 1841, were attached to President Tyler's Message to Congress of June 1, 1841.

26. In an ironic twist, in March 1840, the US Supreme Court found that the federal power over foreign affairs was exclusive, and therefore the state of Vermont had no power to surrender fugitives to a foreign government (Canada). See *Holmes v. Jennison*, 39 US 540 (1840).

27. In August 1962, as the Cuban Missile Crisis was beginning, a Justice Department Memorandum for Attorney General Robert Kennedy highlighted the *Caroline* incident, and the position taken by Secretary of State Webster. The memorandum also noted that the Webster statement on self-defense was also quoted with approval by the International Military Tribunal at Nuremberg. Abram Chayes, *The Cuban Missile Crisis: International Crises and the Role of Law* (New York: Oxford University Press, 1974), appendix I. Webster's Rule is still followed, for example, by Israeli scholars of international law in the twenty-first century in the context of use of force against terrorists. See Noyes, "*The Caroline*," 301.

28. Edward P. Crapol, *John Tyler: the Accidental President* (Chapel Hill: University of North Carolina Press, 2006), 91.

29. David S. Reynolds, *Waking Giant: America in the Age of Jackson* (New York: HarperCollins, 2008), 313.

30. Jones, *To The Webster-Ashburton Treaty*, 40.

31. George C. Herring, *From Colony to Superpower: US Foreign Relations Since 1776* (New York: Oxford University Press, 2008), 186.

32. Kathleen Burk, *Old World, New World: Great Britain and America from the Beginning* (New York: Atlantic Monthly Press, 2007), 264.

33. Paul Albury, *The Story of the Bahamas* (London: MacMillan Education, 1975), 135. The author notes that by 1856, there were 302 ships licensed to engage in salvage, and, astonishingly, that nearly one-half of the able-bodied men of the colony were engaged in wrecking.

34. Don E. Fehrenbacher, *The Slaveholding Republic: An Account of the United States Government's Relations to Slavery* (New York: Oxford University Press, 2001), 104.

35. Ibid, 107.

36. It was not until 1846 that Alexandria was retroceded to Virginia and was no longer part of the District of Columbia.

37. From the Statement of the Umpire Bates in the case of the *Enterprise,* January 15, 1855, as reported in *Report of Decisions of the Commission of Claims Under the Convention of February 8, 1853.*

38. For a review of the history of the writ, see Arthur T. Downey, *Civil War Lawyers: Constitutional Questions, Courtroom Dramas, and the Men Behind Them* (Chicago: ABA Books, 2010), 135.

39. Edward Bartlett Rugemer, *The Problem of Emancipation: The Caribbean Roots of the American Civil War* (Baton Rouge: Louisiana State University Press, 2008), 201.

40. 24 Cong. 1st Sess, 727. Quoted in Fehrenbacher, *The Slaveholding Republic*, 106.

41. Rugemer, *The Problem of Emancipation*, 202.

42. Rugemer, *The Problem of Emancipation*, 202n58.

43. Bahamas National Archives, Nassau, Box 8, Governor's Despatches, 1839–1844.

44. The treaty was formally proclaimed in the United States on February 18, 1815. The tenth article provided: "Whereas the Traffic in Slaves is irreconcilable with the principles of human-

ity and Justice, and whereas both His Majesty and the United States are desirous of continuing their efforts to promote its abolition, it is hereby agreed that both the contracting parties shall use their best endeavours to accomplish so desirable an object."

45. A special session of the Senate was called by outgoing president Martin Van Buren on January 6, 1841. It convened on March 4 and adjourned on March 15. The "extra" session of the 27th Congress was called by President Harrison on March 17. It convened on May 31 and adjourned on September 13. The second session—the so-called long session—convened on December 6, 1841 and did not adjourn until August 31, 1842.

46. This was also the formal title of the first US envoy to the United Kingdom after the War of 1812, John Quincy Adams, who was appointed on February 28, 1815, and presented his credentials in London on August 8, 1815. The first US ambassador was Thomas Bayard, who presented his credentials to the Court of St. James and opened the first US embassy in London, on June 22, 1893.

47. Fehrenbacher, *The Slaveholding Republic*, 107.

48. The people of Richmond gave Stevenson a grand dinner in early January 1842, at which he was hailed as "a man of the purest private character, of undoubted political integrity; one of the best Speakers the House of Representatives ever had, and above all he has managed our various difficulties with England in a manner so satisfactory to the country . . . that even Webster himself says 'he is an honor to his country.'" *Richmond Enquirer*, January 11, 1842.

49. Dickens's novels were initially published as serials in monthly papers. For example, *Oliver Twist* was serialized in monthly numbers of *Bentley's Miscellany* beginning in February 1837 and ending in April 1839.

50. Jill Lepore, "Dickens in Eden," *The New Yorker*, August 29, 2011, 52.

3. THE BRITISH BAHAMAS

1. Wendell K. Jones, "The History of the Clifton Plantation, 1788–2000," *Journal of the Bahamas Historical Society* 22 (October 2000): 4.

2. John D. Burton, "American Loyalists, Slaves and the Creation of an Afro-Bahamian World: Sandy Point Plantation and the Prince Storr Murder Case," *Journal of the Bahamas Historical Society* 26 (October 2004): 14. See also John Burton, "From Slave to Student: Education on San Salvador, The Bahamas," *Journal of the Bahamas Historical Society* 35 (2013): 39.

3. Newsletter of the Bahamas Historical Society, October 23, 2010.

4. Ross Hassig, "The Bahamas, POWs, and the War of 1812," *Journal of the Bahamas Historical Society* 35 (October 2013): 13–21. The other three Caribbean POW depots were located in Barbados, Bermuda, and Jamaica.

5. "An Act for the Abolition of the Slave Trade," 47 Geo. III, c. 36, sess. I, Statutes of the United Kingdom and Ireland: 1807–1869.

6. Darius D. Williams, "Resettlement Villages of Liberated Africans & Emancipated Slaves in the Northern Bahamas," *Journal of the Bahamas Historical Society* 32 (2010): 32.

7. The 1817 Anglo-Spanish Treaty banned the import of African slaves into Cuba.

8. Gail Saunders, "The Impact on the Bahamas of the Abolition of the Transatlantic Slave Trade," *Journal of the Bahamas Historical Society* 30 (2008): 34.

9. Bahamas National Archives, Box 8, Governor's Dispatches, 1839–1844.

10. Saunders, "Impact on the Bahamas," 35. The author claims that one of the slave leaders from the *Creole*, Elijah Morris, settled in Gambier after he was freed from jail in Nassau in April 1842.

11. Whittington B. Johnson, "The Amelioration Acts in the Bahamas, 1823–1833: A Middle Ground Between Freedom and Antebellum Slave Codes," *Journal of the Bahamas Historical Society* 18 (October 1996): 23.

12. However, African natives were not permitted to give evidence, but Creoles were. This may have been because the whites believed that the Africans were not yet ready to understand traditional British values. Johnson, "Amelioration Acts," 26.

13. The full title was "An Act for the Abolition of Slavery throughout the British Colonies; for promoting the Industry of the manumitted Slaves; and for compensating the Persons hitherto entitled to the Services of such Slaves." Ceylon and the possessions of the East India Company were exempted.

14. Edward B. Rugemer, "Slave Rebels and Abolitionists: The Black Atlantic and the Coming of the Civil War," *Journal of the Civil War Era* 2, no. 2 (June 2012): 188.

15. See Patrice M. Williams, "Social Reconstruction of Bahamian Society After Emancipation 1838–1850," *Journal of the Bahamas Historical Society* 26 (2004): 24.

16. Peter T. Dalleo, "Montell & Co., The *James Power* and the Baltimore-Bahamas Packet Trade 1838–1845," *Journal of the Bahamas Historical Society* 30 (2008): 6–7.

17. Ibid., 7.

18. Tyler wrote this to Daniel Webster, then a senator from Massachusetts, on March 12, 1846. Edward P. Crapol, *Tyler: The Accidental President* (Chapel Hill: University of North Carolina Press, 2006), 90.

4. IN NASSAU

1. *We, the People: The Story of the United States Capitol* (Washington, DC: US Capitol Historical Society, 1991), 28.

2. Joyce Appleby, "A Stumbling, Fiery End to War of 1812," review of Steve Vogel, *Through the Perilous Fight: Six Weeks that Saved the Nation*, in the *Washington Post*, May 5, 2013, B-6. Sir George's assignment, after the burning of Washington, was to convey Napoleon to St. Helena in the South Atlantic; he remained as governor of that British possession for a few months. See also Stuart Butler, "Defending Norfolk: An Early Battle with the British in 1813 Saves a Thriving American Port," *Prologue* 45 (2013): 10–18. A photo of a portrait of Sir George appears on p. 16.

3. In the report of the investigations by the magistrate, Robert Duncome, the slaves are identified as "one hundred and thirty-five black passengers" along with four white passengers.

4. This dramatic encounter is not mentioned in Woodside's deposition, but is detailed in the formal protest made by Gifford on December 2, 1841, in New Orleans.

5. This narrative is taken from the deposition sworn to by Woodside in front of Bacon on that same Friday, November 13, 1841.

6. According to Gifford's testimony in the later Louisiana Supreme Court case, two of the slaves had stayed in the cabin, Rachael Glover (about thirty years old) and Mary, a mulatto girl of about thirteen years; the boy was the son of one of those two. The other two women had been in the hold during the voyage and until after the others had left the ship.

7. Edward Eden, "The Revolt on the Slave Ship *Creole*: Popular resistance to slavery in Post-Emancipation Nassau," *Journal of the Bahamas Historical Society* 22 (2000): 16.

8. This report is taken from the deposition sworn to by Gifford in front of Bacon on that same Friday, November 13, 1841. It is consistent with the depositions given by Merritt and by Stevens, the second mate, on the same day.

9. A letter reprinted from the *Charleston Courier* provided a report from a passenger on a ship recently returned from Kingston, Jamaica, that a schooner had arrived from Nassau "with about 60 or 70 Negroes . . . and they were a portion of those taken into Nassau by the brig *Creole*." Quoted in the *Richmond Enquirer*, January 1, 1842, 3.

10. This idea is suggested by Eden, "The Revolt on the Slave Ship *Creole*," 16.

11. These figures are not from a census in Nassau, but rather come from the formal protest of the Americans, and was undoubtedly information supplied by the US consul.

12. One scholar identified this likelihood. See Maggie Montesinos Sale, *The Slumbering Volcano: American Slave Ship Revolts and the Production of Rebellious Masculinity* (Durham: Duke University Press, 1997), 126. Ms. Sale also put a negative twist on the protest, arguing that it "discursively erased the agency, activity, and power of the people of Nassau, and the threat they posed to British authorities had they attempted to produce a different outcome, as well as to the US crew and their supporters" (127).

13. Eden, "The Revolt on the Slave Ship *Creole*," 15.

14. It is unclear what happened to Captain Ensor. Presumably, he returned to the United States on another vessel once he was well enough to travel. On January 27, 1842, there was a meeting of Richmond citizens in the grand ballroom of the Exchange Hotel, and the *Richmond Enquirer* of January 29, 1842, reports, "The Captain of the *Creole* was present." The 1840 census shows a Robert T. Ensor living in Richmond (Henrico County), with two white females under age five (perhaps his daughter and niece), and a white female age twenty to thirty-nine, perhaps his wife. The 1850 census does not reveal any Robert Ensor, but there is an Eliza Ensor, age thirty, in Richmond, perhaps his wife (or widow) along with three children ranging from age twelve to eleven months. Perhaps the captain had died from his injuries, or perhaps he was simply at sea when the census was taken. Cathy Morgan of the Virginia Historical Society, December 10, 2010, provided this census research.

15. Bahamas National Archives, Secretary of State Correspondence (loose papers, 1832–1921—Gov. 15/1).

16. These were John Dodson, a former member of Parliament, and king's advocate in the Melbourne administration, and an Oxford graduate; Frederick Pollack, a Cambridge graduate, Member of Parliament (1831–1844), and attorney general 1834–1835 and 1841–1844 in the Peel administrations; and Sir W. W. Follett.

17. Charles Dickens satirized Doctors' Commons in *Sketches by Boz* (1836) and *David Copperfield* (1850).

18. There is evidence that one of the leaders, Elijah Morris, settled in the Village of Gambier, nine miles west of Nassau. It was this settlement where the British Navy brought Africans after the abolition of slavery. See Gail Saunders, *Gambier Village: A Brief History* (Nassau: 2007), 9.

5. IN THE UNITED STATES

1. In the penultimate paragraph, Tyler urged Congress to move more quickly to apply the funds received under the will of "Mr. Smithson, of England, for the diffusion of knowledge." Ultimately, this led to the formation of the great Smithsonian Institution in Washington, DC.

2. Webster had written to Edward Everett, the US minister in London, on November 20 about all of these issues as outlined by the president.

3. For an excellent description of New Orleans and the slave life there in the 1840s, see John Bailey, *The Lost German Slave Girl* (New York: Grove Press, 2003).

4. Edward B. Rugemer, "Slave Rebels and Abolitionists: The Black Atlantic and the Coming of the Civil War," *Journal of the Civil War Era* 2, no. 2 (June 2012): 204.

5. *Black's Law Dictionary*, 5th ed. (St. Paul: West Publishing, 1979), 1101.

6. See, for example, the *Richmond Enquirer* of December 21 and 22, 1841.

7. Quoted in the *Richmond Enquirer*, December 25, 1841, 2.

8. Rugemer, "Slave Rebels and Abolitionists," 203.

9. As quoted in the *Richmond Enquirer*, December 25, 1841, 2.

10. The *Richmond Enquirer* of January 6, 1842.

11. *Journal of the Senate of the United States of America, 1789–1873*, Monday, January 10, 1842, 77.

12. Quoted in the *Richmond Enquirer* of January 27, 1842, 3.

13. One scholar views Webster's dispatch in a sinister fashion, in that it "coded the conflict as a property dispute between national powers and discursively erased both the control of the rebels over the vessel and the agency of the people of Nassau. . . . Webster's dispatch defended the property claims of slaveholders over the rebels' struggle for personal liberty." Maggie Montesinos Sale, *The Slumbering Volcano: American Slave Ship Revolts and the Production of Rebellious Masculinity* (Durham: Duke University Press, 1997), 131.

14. The *Richmond Enquirer*, February 22, 1842.

15. From Webster's diary, as quoted in Robert V. Remini, *Daniel Webster: The Man and His Time* (New York: Norton, 1997), 541.

16. Joseph Wheelan, *Mr. Adams's Last Crusade: John Quincy Adams's Extraordinary Post-Presidential Life in Congress* (New York: Public Affairs, 2008), 189.

17. Harlow Giles Unger, *John Quincy Adams* (Boston: Da Capo, 2012), 297.

18. The rule had been expanded at each session, and now provided that "No petition, memorial, resolution or other paper, praying for the abolition of slavery in the District of Columbia, or any other state or territory, *or the slave trade between the states and territories of the United States where it exists* shall be received by this House or entertained in any way whatsoever." See Unger, *John Quincy Adams*, 298.

19. See the *Richmond Enquirer*, February 10, 1842, 2.

20. Thomas Marshall, a Kentucky congressman and nephew of Chief Justice John Marshall, moved to censure Adams for having committed high treason for having submitted such a petition, but Adams demanded that the clerk read from the Declaration of Independence pointing to the right and duty to "throw off" injurious government. See Unger, *John Quincy Adams*, 298–99.

21. William Lee Miller, *Arguing About Slavery: The Great Battle in the United States Congress* (New York: Knopf, 1996), 449.

22. Ibid.

23. Don E. Fehrenbacher, *The Slaveholding Republic: An Account of the United States Government's Relations to Slavery* (New York: Oxford University Press, 2001), 111.

24. In contrast, an "expulsion" requires a two-thirds vote. There have only been five expulsions, the first three of which took place during the first year of the Civil War.

25. The first member censured was Rep. William Stanberry, also of Ohio, in 1832, for insulting the Speaker, Andrew Stevenson, later the American minister to Great Britain (1836–1841). The most recent member censured was Rep. Daniel B. Crane of Illinois, in 1983, for sexual misconduct with a page.

26. The text of the letter, along with Adams's diary entry, is found in Miller, *Arguing About Slavery*, 453.

27. *Joshua R. Giddings: Life, Liberty and the Pursuit of Happiness* (Ashtabula, OH: Ashtabula Historical Society, 2006), 8–9.

28. House Document No. 215, 27th Congress, second session.

29. Fehrenbacher, *The Slaveholding Republic*, 109.

30. William Glyde Wilkins, ed., *Charles Dickens in America* (Honolulu: University Press of the Pacific, 2005; 1911), 153.

31. Jessica M. Lepler, *The Many Panics of 1837: People, Politics, and the Creation of a Transatlantic Financial Crisis* (New York: Cambridge University Press, 2013), 166. (The author erroneously dates Dickens's visit in 1841, rather than 1842.

32. Charles Dickens, *American Notes* (New York: Oxford University Press, 1987), 125.

33. Dickens was unhappy with Fuller's, along with almost everything else in Washington. Dickens described the backyard of the hotel: "Clothes are drying in this same yard; female slaves, with cotton handkerchiefs twisted round their heads, are running to and fro on the hotel business; black waiters cross and recross with dishes in their hands; two great dogs are playing upon a mound of loose bricks in the center of the square; a pig is turning up his stomach in the sun, and grunting 'that's comfortable'; and neither the men, nor the women, nor the dogs, nor the pigs, nor any exalted creatures takes any notice" of the residents' call for a servant. *The Surratt Courier* XXXVII (2012), 7.

34. An interesting fictional account portrays Dickens's view of Daniel Webster, after Webster called on Dickens at the hotel, that, of all the famous people who have called on Dickens since his arrival in the United States, "Mr. Webster was the most artificial, the most posturing, the most self involved of the lot." In contrast, Dickens found Henry Clay to be "the warmest, kindest, most self-effacing (despite his considerable political power) man you could ever wish to meet." The account is taken from a fictional lost diary of Mrs. Dickens: Daniel Panger, *Hard Times: The Lost Diary of Mrs. Charles Dickens* (Berkeley, CA: Creative Arts, 2000), 63–64.

35. Dickens, *American Notes*, 116.

36. For an interesting and full account of her role as hostess, see Christopher J. Leahy, "Playing Her Greatest Role: Priscilla Cooper Tyler and the Politics of the White House Social Scene, 1841–44," *Virginia Magazine of History and Biography* 120 (2012): 237.

37. Wilkins, *Charles Dickens in America*, 167.
38. Ibid., 178.
39. The nasty habit of tobacco chewing, and spitting, so upset Dickens that he devoted as much time in his letters and in *American Notes* to it as he did to slavery. See Jon Acheson, "Charles Dickens in America: The Baltimore Letters," *Maryland Historical Magazine* 102 (2007): 329.
40. Acheson, "Charles Dickens in America," 321.
41. Ibid., 325.
42. Ibid., 331.
43. Ibid., 186 and 189.
44. Peter Ackroyd, *Dickens* (London: Vintage, 1999), 380.
45. Dickens, *American Notes*, 120. Dickens's view of Washington's political life was not rosy. He said he saw "Despicable trickery at elections; under-handed tampering with public officers; cowardly attacks upon opponents, with scurrilous newspapers for shield, etc."
46. Chief Justice Hughes laid the cornerstone for the Supreme Court's building on October 13, 1932, and it opened in 1935.
47. The noted legal scholar, especially with respect to slavery, Prof. Paul Finkelman, suggests that the *Prigg* case represented the first example of the modern notion of "unfunded mandates." Paul Finkelman, "Teaching Slavery in American Constitutional Law," *Akron Law Review* 34 (2000): 280.
48. This sensible suggestion is made by H. Robert Baker in his superb *Prigg v. Pennsylvania: Slavery, the Supreme Court, and the Ambivalent Constitution* (Lawrence: University of Kansas Press, 2012), 139.
49. Baker, *Prigg v. Pennsylvania*, 152.
50. Ibid.
51. Akhil Reed Amar, *America's Constitution: A Biography* (New York: Random House, 2005), 263.

6. ENTER DIPLOMACY; CRISIS AVERTED

1. Kathleen Burk, *Old World, New World: Great Britain and America from the Beginning* (New York: Atlantic Monthly Press, 2007), 265.
2. Robert V. Remini, *Daniel Webster: The Man and His Time* (New York: Norton, 1997), 491.
3. Ibid.
4. Ephraim Douglass Adams, "Lord Ashburton and the Treaty of Washington," *American Historical Review* 17, no. 4 (July 1912): 764.
5. Remini, *Daniel Webster*, 545.
6. Adams, "Lord Ashburton," 766.
7. Ibid., 767n3.
8. George C, Herring, *From Colony to Superpower: US Foreign Relations Since 1776* (New York: Oxford University Press, 2008), 187.
9. It is not clear whether they visited both the House and the Senate, or only the Senate—the chamber that would have to give advice and consent to any resulting treaty.
10. Exactly ten years earlier, the Great Reform Bill became law in the United Kingdom; it swept away ancient abuses of parliamentary representation and greatly increased the size of the British electorate. Prior to that act, for example, the great industrial cities of Manchester and Birmingham, with populations of 310,000 and 145,000 respectively, had no representation in Parliament. On the other hand, thinly populated Cornwall had forty-four representatives. See Alan Ryan, "A Big British Moment," review of Antonia Fraser, *Perilous Question: Reform or Revolution? Britain on the Brink, 1832* in *New York Review of Books*, January 9, 2014, 45.
11. Erik J. Chaput, *The People's Martyr: Thomas Wilson Dorr and His 1842 Rhode Island Rebellion* (Lawrence: University Press of Kansas, 2013), 88.
12. Ibid., 89.

13. Ibid., 132.
14. Ibid., 146.
15. Gary May, *John Tyler* (New York: Times Books/Henry Holt, 2008), 103.
16. William H. Rehnquist, "Daniel Webster and the Oratorical Tradition," *1989 Yearbook* (Supreme Court Historical Society, 2008), 14.
17. Webster's great biographer, Robert V. Remini, notes that Webster was not shy about selling diplomatic appointments, and that, following a loan by Isaac Jackson (a Philadelphia merchant) to enable him to buy Swann House, Jackson was appointed to a diplomatic post in Denmark. Remini, *Daniel Webster*, 513.
18. Swann House was razed in 1922, and a new building was constructed to house the US Chamber of Commerce, which is still in use by the chamber.
19. The "Ashburton House" came into the possession of John Nelson, later Tyler's attorney general, and then became the British Legation until 1852. Beginning in the twentieth century, the house became the parish house of St. John's Episcopal Church, and in 1974, it was designated as a National Historic Landmark.
20. Today, the State Department has about 19,000 American employees, many of whom are stationed overseas.
21. A plaque commemorating the signing of the treaty on August 9, 1842, was placed at the site of the Old State Department in 1929.
22. Remini, *Daniel Webster*, 517–18.
23. Howard Jones, *To The Webster-Ashburton Treaty: A Study in Anglo-American Relations, 1783–1843* (Chapel Hill: University of North Carolina Press, 1977), 145–46.
24. Remini, *Daniel Webster*, 547–48.
25. Adams, "Lord Ashburton," 773.
26. *Richmond Enquirer*, May 17, 1842, 2.
27. *Richmond Enquirer*, May 20, 1842, 2. See generally, Wilbur Devereux Jones, "The Influence of Slavery on the Webster-Ashburton Negotiations," *Journal of Southern History* 22, no. 1 (February 1956): 48–58.
28. *Richmond Enquirer*, June 7, 1842, 3.
29. Adams, "Lord Ashburton," 777.
30. Ibid., 778.
31. Congress rather quickly solved the McLeod problem by enacting legislation to permit rapid removal from state courts to federal courts in the future. Act of August 29, 1842; 5 Statutes at Large, 539–40.
32. Remini, *Daniel Webster*, 551.
33. Jones, *To The Webster-Ashburton Treaty*, 147.
34. *Opinions of the Attorney General* 4, no. 101 (1841–48).
35. Legare died less than a year later while he was accompanying President Tyler to the dedication of the monument at Bunker Hill in Boston.
36. Remini, *Daniel Webster*, 563.
37. At about the same time, British and Chinese negotiators were sitting in oppressive August heat and humidity half a world away, putting the finishing touches on the Treaty of Nanjing, the first of the so-called Unequal Treaties, which ended the First Opium War and reflected the capitulation of the Qing Dynasty to the British.
38. Adams, "Lord Ashburton," 779.
39. Oxford defines the adjective as "assertive of authority in an annoyingly domineering way, especially with regard to petty or trivial matters"; Merriam-Webster defines it as "volunteering one's services where they are neither asked nor needed."
40. The term was coined by National Security Adviser Henry Kissinger in reference to the Joint Statement Following Discussions With Leaders of the People's Republic of China in Shanghai, February 27, 1972.
41. Adams, "Lord Ashburton," 779.
42. Ibid.
43. Remini, *Daniel Webster*, 559.
44. Remini, *Daniel Webster*, 566. Robert V. Remini, the award-winning historian, biographer, and official House historian, died on March 28, 2013, at age 91.

45. Jones, *To The Webster-Ashburton Treaty*, 162–63.
46. Remini, *Daniel Webster*, 567.
47. Hugh Taylor Gordon, "The Treaty of Washington," the James Bryce Historical Prize essay for 1907 (Berkeley, CA: University Press, 1908), 217. See also Remini, *Daniel Webster*, 564n1.
48. 15 Congressional Globe, 29th Cong, 1st Sess., April 6, 1846, 609.
49. Ibid., 621.

7. INSURANCE FOR SLAVE "PROPERTY"

1. The seven are: *McCargo v. New Orleans Insurance Co.* (twenty-six slaves); *Andrews v. The Ocean Insurance Co.* (eight slaves); *Lockett v. Fireman's Insurance Co., of New Orleans* (twenty-eight slaves); *Hagan v. The Ocean Insurance Co.* (nine slaves); *Johnson v. The Ocean Insurance Co.* (twenty-three slaves); *McCargo v. The Merchants Insurance Co., of New Orleans* (nineteen slaves); and *Lockett v. The Merchants Insurance Co. of New Orleans*.
2. For an interesting courtroom thriller set in New Orleans in 1843, which reconstructs the sights and sounds and smells of that city, especially the slavery issue, see John Bailey, *The Lost German Slave Girl: The Extraordinary True Story of Sally Miller and Her Fight for Freedom in Old New Orleans* (New York: Grove Press, 2003).
3. Sometimes it is suggested that Slidell and Benjamin had a partnership, but the earliest scholar who studied the matter claims there is no authority supporting a formal partnership, and family sources confirmed that. See Pierce Butler, *Judah P. Benjamin* (Philadelphia: G. W. Jacobs, 1907; New York and London, 1980), 37.
4. Justice Ruth Bader Ginsburg, "From Benjamin to Breyer: Is There a Jewish Seat?" *Supreme Court Historical Society Quarterly* 24, no. 3 (2003): 4.
5. Eli N. Evans, *Judah P. Benjamin: The Jewish Confederate* (New York: Free Press, 1988), 27.
6. Ibid., 28.
7. Butler, *Judah P. Benjamin*, 43.
8. *Thomas McCargo v. The New Orleans Insurance Company*, vol. X, Louisiana Reports 202 (1845).
9. Ibid., 312.
10. Ibid., 260.
11. Ibid., 277.
12. Ibid., 279.
13. Ibid., 251.
14. Ibid., 254.
15. Ibid., 317.
16. Ibid., 330.
17. Ibid., 326.
18. Ibid., 332. The other six cases were summarily treated in the same way, since the same facts and questions of law were presented. There was an application for rehearing in one case, but that was denied.
19. In two of the cases, *McCargo v. The Merchant's Insurance Co of New Orleans* and *Lockett v. The Merchants Insurance Co. of New Orleans*, the jury in the lower court awarded compensation, in part on the "seaworthy" issue and in part due to technically different provisions in their contract. Judge Bullard explained that the evidence was not sufficient for him to overturn the two jury verdicts. These same two cases were later dealt with by the US Supreme Court.

8. SHOULD THE BRITISH HAVE FREED THE SLAVES?

1. The Senate gave its advice and consent on March 15, 1853. It was ratified by the United States and the United Kingdom on March 17 and June 29, respectively, and ratifications were exchanged in London on July 26, 1853.

2. Sir Edmund in 1865 would become the first chief judge of the British Supreme Court for China and Japan, which dealt with cases involving British subjects, in accordance with extraterritorial rights the United Kingdom acquired by treaty.

3. Jessica M. Lepler, *The Many Panics of 1837: People, Politics, and the Creation of a Transatlantic Financial Crisis* (New York: Cambridge University Press, 2013), 11. The author does not identify Francis Baring as Alexander Baring's second son, but his grandfather, Francis Baring, died in 1810.

4. John E. Noyes, "*The Caroline*: International Law Limits on Resort to Force," in *International Law Stories* (New York: Foundation Press, 2007), 293.

5. The division was as follows: Edward Lockett = $22,250; John Hogun = $8,000; William H. Goodwin, for self and Thomas McCargo = $23,140; John Pemberton, as liquidator of the Merchants' Insurance Company of New Orleans (first claim) = $12,460; G. H. Apperson and Sherman Johnson = $20,470; P. Botchford = $2,136; John Pemberton, as liquidator of the Merchants' Insurance Company of New Orleans (second claim) = $16,000; and James Andrews = $5,874.

6. David Brion Davis, *Inhuman Bondage: The Rise and Fall of Slavery in the New World* (New York: Oxford University Press, 2006), 269. Dr. Davis is Sterling Professor of History Emeritus at Yale University, and a Pulitzer Prize winner.

7. Maggie Montesinos Sale, *The Slumbering Volcano: American Slave Ship Revolts and the Production of Rebellious Masculinity* (Durham: Duke University Press, 1997), 144.

8. These two cases were brought by McCargo (for nineteen slaves) and Lockett (for fifteen slaves). In the Louisiana Supreme Court case (treated in chapter 7), these two claims won in the Commercial Court, and those verdicts were affirmed by the Supreme Court.

9. *John Pemberton, Liquidator of the Merchants' Insurance Company v. Edward Lockett, James G. Berret, and Henry D. Johnson*, 62 US 257 (1858).

10. In 1871, President Grant appointed Justice Nelson to serve on the US-UK Claims Commission in London, with respect to the *Alabama* claims arising out of the Civil War.

9. A FORMER SLAVE'S HEROIC SLAVE

1. For an interesting review of Douglass's visit, see Tom Chaffin, "Frederick Douglass's Irish Liberty," Opinionator.blogs.nytimes.com/2011/02/25. Chaffin is Research Professor of History at the University of Tennessee, Knoxville.

2. Colum McCann, *Trans-Atlantic* (New York: Random House, 2013), 62–63. The National Book Award author carefully noted: "Scholars of Douglass should know that I have sometimes combined, conflated, and on occasion fictionalized quotes in order to create the texture of truth."

3. One eminent historian prefers to use the term "Armistice" rather than "Compromise." See William W. Freehling, *The Road to Disunion: Secessionists at Bay: 1776–1854* (New York: Oxford University Press, 1990), 511.

4. See Arthur T. Downey, *Civil War Lawyers: Constitutional Questions, Courtroom Dramas and the Men Behind Them* (Chicago: ABA Books, 2010), 11.

5. Forrest McDonald, *States' Rights and the Union: Imperium in Imperio* (Lawrence: University Press of Kansas, 2000), 161.

6. For a brilliant review, see Steven Lubet, *Fugitive Justice: Runaways, Rescuers, and Slavery on Trial* (Cambridge: Belknap, 2010).

7. See George Bornstein, "Best Bad Book: Black Notes and White Notes to the Tale of Uncle Tom," *Times Literary Supplement*, March 30, 2007, 3–4. Interestingly, just as Frederick Douglass toured Britain shortly after publishing his autobiography a decade earlier, so also did Mrs. Stowe tour Europe shortly after the publication of her book. That tour produced her book *Sunny Memories of Foreign Lands*, which was sort of a guide of travel etiquette for Americans visiting Europe.

8. Julia Griffiths, ed., *Autographs for Freedom* (Cleveland: John P. Jewett & Co., 1853).

9. Maggie Montesinos Sale, *The Slumbering Volcano: American Slave Ship Revolts and the Production of Rebellious Masculinity* (Durham: Duke University Press: 1997), 241n9.

10. The most complete analysis of the themes in *The Heroic Slave* is found in Sale, *The Slumbering Volcano*.

11. This point is well made by Edward Eden, "The Revolt on the Slave Ship *Creole*: Popular Resistance to Slavery in Post-Emancipation Nassau," *Journal of the Bahamas Historical Society* 22 (October 2000): 18.

12. In 1865, the abolitionist and feminist activist Lydia Maria Child published *The Freedmen' Book* (Cambridge: University Press: Welsh, Bigelow & Co.) She devotes one seven-page chapter to Madison Washington. In it, his wife, Susan, is an octoroon, the daughter of the master. She finds herself on the *Creole* with Madison. He leads the revolt but insists on minimal bloodshed. The story ends upon the arrival in Nassau where the slaves walk off without any involvement of the crew or local British or American authorities.

13. The Abbey was located on the banks of the River Tweed in the Scottish Borders and existed from about 1150 to near 1600. Douglass had lived in the United Kingdom in 1845–1846 and perhaps visited the site of the Abbey.

EPILOGUE

1. Gary May, *John Tyler* (New York: Times Books/Henry Holt, 2008), 104.

2. Quoted by Thomas Fleming, review of Nathaniel Philbrick, *Bunker Hill* in *Wall Street Journal*, April 27–28, 2013, C-7.

3. Lynn Hudson Parsons, *John Quincy Adams* (Lanham, MD: Rowman & Littlefield, 2001), 267.

4. One of Adams's biographers adds the death of Benjamin Franklin, after Washington. Harlow Giles Unger, *John Quincy Adams* (Boston: Da Capo, 2012), 310. Unger concludes that Adams "was an aristocrat of an earlier generation, raised in an age of deference, who spoke the rich language that ordinary people could seldom fathom, but in the end, they sensed that he spoke for their greater good and to protect their rights and freedoms."

5. David Brion Davis, "How They Stopped Slavery: A New Perspective," review of James Oakes, *Freedom National: The Destruction of Slavery in the United States, 1861–1865* in *New York Review of Books*, June 6, 2012, 59–60.

6. Justice Ruth Bader Ginsburg, "From Benjamin to Breyer: Is There a Jewish Seat?" *Supreme Court Historical Society Quarterly* 24, no. 3 (2003): 1.

7. Wade was president pro tem of the Senate during the impeachment trial of President Johnson. Had the attack on Johnson not failed by one vote, Wade would have become president, since Johnson had no vice president.

8. Eli N. Evans, *Judah P. Benjamin: The Jewish Confederate* (New York: The Free Press, 1988), 97.

9. Sandy Prindle, "Judah Benjamin: A Person of Interest," *Surratt Courier* 38 (April 2013): 9. Prindle offers no proof, and makes clear that this is only speculation.

10. Judah Best, "Judah P. Benjamin: Part II: The Queen's Counsel," *Supreme Court Historical Society Quarterly* 33, no. 3 (2011): 9.

11. David Lynch, "Judah Benjamin's Career on the Northern Circuit and at the Bar of England & Wales," *Supreme Court Historical Society Quarterly* 33, no. 4 (2011): 10.

12. Ginsburg, "From Benjamin to Breyer," 4.

13. Jill Lepore, "Dickens in Eden," *The New Yorker*, August 29, 2011, 61.

14. Michael Slater, *The Great Charles Dickens Scandal* (New Haven: Yale University Press, 2013).

15. David Grylls, "What Larks," *Financial Times*, October 17–18, 2009, 16.

16. Ben Pershing, "Douglass Statue Arrives at Capital, His Cause in Tow," *Washington Post*, June 20, 2013, A3.

17. Bob Greene, "The Forgotten Gettysburg Addresser," *Wall Street Journal*, June 22, 2013, A-15.

18. In April 1848, revolution erupted in Germany, Austria, and Italy. Karl Marx and Friedrich Engels had just completed a pamphlet titled *The Communist Manifesto.* An excellent source for this period in Europe is Mike Rapport, *1848: Year of Revolution* (New York: Basic Books, 2008).

19. See generally, Patrice M. Williams, "'Freedom Day': The Emancipation Celebrations in the Bahamas in the 19th Century," *Journal of the Bahamas Historical Society* 17 (1995): 23.

20. Peter T. Dalleo, "Montell & Co., *The James Power* and the Baltimore-Bahamas Packet Trade 1838–1845," *Journal of the Bahamas Historical Society* 30 (2008): 8.

21. Thomas P. Lowry, "The Big Business of Bahamian Blockade Running," *Civil War Times* (May 2007): 59. See also D. Gail Sanders, "The Blockade Running in the Bahamas: Blessing or Curse?" *Journal of the Bahamas Historical Society* 10 (1988): 14.

22. *Economist,* October 5, 2013, 42.

23. For a positive description of the Anaconda Plan, see Tim Rowland, "The Big Squeeze," *America's Civil War* (March 2013): 37–43.

24. Robert D. Shuster and William G. Shuster, "Winfield Scott's Last Mission," *Civil War Times* (June 2013): 58.

25. Marjorie M. Whiteman, *Digest of International Law*, vol. 4 (Washington, DC: Department of State, 1965), vol. 4, 645.

26. May, *John Tyler*, 145.

27. Robert V. Remini, *Daniel Webster: The Man and His Time* (New York: Norton, 1997), 640. See also Erik J. Chaput, *The People's Martyr: Thomas Wilson Dorr and His 1842 Rhode Island Rebellion* (Lawrence: University Press of Kansas, 2013), 198–99.

28. 48 U.S. (7 How.) 1 (1849).

29. "Political Questions are controversies that the US Supreme Court has historically regarded as nonjustifiable and inappropriate for judicial resolution. . . . Although the Court may have jurisdiction over cases involving such questions, it has often chosen not to decide them, preferring instead to allow them to be resolved by the 'political' branches of government." Kermit L. Hall, ed., *The Oxford Companion to the Supreme Court of the United States* (New York: Oxford University Press, 1992), 651.

30. Remini, *Daniel Webster*, 685.

Index

About the Author

Arthur T. Downey has had an eclectic career and each element has contributed to his presentation of the *Creole* story. Having been a diplomat and served on the National Security Council staff under Dr. Kissinger, he brings an understanding of the complexity of international negotiations, such as those between Secretary of State Webster and Lord Ashburton. As an adjunct professor at Georgetown Law School for a dozen years, he cuts through the issues of the legal structures in which slavery lived in the 1840s, in both the United States and the British Bahamas. Finally, his last book was about the Civil War, which brought an understanding of the enormous domestic political pressures that slavery and abolition forces created; those pressures erupted twenty years after the *Creole* in the Civil War.